THE PARLIAMENTARY REPRESENTATION
OF THE ENGLISH BOROUGHS
DURING THE MIDDLE AGES

THE PARLIAMENTARY
REPRESENTATION OF
THE ENGLISH BOROUGHS
DURING THE MIDDLE AGES

By

MAY McKISACK

FRANK CASS & COMPANY LTD

OXFORD UNIVERSITY PRESS

First published by Oxford University Press in 1932

FIRST EDITION 1932
REPRINTED 1962

Published by Frank Cass & Company Ltd.,
10 *Woburn Walk, London, W.C.*1

Printed in Great Britain by
Taylor Garnett Evans & Co. Ltd.,
Watford and London

PREFACE

THE material for these studies was collected during my tenure of the Mary Somerville Research Fellowship, which made it possible for me to inspect a number of municipal records in different parts of England. I am deeply indebted to the Donors of the Fellowship and to the Council of Somerville College for my election as Fellow, and for their generosity in allowing me to retain my tenure of the Fellowship for one year after my appointment at Liverpool.

My interest in medieval parliamentary boroughs was first awakened while preparing a thesis for the degree of B.Litt. under the direction of Mr. Austin Lane-Poole. It is a pleasure to express my gratitude to him, and to two other Oxford friends whose wise counsel has been invaluable to me in the preparation of this book. Miss M.V. Clarke and Mr. J. G. Edwards spared much precious time to read through the manuscript, and both have placed their expert knowledge of medieval parliamentary history freely at my disposal. Their advice has saved me from many blunders and omissions, though they are not to be held responsible for those which still remain.

My thanks are also due to all those who helped me to gain access to the civic and municipal records and advised me as to their use, particularly to Mr. A. H. Thomas at the Guildhall, London, to Dr. Maud Sellers at York, to Mr. J. S. Furley at Winchester, to Mr. Johnston at Norwich, and to the Town Clerks of York, Norwich, King's Lynn, Shrewsbury, Canterbury, Winchester, Salisbury, Exeter, Reading, and Wallingford. Miss Jeffries-Davis allowed me to draw on her wide knowledge of London history; Miss Jean Rowntree gave me some interesting information relating to the representatives of Scarborough; and conversation with Colonel Wedgwood threw much light on the personnel of the medieval parliament. My colleague Mr. L. J. H. Bradley, of the University Library at Liverpool, helped to solve several linguistic difficulties; another colleague,

Mr. R. R. Betts, kindly verified some references in the Norwich records. To Professor Powicke and to the readers of the Press I am greatly indebted for help and advice in the correction of proofs. Lastly, it was my good fortune, as a beginner, to receive some advice and criticism from the late Professor Tout. His enthusiasm for my subject, and his great kindliness towards a student for whom he was in no way responsible, were in themselves an inspiration. It is my privilege to conclude the list of those who have helped me with his name.

M. McK.

1931

CONTENTS

PAGE

INTRODUCTION ix

I. BOROUGH REPRESENTATION IN THE THIR-
TEENTH CENTURY 1

II. BOROUGH REPRESENTATION IN THE FOUR-
TEENTH CENTURY 24

III. BOROUGH REPRESENTATION IN THE FIF-
TEENTH CENTURY 44

IV. THE PROBLEM OF ATTENDANCE . . . 66

V. THE PAYMENT OF THE PARLIAMENTARY
BURGESSES 82

VI. THE BURGESS PERSONNEL OF THE MEDIEVAL
PARLIAMENT 100

VII. THE BURGESSES IN PARLIAMENT . . . 119

APPENDIX I. SOME NAMES OF BURGESS REPRESENTATIVES NOT
INCLUDED IN THE BLUE BOOK OF 1878 . . 146

II. PARLIAMENTARY RETURNS, ILLUSTRATING ELECTION
METHODS OF THE FIFTEENTH CENTURY . . 158

III. A BILL FOR PARLIAMENTARY EXPENSES (NORWICH,
1445–6) 161

BIBLIOGRAPHY 164

INDEXES 172

INTRODUCTION

THIS book is concerned with one limited aspect of
English parliamentary history. It is an attempt to
correlate some of the evidence bearing on the representation
of the towns in the medieval parliament, to discover how
the citizens and burgesses were elected, paid, and taxed,
what their function in parliament was, and what type of
men they were. Yet from whatever angle the history of
parliament is approached, one fundamental problem is in-
escapable. An attempt must be made to decide what, in
the reigns of the first two Edwards, constituted a parliament. Was it a meeting of 'three estates' of the realm
convened by a wise and far-seeing king for purposes of
deliberation, legislation, and taxation? Or was it a meeting
of magnates to which the king summoned representatives
of the commons in order to obtain grants of money and to
appoint collectors of taxes? Or was it a meeting of a royal
and feudal council, before which representatives of the
commons were summoned in order to supply the king and
his ministers with information as to the administration of
the country? Or, again, was parliament a supreme court
of justice, held at regular terms, where the commons
appeared chiefly as petitioners, their presence or absence
being merely incidental and in no way affecting the function of the court? Each of these theories as to the nature
of parliament has found supporters among eminent scholars,
well acquainted with the literature of the period of which
they write, but no one solution has been generally accepted
as conclusive. The student of the subject cannot, therefore,
escape the necessity of making a choice from among the
alternatives thus offered to him.

It is now universally acknowledged that anxiety to discover exact dates for the origins of our great institutions
misled many among the older generation of historians.
Anxiety to discover exact definitions may, possibly, prove
little less misleading. At least it seems clear that, to the

ordinary, educated man living in the last quarter of the thirteenth century, the word *parliamentum* conveyed no specific technical meaning. Writers of this period use it indifferently to describe gatherings of clergy, of soldiers, of tenants-in-chief, of king's counsellors.[1] Attempts to find an exclusive definition for the parliaments of the thirteenth century are not altogether successful. Regular ceremonial meetings were the king's inheritance from his remote ancestors, and one of the main purposes of such gatherings had been a demonstration of the royal authority, a ' crown-wearing ' to be witnessed by the chief persons of the realm. As the prestige of the king developed and his functions increased, these gatherings were turned to serve many purposes. There the king might meet his tenants-in-chief or other counsellors, to discuss with them questions of general policy and to ask for financial aid. There petitioners both great and small might come with such cases as should properly be heard in the supreme court of the realm. Nor was it remarkable that the king should, on occasions, summon representatives of shires, or towns, or both, to strike a financial bargain, to obtain information on specific points, to test the feeling of the country generally, or to obtain the support of numbers for a policy. It is unnecessary to suppose that the king by so doing intended to delegate or limit any of his own powers, or that he had conceived a new type of legislative assembly, to which the presence of representatives should be essential. Regular meetings of the king's court continued to be held, with or without representatives of the commons, and the judicial business of the court proceeded independently of such summonses. None the less, a shrewd observer at the end of the reign of Edward I might have perceived that the king, for one reason or another, was finding it increasingly difficult to dispense with the presence of elected representatives for long periods at a time. Slowly, and almost imperceptibly, some distinction between 'full' parliaments, which included representatives of the commons, and other parliaments, which did not, was beginning to penetrate to the outside

[1] See the references in *Bulletin of the Institute of Historical Research*, v, no. 15, p. 150.

world.[1] But at the close of the thirteenth century no clear-cut distinction was generally recognized.

For the purpose of this study, Maitland's definition of an early parliament as 'any meeting of the King's Council that has been solemnly summoned for general business',[2] has been accepted. Any such meeting in which representatives of the towns met together with the magnates has been regarded as a proper subject for investigation. The valuable work of Messrs. Richardson and Sayles in recent numbers of the *Bulletin* of the *Institute of Historical Research*[3] has shown that the meetings of councils or parliaments for judicial purposes were, under Edward I and Edward II, held with much greater regularity than has hitherto been supposed; but no really satisfactory reason has yet been shown why we should refuse the designation 'parliament' to other meetings of the King's Council which did not assemble at these regular sessions. For instance, the assemblies of 1283 and May 1298 have here been treated as parliaments though they do not comply with the definition suggested by these writers. That a specific technical test can, in Edward I's reign, be applied to the word still seems doubtful. If such a test existed, it was not generally recognized. *Parliamentum* may be used, and is used, albeit loosely, to describe any formal meeting of the King's Council, whether or not such a meeting includes representatives of the commons, and whether or not it conforms in every particular to the regular judicial sessions of the Council.

The new material used in these studies has been found mainly in local archives. As a source for medieval parliamentary history, the borough records have been hitherto almost entirely neglected.[4] Yet these records supply us not only with many names of members of parliament which are missing from the official returns, but also with valuable information on methods of election and taxation, on the

[1] *Studies Supplementary to Stubbs' Constitutional History*, vol. iii, p. 482, n. 1.
[2] *Memoranda de Parliamento*, p. lxvii.
[3] Vol. v, no. 15; vol. vi, nos. 17 and 18.
[4] This defect is now being remedied by the initiation of the official history of parliament, which is to include a thorough search of the borough records by various scholars.

payment of parliamentary wages, and on the use made of their representatives by the town communities. Outside London, the most interesting records for this purpose have been found at King's Lynn. Scarcely less valuable are the collections at Norwich, Canterbury, Winchester, Salisbury, and Exeter ; and there can be little doubt that much still remains to be discovered. It need hardly be said that this short book does not pretend to be exhaustive in its survey of the material for parliamentary history which lies hidden in the borough records. It will have served its purpose if it helps to draw attention to the existence of such material, and to elucidate one or two of the more obscure passages in the history of the English parliament.

BOROUGH REPRESENTATION IN THE THIRTEENTH CENTURY

THE parliament convened under the influence of Simon de Montfort, in 1265, is the first to which a number of English boroughs are known to have been summoned, through their representatives, for a general political purpose. On a number of occasions before this date, representatives of certain towns had been summoned before the King and his Council for a specific purpose,[1] but de Montfort's parliament is the first, the motive of summons to which is stated in general terms. The purpose, as stated in the writ, is to treat with the King and the magnates and to give counsel on the subject of the liberation of the Lord Edward and as to the best means of providing for the future security of the kingdom.[2] De Montfort's motive in thus summoning representatives of the towns to afforce the Council was, almost certainly, a desire to find moral support for his policy. He had shown a similar intention in the previous year when he had required the mayor of London to place his seal beside those of the bishops and barons, at the bottom of the *forma regiminis domini regis et regni*.[3] In 1265 he sought the support of certain other towns, besides London, which he probably believed to be favourable to his cause. We do not, unfortunately, know which these towns were, but that their numbers were considerable may be inferred from the wording of the Close Roll—*in forma predicta scribitur civibus Ebor'*, *civibus Lincoln et caeteris burgis Anglie*—as well as from the statement of Fitz Thedmar that there were present representatives *de qualibet civitate et burgo*.[4] It is just possible that all towns of any size were asked to send representatives; but the fact that letters were sent directly to the citizens and not through the sheriffs, seems to suggest that de Montfort and his friends wished to retain, as regards the towns, the

---

[1] These instances have been collected by Professor A. B. White in *American Historical Review*, xix. 742 sq.

[2] *Rep. Dig. Peer.* i. 142–3.   [3] Rymer, *Foedera*, i. 143.

[4] *Rep. Dig. Peer.* i. 143 ; *Liber de antiquis legibus*, p. 71.

power of selection which they had already freely exercised as regards the bishops and barons. No writ seems to have been sent to London, probably because it would have been superfluous. The parliament was to meet in London, and the mass of the citizens had, throughout the war, shown themselves to be ardent supporters of the baronial cause.[1]

The support of the towns, for both financial and military reasons, was of the greatest importance to either party, but it is probable that the part which knights and burgesses were called on to play in this parliament was mainly spectacular. The knights received their expenses writs on 15 February, the day following the King's solemn oath to maintain the new form of government,[2] and the majority of the burgesses would naturally have been dismissed at the same time. The mayor and aldermen of London probably remained. On 17 March they took the oath of fealty to the King at St. Paul's, in common with all those who had adhered to de Montfort's party at Lewes.[3] De Montfort had obtained what he required—the approval of his new constitution by an assembly impressive in size if not in strength. The absence of many lay barons had been counterbalanced by the presence of an unprecedentedly large number of higher clergy, knights, and burgesses. The whole assembly has been well described as ' the convention of a party rather than a true parliament ',[4] and to see in it evidence of de Montfort's wish to apply the representative principle to the summoning of the Great Council is to misunderstand the nature of his opposition to the Crown. None the less, the venture had been successful enough to justify its repetition ; and the experiment was renewed, in modified form, three years after de Montfort's death.

In March 1268, the mayor, the bailiffs, and six representatives from each of twenty-seven selected towns were summoned before the Council to treat of matters touching the King, the Kingdom, and themselves.[5] As selection was

---

[1] Ibid., p. 91.   [2] Rep. Dig. Peer., Appendix, p. 35.
[3] Liber de antiquis legibus, pp. 72-3.
[4] Pasquet, Origins of the House of Commons, p. 56.
[5] For our knowledge of this assembly we are indebted to the interesting document discovered by Mr. G. O. Sayles in the Public Record Office. English Historical Review, xl, pp. 580 sq.

desired, the writs were again addressed directly to the towns. The representatives were to be chosen from the better, richer, more discreet, and more powerful men of the city; and they were to bring with them letters patent, under the seal of the town, giving them what was virtually power of attorney. The business in hand was the general work of reconstruction after the acceptance of the Dictum of Kenilworth, and included the sealing of the charter restoring the privileges of London. It may be conjectured that the towns summoned were those which, with London, had been most active in support of de Montfort, and which were now to be admitted to full restitution of their rights. York and Lincoln head the list, as they headed those summoned by de Montfort in 1265, and the list includes those towns of the Welsh March which we know to have been active on de Montfort's side. Further, the writ states definitely that the matters to be discussed affect the towns themselves.[1] Unfortunately, we know nothing of what took place in this assembly and, like the other early meetings of representatives in parliament, it excited no comment among contemporary chroniclers. The towns summoned were York, Lincoln, Northampton, Stamford, Norwich, Cambridge, Lynn, Oxford, Worcester, Gloucester, Shrewsbury, Hereford, Bristol, Winchester, Southampton, Canterbury, Chichester, Rochester, Bath, Coventry, Lichfield, Exeter, Ely, Bury St. Edmunds, Yarmouth, Ipswich, and Dunwich, all of which are known to have received summonses to the parliament of 1295, except Lichfield, which did not send representatives again until 1305.[2]

The important parliament of 1275 is the next which can be proved definitely to have included representatives of the towns. But as the discovery of the evidence for the composition of this parliament as well as for that of 1268 was accidental, it is obvious that lack of evidence is an unsafe basis for any argument on the subject. The probability is that representatives of the cities and boroughs continued to

[1] '. . . super arduissimis negociis nos et regnum nostrum, statum et communitatem regni nostri et vos tangentibus.' Ibid.
[2] *Names of Members of Parliament*, i. 20 ; *Bulletin of the Institute of Historical Research*, iii. 8, pp. 110–15.

be summoned to parliament between 1268 and 1275. In the autumn of 1269, the relics of St. Edward were solemnly transferred to Westminster Abbey, and on that occasion, according to the chronicler, there were present the more powerful men of the cities and boroughs (*civitatum pariter et burgorum potentiores*) ; and after the ceremony the nobles (*nobiles*) began to discuss the affairs of the King and the Kingdom in parliament, the greater men (*majores*) agreeing with them, or not daring to contradict them. It was there agreed that one-twentieth of the movables of the laity should be granted to the King.[1] It seems reasonable to infer that the *majores*, who are here contrasted with the magnates or *nobiles* whom they did not dare to contradict, are synonymous with the *potentiores* of the cities and boroughs already mentioned, who may well have been asked to remain for the debate on the raising of a subsidy and to give their formal assent. Again, in 1273, while the King was still on Crusade, a solemn assembly (*convocatio*) was held at Westminster, which is interesting as showing how the practice of doing business with the towns through their representatives at a central assembly was becoming habitual. To this gathering were summoned archbishops, bishops, earls, barons, abbots, priors, and from every shire and from every city four men (*et de qualibet civitate quatuor*), to take the oath of fealty to Edward I.[2]

The important statutes of the spring of 1275 were enacted, we are told, *par le assentement des Erceveskes, Eveskes, Abbes, Priurs, Contes, Barons, et la Communaute de la tere ileokes somons*.[3] That the *communaute de la tere* included representatives of the shires and boroughs was proved by the discovery of the writ addressed to the sheriff of Middlesex and of fragments of the writs addressed to three other sheriffs together with lists of knights and burgesses for several counties.[4] These writs direct the sheriff to cause six or four citizens, burgesses, or other good men to come from every city, borough, and town of merchants (*villa mercatoria*) in his bailiwick. The wording and the fact that the writs were

[1] *Ann. Wykes*, pp. 226–7.	[2] *Ann. Winton.*, p. 113.
[3] Ibid., p. 442.
[4] *English Historical Review*, xxv, pp. 231 sq.

sent to the sheriffs, not directly to the towns, suggests that a comprehensive summons was intended, and it was probably the King's desire that all communities of any mercantile significance should be represented at a parliament in which the regulation of the tax on wool and leather was to be discussed.[1] The sheriffs certainly seem to have interpreted the writ in its widest sense. If the fragmentary lists which remain to us may be taken as typical of the returns made throughout the country, more towns must have been represented in this parliament of 1275 than in any subsequent parliament before 1500. The three Bedfordshire *villatae* of Biggleswade, Shefford, and Odell each made a return, although in all subsequent parliaments, save two, the borough of Bedford was the only town in the county represented in parliament.[2] The return of representatives from Uxbridge and Staines to this parliament marks, so far as we know, the only occasion on which these Middlesex *villae* were represented. The Warwickshire returns are still more remarkable. Warwick and, more rarely, Coventry were the only towns in the county which returned representatives to later parliaments ; but in 1275 eight town-communities within the shire made returns. Besides Warwick and Coventry, Nuneaton, Birmingham, Tamworth, Coleshill, Alcester, and Stratford-on-Avon were all represented.[3] These three instances alone suggest that the small towns of the country must have been much more fully represented in the parliament of 1275 than in the so-called 'model' parliament of 1295. In spite of the direction in the writ to send six or four men from every town, those whose names are here preserved sent only four, and Cricklade sent only three. But to later parliaments no town (except London) sent more than two representatives, so that the parliament of 1275 must have been more than double the size of any normal parliament of the fourteenth century.[4] Thus the statement that the new duty on wool was accorded 'at the request

---

[1] Cf. Professor Tait's article on 'The Study of Early Municipal History', in *Proceedings of the British Academy*, vol. x, 1922.

[2] Dunstable was represented in the parliaments of August 1311 and July 1312.

[3] With the exception of the borough of Warwick, all these are described as *villatae*. Cf. Tait, *British Borough Charters*, ii, pp. xlix–liv.

[4] *English Historical Review*, loc. cit.

of the communities of merchants of all England' probably
contains little exaggeration.[1]

No burgesses came with the knights to the second parliament of 1275, and no further evidence as to the representation of the towns is available until the year 1283. In January
of that year, Edward I issued writs from Rhuddlan ordering
the sheriffs to send to Northampton or to York (according
to the locality of the shire) four knights from every county,
and from every city, borough, and town of merchants two
men having full power on behalf of their communities ' to
hear and to do those things which we for our part shall
cause to be disclosed to them '.[2] The object of the summons was the raising of money for the campaign in Wales.
Edward I had, in the previous year, reverted to the older
method of sending his Treasurer round the shires and towns
instead of causing the latter to send their representatives
to a central assembly. Doubtless the coercion of the town
by the Treasurer proved less simple than the overawing of
isolated delegates before the King's Council, for the con-
tributions offered were found inadequate.[3] The subsequent
summons to York and Northampton affords an interesting
illustration of the way in which the representative principle
was coming to be applied more and more frequently (not
indeed as a principle, but rather as an expedient) for both
political and financial purposes. No returns are extant for
these assemblies, so it is not possible to compare the interpretation of *villa mercatoria* with that given to it in 1275.
At Shrewsbury, in September of the same year (1283), a
parliament was held which pronounced sentence on David
of Wales. To this parliament were summoned two knights
from every shire and two of the wiser and fitter burgesses
from London and each of twenty other specified towns.[4] The
towns being specially selected, the writs were again sent direct
to the mayors or bailiffs. Thirteen of these towns were among
those similarly summoned to the parliament of 1268 (York,
Lincoln, Northampton, Norwich, Lynn, Worcester, Shrewsbury, Hereford, Bristol, Winchester, Canterbury, Exeter,
and Yarmouth). The remaining seven were all important

[1] *Parl. Writs,* i, p. 1.   [2] *Rep. Dig. Peer.* i. 186.
[3] Pasquet, op. cit., p. 84.   [4] *Parl. Writs,* i, p. 16.

chartered towns—Newcastle-on-Tyne, Carlisle, Nottingham, Scarborough, Grimsby, Colchester, and Chester. London, we know from another source, sent six representatives to this parliament.[1] The motive which led Edward to summon representatives of the chief towns with the knights may have been, as Dr. Pasquet suggests, the preparation of the Statute of Merchants,[2] or possibly a motive similar to that which actuated de Montfort in 1265, the desire for moral support in carrying out a difficult policy. The distribution of the remains of the unfortunate David to the four towns at the four corners of England suggests that Edward wished to make his conquest of Wales a reality in the eyes of the whole country.[3] The London Chronicle, at all events, makes no reference to the Statute of Merchants, but carefully records the return of the representatives with David's head.[4]

The cities and boroughs are not again found returning representatives until the famous parliament of November 1295. The returns for Norfolk and Suffolk having been lately discovered,[5] the list of representatives is, so far as we know, complete (except for the London returns), and is of very great interest, as being the earliest of such complete lists that we possess. The summonses to the towns were sent through the sheriffs, no selection being desired, but a narrowing of the scope of the writ was probably intended by the omission of any reference to the *villae mercatoriae*. The sheriff is to cause to be elected, without delay, two knights of his shire, and from every city of the same shire two citizens, and from every borough two burgesses from among the more discreet and capable. The purpose of summoning the representatives is said to be the holding of a colloquy to provide a remedy for the dangers which threaten the kingdom. Both knights and burgesses are to appear with full and sufficient powers to do what shall be ordained by common counsel, so that business may not be hindered by their lack of any such powers.[6]

[1] *Ann. Lond.*, p. 92.   [2] Pasquet, op. cit., p. 88.

[3] *Ann. Oseney*, p. 294.   [4] *Ann. Lond.*, loc. cit.

[5] *Bulletin of the Institute of Historical Research*, iii. 8, pp. 110 sq.

[6] *Rep. Dig. Peer.*, App. i, p. 66.

Excluding London (which, although their names are lacking, must certainly have elected representatives) 114 towns made returns to this parliament. The sheriffs of Buckinghamshire, Hertfordshire, Middlesex, and Rutland, either reported that there were no boroughs within their bailiwicks, or implied it by their failure to return the names of burgesses. The greatest number of burgess returns came from Wiltshire, where thirteen boroughs in all elected representatives;[1] Yorkshire came next with eleven;[2] then Hampshire with ten.[3] Bedfordshire has returns from one borough only, as against three in 1275; Middlesex none, as against two; Warwick and Leicester three, as against nine. These figures seem to suggest that the sheriffs were definitely interpreting ' cities and boroughs ' in a narrower sense than ' cities, boroughs, and towns of merchants '. On the other hand, the returns from the sheriff of Somerset and Dorset show only five boroughs in the two shires returning representatives in 1275, while nine made returns in 1295. Again, of the thirteen Wiltshire boroughs of 1295 only five made returns in 1275. These discrepancies can be accounted for only by the scope given to each sheriff to interpret royal writs as seemed best to himself.

The following year (1296), a parliament was summoned to meet at Bury St. Edmunds on the morrow of All Saints' Day, the writs to the sheriffs being similar in form to those of 1295.[4] On 21 and 24 September new writs were issued, addressed to twenty-four important towns ordering them each to elect two citizens[5] capable of helping in the organization of a new town (*qui melius sciant quandam novam villam disponere et ordinare*) and to send them to Bury St. Edmunds on the same day.[6] All these towns except Chester[7] and

---

[1] Bedwyn, Bradford, Calne, Chippenham, Cricklade, Devizes, Downton, Ludgershall, Malmesbury, Marlborough, Old Sarum, Salisbury, Wilton.

[2] Beverley, Hedon, Malton, Pickering, Pontefract, Ripon, Scarborough, Thirsk, Tickhill, Yarm, York.

[3] Alresford, Alton, Andover, Basingstoke, Overton, Portsmouth, Southampton, Winchester, Newport (I. of W.), Yarmouth (I. of W.).

[4] *Parl. Writs*, i, p. 48.   [5] London was ordered to elect four.

[6] *Parl. Writs*, i, p. 49. The *nova villa* was Berwick, cf. Tout, *Medieval Town Planning*, pp. 28–9.

[7] Chester, as a palatine borough, was not represented in any medieval parliament except the Shrewsbury parliament of 1283, to which it received a special summons.

Dunwich [1] had been represented in the parliament of 1295, but the purpose of this writ was, clearly, to cause them to choose experts to attend a special council distinct from the parliament which was sitting at the same time. None of the returns for this parliament have been discovered, but local records provide us with the names of the London representatives,[2] and of one of the representatives elected by the borough of Wallingford (Berks.).[3]

An interval of eighteen months elapsed before the towns were again summoned, although two knights from each county were summoned in October 1297. On 13 April 1298 writs were issued to the sheriffs, similar in form to those of 1295, for a parliament to meet at York on 25 May.[4] The number of towns reported by the sheriffs to have returned representatives was considerably smaller than in 1295—seventy-eight instead of 114, and the lost returns from Berkshire, Cumberland, and Leicestershire could hardly have provided more than six additional towns. The Wiltshire boroughs have dropped from thirteen to five, those of Yorkshire from eleven to six, those of Hampshire from ten to three. Buckinghamshire, Middlesex, and Rutland again returned no burgesses, the sheriff of Buckinghamshire stating definitely in his endorsement of the writ that there is no city nor borough in the county.[5] Among the towns represented in 1295 which did not appear in the returns of 1298 were Ely, Tonbridge, Lyme Regis, Liverpool, Wigan, Yarmouth, Stafford, and the five Worcestershire boroughs of Bromsgrove, Dudley, Evesham, Kidderminster, and Pershore.

Although the parliament of March 1300 was summoned by writs similar to those of 1295, no returns except that for Yorkshire survive. Eight boroughs appear on this return. The only other evidence as to the returns from the towns is contained in the writs *de expensis*, which were issued to twenty boroughs, and in an extract from the Leicester

---

[1] The Bailiff of Dunwich had made no reply in 1295, *Bulletin of the Institute of Historical Research*, loc. cit.
[2] *Cal. Letter Book C.*, p. 24 ; *Parl. Writs*, i, p. 49.
[3] *Hist. MSS. Comm.*, *6th Report*, Appendix, p. 591.
[4] *Parl. Writs*, i, p. 65.   [5] Ibid. i, p. 66.

records proving that Leicester was represented.[1] The lists for the parliament held at Lincoln in January 1301 show returns from seventy-three towns.[2] There are none for the Cornish boroughs or for Gloucester, and the towns of St. Albans, Canterbury, Andover, Basingstoke, Odiham, and Southampton, are declared to have made none. It is, however, noteworthy that the sheriff of Buckinghamshire confesses, for the first time, to the existence of boroughs within his county, and returns exist from Amersham, Marlow, Wendover, and Wycombe. For the parliament of October 1302 we have the names of seventy towns returning representatives. Bristol, Lynn, Yarmouth, and Bury St. Edmunds, are stated to have made no returns, but the defaulting towns of the previous parliament appear in this, except St. Albans and Odiham. Only one borough in Buckinghamshire makes a return. Ninety-three boroughs made returns to the parliament of February 1305.[3] Twelve towns are entered on the writs as having made no return —Windsor, Lyme Regis, Melcombe Regis, Colchester, Hertford, St. Albans, Bath, Taunton, Alton, Basingstoke, Portsmouth, and Southampton—but it is noteworthy that in spite of the sheriff's statement as to the absence of a return from Colchester, one Elias Fitzjohn received his expenses for representing Colchester in this parliament. Probably the return had been received too late for the sheriff to enrol the names on his writ. The Buckinghamshire boroughs of Marlow and Wycombe made returns to this parliament.

The writs for the parliament which met to grant an aid at the knighting of Prince Edward in May 1306 directed the sheriffs to procure the election of two knights from each shire, two citizens from each city and two burgesses from each borough, or one only, if the borough were small.[4] Of the seventy-eight towns which made returns twenty-four sent one burgess only. Besides the small

---

[1] *Records of the Borough of Leicester*, i. 235.
[2] The Bedford and Reading names are taken from the writs *de expensis*.
[3] Representatives of the towns were summoned to a *colloquium* at York, in June 1303, to discuss an increase in the customs.
[4] *Parl. Writs*, i, p. 164; cf. *Bulletin of the Institute of Historical Research*, v. 15, pp. 147–8.

boroughs of Somerset and Wiltshire, such relatively important towns as Carlisle, Colchester, Southampton, Dunwich,
and Ipswich returned one representative only instead of
two. To the last parliament of Edward I (January 1307)
eighty-seven towns made returns. The sheriffs noted that
they had received no returns from Lyme Regis, Grimsby,
Alton, Basingstoke, Christchurch, and Odiham. Eleven
boroughs in Wiltshire made returns, eight in Somerset, and
eight in Hampshire. The names for Cumberland and
Northamptonshire are missing.

These figures show clearly that there was considerable
fluctuation in the towns and number of the towns attending Edward I's parliaments. Dr. Riess has calculated that
although 166 towns were represented in one or more of
these parliaments, the average number appearing in each
was only seventy-five.[1] His calculations are based on the
returns for the eight parliaments of Edward I's reign for
which he considers sufficient material to exist, namely
those of 1295, 1298, 1300, 1301, 1302, 1305, 1306, and
1307. Such an estimate gives a false impression by ignor-
ing the loss of numerous returns. As we have seen, all the
returns, but one, for the parliament of 1300 have been
lost, and the list of names has been compiled from the
expenses writs, which do not in any sense correspond with
the returns.[2] To include this list of twenty-eight towns in
such a calculation is at once to bring down the average.
A more accurate estimate can be reached by taking the
average for the remaining seven parliaments, for which
most of the returns are extant. This gives the figure 84·7.
Even then, we still have to allow for twelve single instances
in which the returns for a county have been lost; if these
were traced the correct average could hardly be less than 86.

One of the most difficult problems arising from a study
of these early parliaments is to discover how the borough
elections were made. The wording both of the writs of
summons and of the sheriffs' returns suggests that the
normal procedure was for each town to make its own

---

[1] Riess, *Geschichte des Wahlrechts zum englischen Parlament*, p. 19.
[2] The point at issue is, of course, the number of returns, not the number of
actual attendances. For a discussion of the latter see below, Chap. IV.

election, locally, and to communicate the result to the sheriff. Thus the writs to the sheriff, as we have seen, order him to provide for the election of two citizens and two burgesses from every city and borough in the shire, to be chosen from among the more discreet citizens or burgesses, and having full power to act on behalf of the communities which they represent. The sheriff is to return the writ, together with the names of the knights, citizens, and burgesses.[1] These directions could hardly have been carried out otherwise than by the holding of separate elections in each town, and the returns show that it was in this sense that the sheriff interpreted the writ. Thus, a characteristic return from the sheriff of Worcestershire (1305), states, after giving the names of the knights, ' As for the citizens of Worcester, this writ was returned to the bailiffs of the liberty of that city, who have full return of writs, who replied to me that two citizens have been elected in accordance with the tenor of the writ '.[2] If no reply was made, the sheriff was equally careful to record the fact so as to clear himself of responsibility for the non-attendance of the citizens or burgesses. In 1306, the sheriff of Dorset and Somerset writes, ' In order to cause two burgesses to be elected from the liberties of Lyme and Melcumb, the lord king's writ was returned to the mayor and bailiffs of those liberties, who have not troubled to send me any reply ' (*qui nullum mihi responsum dare curaverunt*).[3] Again, in 1305, the sheriff of Hertford and Essex reports : ' Return of this mandate was made to the bailiffs of St. Albans, the bailiffs of the town of Hertford, and the bailiffs of the town of Colchester, who have the return of all writs, who have given me no answer in the matter; and there is no other city or borough within my bailiwick.'[4] The form of these answers seems to place it beyond doubt that, at least in those towns which enjoyed the privilege of ' return of writs '—a privilege freely granted by royal charter during the thirteenth century—there can have been no interference from the sheriff with the elections to parliament. If there was

[1] *Rep. Dig. Peer.*, App. i, p. 66.
[2] *Parl. Writs*, i, p. 155.
[3] Ibid., p. 175.
[4] *Parl. Writs*, i, p. 143.

any valid reason for a town's failure to send representatives, that, too, was sometimes noted. In 1295, the sheriff of Westmorland, after giving the names of the elected knights and burgesses, added, 'But these cannot come on the day named in the writ because all men of my bailiwick between the ages of fifteen and sixty, both knights, freeholders and foot-soldiers, have been charged to appear before the lord bishop of Durham and John, Earl Warenne, and their lieutenants.'[1] Sometimes the names of the elected burgesses were received by the sheriff after the writ had been already endorsed and returned, as in the Colchester case to which reference has been made. Dr. Riess has drawn attention to the Yorkshire return in which the formula *nullum mihi dederunt responsum* has been crossed through and the names of the Scarborough representatives entered below, presumably at the last minute.[2] When the writs had been finally endorsed with the names of the knights and burgesses, and with any information concerning them which the sheriff wished to impart, they were returned into the Chancery.

It has been suggested that the representatives of the towns were sometimes elected in the county court, but there is no positive evidence of any such practice in this period.[3] The wording of some of the returns is, indeed, sufficiently ambiguous to have given rise to such a suggestion. Thus, the sheriff of Somerset and Dorset writes, in 1295, 'In full county courts of Somerset and Dorset by the community of the said counties I have caused four knights to be elected and by each city two citizens and by each borough two burgesses, according to the tenor of this writ'.[4] Such a return may be held to mean that the election of the borough representatives actually took place in the county court; but we know that in the fifteenth century it was customary in some of the shires which included a large number of boroughs for deputies from each to proclaim the election in the county court, and it is

[1] Ibid., p. 44.   [2] Riess, *Geschichte des Wahlrechts*, p. 61.
[3] The suggestion is made by both Gneist (*Englische Verfassungsgeschichte*, p. 385) and Stubbs (*Constitutional History*, ii. 247).
[4] *Parl. Writs*, i, p. 41.

probable that the reference here is to a similar practice.[1]
Riess has shown that burgesses of several towns within the
same county occasionally had the same sureties.[2] But the
instances which he has collected are admittedly exceptions
and may be explained by the occasional failure of a given
town to find sureties for its representatives. Sometimes
such a failure was noted on the writ [3] but sometimes to
prevent delay the sheriff may possibly have filled in the
gap by an arbitrary selection from the names of other
sureties already before him. It was probably rare for a
surety to be called to account, and the sheriff had little
reason to be over-scrupulous. A study of the returns for
this period as a whole seems to place it beyond doubt that
the normal practice was for the sheriffs to send the order
to elect to the different boroughs and to await their
replies.

But when we proceed to inquire how the towns carried
out the order to elect representatives, we are at once baffled
by lack of evidence. Our knowledge of borough elections
for the earliest period of parliamentary history is very slight.
The London records alone afford some information as to the
conduct of elections in the city. London was a shire incorporate, and the writ of summons was sent directly to the
sheriffs. The earliest elections to parliament were made by
the aldermen and deputations from the wards. The election
of 1296 is described in some detail in one of the city's Letter
Books and has been printed by Palgrave.[4] The passage contains the earliest known description of a parliamentary election in London. By virtue of the writ of summons, all the
aldermen of the city and four men from each ward were
called together on 26 September 1296, and they unanimously elected Stephen Aschewy and William de Hereford to go
to the parliament, granting them twenty shillings a day for
their expenses. On 8 October, in the presence of John le
Breton, Warden of the City, and ten aldermen, the community was called together (that is to say six of the better
and more discreet persons from each ward), and these again

---

[1] *Infra,* Chap. III.   [2] *Op. cit.,* p. 104.
[3] E.g. in the case of Chichester (1298). *Parl. Writs,* i, p. 76.
[4] *Parl. Writs,* i, p. 49.

elected Aschewy and Hereford and appointed their sureties. The double process of election is puzzling, but it appears to have been exceptional and may very probably be explained by the peculiar circumstances of the time. Since 1285, the citizens had been deprived of their liberties, and the city placed in the custody of a royal warden, John le Breton.[1] As the first election apparently took place without reference to the warden, the second may have been the result of his refusal to recognize its validity. It may even have been by his orders and in the hope of reversing the original election that six instead of four citizens attended from each ward.[2]

The document printed, with a note by Miss Jeffries-Davis, in the *Bulletin of the Institute of Historical Research*,[3] shows that the election of 1298 was made by twelve of the aldermen and six citizens from each ward. The votes of eight aldermen are recorded, but not that of the mayor, who may, perhaps, have limited himself to a casting vote. But the document printed in the *Bulletin* gives rise to further speculation. It comes from one of the *interlocutoria* membranes of the Husting Roll, and these, as Miss Jeffries-Davis explains, were used for noting miscellaneous business of the Husting Court which could not be dealt with at the regular meeting. Now, the Husting was the county court of London, 'the King's Court in the City', as a fifteenth-century writ describes it. Royal writs, including the writs of summons to parliament, would here be proclaimed by the sheriffs, just as they were proclaimed in other county courts throughout the kingdom ; and in London, as often in the provincial boroughs, it was found convenient to entrust the actual election to a smaller body, which subsequently reported its choice to the sheriffs. Officially, the Husting was the electing body ; in practice, the choice was made by a much narrower group.[4] The later elections of Edward I's reign were made in the same way. On 3 February 1300, before the mayor and aldermen, there were assembled six of the 'better and more discreet' persons of each ward to elect

---

[1] Sharpe, *London and the Kingdom*, i. 122.
[2] Stephen Aschewy had been imprisoned by the King's orders in 1285. Possibly the failure to appoint sureties rendered the first election invalid, ibid.
[3] Vol. iii, no. 7, pp. 45, 46.   [4] See below, pp. 30-32.

two citizens to attend parliament, for whom the aforesaid commonalty would be ready to answer. Four were chosen (two aldermen and two others) to have full power of the City, so that whatever should be done by them the commonalty would ratify and confirm;[1] but in the commission dated 28 February and addressed to the King only the two aldermen are mentioned as having full powers.[2] The writ for the parliament of 1305 ordered the election of two citizens from London; and two only were elected.[3] Yet, although these details of parliamentary elections in London are of very great interest, they cannot be regarded as in any sense characteristic of what happened elsewhere. No material has yet been discovered which throws any light on the conduct of elections in other towns during the reign of Edward I.

It has already been noticed that the towns sometimes failed to make an election when directed to do so. To discover, if possible, to what extent such omissions were general is a matter of some importance for the parliamentary history of the time. First of all, we may observe the elaborate precautions taken by the Crown to ensure the carrying out of its decrees. Sureties had to be found for the attendance of every elected representative; the sheriff had to enter the names of the sureties on his return. If none were forthcoming the sheriff was allowed to take over some of the representative's chattels as security. Any elected representative who was unable to attend from illness or other cause was obliged to send his excuses to the sheriff. But these precautions to ensure the attendance of elected deputies did not meet the case where a town simply omitted to make any election at all. The abandonment, during Edward I's reign, of the direct individual summons to the towns in favour of a general summons meant that the sheriff must be the ultimate arbiter as to which towns should be called to parliament and which should not. The interpretation which the sheriff would put upon the words 'every city and borough within your bailiwick' depended upon himself. Modern scholarship has failed to find any satisfactory general defini-

---

[1] *Cal. Letter Book C.*, pp. 59–60.
[2] *Parl. Writs*, i, p. 85.   [3] *Cal. Letter Book C.*, p. 142.

tion for a thirteenth-century borough, and it is hardly possible that Edward I's sheriffs, living at a time when the borough was still in process of formation, were able to apply any general technical test to the words of the King's writ. The fact that they did not do so seems abundantly proved by an examination of the returns. For example, the sheriff of Cornwall, in 1295, sent the summons to an insignificant little merchant community such as Tregony, which, if a borough, had never received a charter, while the sheriff of Buckingham declared that there was no borough in a county which included the town of Wycombe, enfranchised by Henry III. It is not necessary to accuse the sheriffs of deliberate falsehood in order to explain these variations. The general summons was a novelty in Edward I's reign, and the sheriffs may well have been genuinely puzzled as to how they should interpret it. Some took the safe course of including any community that could possibly be classed as a borough. Others hesitated to send the summons to petty communities, even though the inhabitants had received a royal charter. The ambiguity of the term borough also explains the discrepancies in the returns made by successive sheriffs of the same shire, notably that of Buckinghamshire, to which attention has already been drawn.

There is, then, no general standard by which to test whether a town should, or should not, have been summoned to parliament by the sheriff. The only means of discovering which towns failed to elect is to discover which towns were selected for summons by the sheriff and which failed to reply. Now the sheriffs, as we have seen, frequently endorsed the writs with a note stating that such-and-such a town had been summoned but had made no answer. Notes of this kind are fairly frequent on the returns of Edward I's reign. St. Albans, Hertford, and Colchester [1] are entered as having failed to reply in 1305, Bristol [2] in 1302, Grimsby [3] in 1307, Yarmouth and Lynn [4] in 1302, Bath and Taunton [5] in 1305, Southampton, Andover, Odiham, and Basingstoke [6] in 1301, to cite a few examples. Unfortunately, these notes

---

[1] *Parl. Writs*, i, p. 143.
[2] Ibid., p. 121.
[3] Ibid., p. 190.
[4] Ibid., p. 123.
[5] Ibid., pp. 151-2.
[6] Ibid., p. 100.

cannot be taken as giving either a full or an accurate answer to the questions at issue. In the first place, it does not follow that, because a town is stated by the sheriff to have made no answer, the town had failed to elect. Colchester, as we have seen, returned at least one burgess to the Parliament of 1305 in spite of the sheriff's statement that no reply had been given; and comparing this with other similar instances we are bound to recognize that owing to some delay in communication it might often happen that the results of an election reached the sheriff too late to be entered on the return. On the other hand, we cannot assume that the number of times the sheriffs entered *nullum dederunt responsum* on the returns represents the maximum number of failures to elect. As Riess[1] and Pasquet[2] point out, the sheriff often passed over in silence the fact that his summons had been ignored. Riess has put forward a convincing argument to show that the sheriff generally jotted down on the back of the writ abbreviated forms of the names of towns, or of hundreds or liberties containing towns, to which he had sent a summons. A comparison of these notes with the returns shows that a considerable number of towns failed to make any return.[3] The list of such towns includes, as Pasquet points out, not only small country towns, but important centres such as Bristol.

From these facts some historians have deduced a general reluctance to attend parliament on the part of the towns, coupled with very frequent evasions of the onerous duty of making elections. It does not seem clear that the evidence is sufficient to warrant such a conclusion. That attendance at the King's court was regarded by the thirteenth-century burgess as a privilege is a view which has long since been dispelled; but it is going too far in the other direction to suppose that so effective an administration as that of Edward I would be content with widespread evasion.[4] There are seven parliaments in Edward I's reign the returns for which are

---

[1] Op. cit., pp. 18–19. [2] Op. cit., p. 160.
[3] E.g. the case of Yorkshire quoted by Pasquet, op. cit., p. 160.
[4] Cf. Mr. J. G. Edwards's article on 'The Personnel of the Commons in Parliament under Edward I and Edward II' in *Essays in Medieval History presented to Thomas Frederick Tout*, pp. 197–214.

complete enough to allow of their being used as evidence. An examination of these seven lists gives us the following results. Twenty-two towns are known to have made elections to each of these seven parliaments. The twenty-two are Bedford, Cambridge, Derby, Barnstaple, Exeter, Totnes, Colchester, Hereford, Leominster, Huntingdon, Leicester, Lincoln, Norwich, Nottingham, Oxford, Shrewsbury, Bridgwater, Winchester, Ipswich, Warwick, Salisbury, and Worcester. Thirteen others are absent from the lists only when the returns have been lost. These are Reading,[1] Bodmin, Launceston,[2] Carlisle,[3] Gloucester,[4] Rochester,[5] Northampton,[6] Newcastle-on-Tyne,[7] Guildford, Southwark,[8] Appleby,[9] Scarborough, York.[10] A few important towns apparently failed to make a return to one of these seven parliaments. There is no return from Canterbury in 1301, from Bristol, Dorchester, Lynn, or Chippenham in 1302, from Coventry or Grimsby in 1307. Yarmouth, Southampton, and Portsmouth twice failed to make returns. But the great majority of those towns which several times failed to return must have been insignificant villages, judged even by contemporary standards. Cockermouth, Egremont, Torrington, Ledbury, Axbridge, are typical names drawn from the list of those whose absences outweigh their attendances. An analysis of all the lists of returns suggests experiment on the part of the sheriffs rather than persistent evasion on the part of the towns. The sheriffs seem to have been feeling their way towards a workable interpretation of the words of the writ. At first many of them tried to cast their nets as widely as possible, but a few years' experience usually convinced them that no good purpose was served by attempting to impose the strain of representation upon villages unable to sustain it materially.

---

[1] Berks. returns missing 1298.
[2] Cornwall returns missing 1301, defaced 1306.
[3] Cumberland returns missing 1298, 1301, 1307.
[4] Return for Gloucester missing 1301.   [5] Kent returns missing 1302.
[6] Northamptonshire returns lost 1307.
[7] Northumberland returns missing 1301.
[8] Surrey returns missing 1306.
[9] Westmorland returns missing 1301 and 1306.
[10] Yorkshire returns missing 1302.

Consequently a great number of the towns which have been described as evading the summonses of Edward I's reign disappear altogether from later lists. It is certainly unjustifiable to base generalizations as to the reluctance of the medieval burgess to attend parliament on facts taken from a reign which was inevitably a period of experiment.

Riess argues that those towns which eventually escaped parliamentary obligations were, as a rule, those which received the summons, not directly from the sheriff, but from the bailiff of the liberty or hundred within which the town lay. Undoubtedly, when a sheriff was unable to make a return, he tended to lay the blame on the bailiffs to whom he had transferred the summons.[1] That this should be so was only natural in view of the right to exclude the sheriff which was the cherished privilege of the liberties. On the other hand, it was probably the sheriff's duty to enter a liberty and to enforce the King's command, if the bailiffs of that liberty had failed to execute a writ.[2] When the sheriff failed to use his power in connexion with a summons to parliament, it may often have been because he was sufficiently convinced of the inability of the town to sustain the expense of representation. It is true that an important town like Bury St. Edmunds sent no representatives to the medieval parliament, a fact which augurs successful resistance on the part of the abbot. Yet Dr. Riess himself admits that the counties of Wilts, Devon, Somerset, Dorset, and Cornwall must be excepted from his general hypothesis that all towns lying within large franchises or liberties, exempt from the sheriff's jurisdiction, ultimately escaped representation. We know

[1] Examples quoted by Riess, op. cit., pp. 32–5.

[2] The evidence on this point is not clear. Most of the *non-intromittat* clauses in the borough charters contain a saving clause permitting the sheriff to enter if the town failed to do its duty. Dr. Tait thinks that ' even then the sheriff seems to have needed a special royal mandate ' (*British Borough Charters*, ii. p. lxiv). I have found no specific instance of a sheriff entering a liberty to execute a parliamentary writ, and that the sheriffs were chary of entering the great liberties seems indicated by the defence offered by the under-sheriff of Suffolk in an Exchequer plea of 1308. He stated that he had been unable to raise the parliamentary wages of the knights because two parts of the county were in the liberties of St. Edmund and St. Etheldreda, which he could not enter. The plaintiff, however, urged that it was his duty to enter, and cited the words of the writ ordering the sheriff not to omit to levy the money on account of any liberty. (Madox, *Firma Burgi*, p. 100).

that a small borough like Midhurst, the property of the
Arundels, made frequent returns to the medieval parliament. It is probably unwise, with this as with so many
other disputed questions of medieval history, to hope that
a general statement will provide the answer to what is
essentially a particular problem. All that we may venture to
assert is that towns which lay within great 'liberties' were
more likely to escape representation than the royal boroughs
were.[1]

There remains the problem how often the borough
representatives were re-elected[2] to parliament in this reign.
The point is of more than purely antiquarian interest, for on
it hangs the question of the parliamentary experience of the
representatives. Was each of Edward I's parliaments an
assembly of novices, bewildered by utterly unfamiliar sur-
roundings, or was there in each parliament a nucleus of men
who had been there before, who, although they could not
in any sense be described as political experts, yet had some
familiarity with the procedure of the great assembly, some
inkling, perhaps, of the real purpose for which the commons
were thus summoned before the King and his Council?
Although the incompleteness of the returns prevents us
from giving any precise figures as to the number of re-elections in the boroughs in this reign, the existing material
is sufficient to show that there must have been in every
parliament some such nucleus of relatively experienced men.
The great majority of the towns made at least one re-election
during the reign of Edward I, and many of them made more
than one.[3] Oxford returned one Andrew de Pyrie to seven
parliaments in this reign; Hereford returned William

---

[1] Cf. *English Historical Review*, v, pp. 146–56.

[2] The word is here used in the sense of election to more than one parliament.
For a discussion of this problem see the articles by Mr. J. G. Edwards in
Essays in Medieval History presented to T. F. Tout, pp. 197–214, and in *History*, xi.
204–10, and by Professor Pollard in *History*, xi. 15–24.

[3] The discussion of the subject is complicated by the difficulty of identifying
many of the burgess representatives in our early parliaments, and by the frequent
recurrences of such 'surnames' as le Clerk or Clericus, le Taillour, fil' Johannis,
&c. It is not always possible to distinguish between father and son. In discussing
the parliaments of the thirteenth and early fourteenth centuries it has here been
generally assumed, in the absence of corroborative evidence, that identity of
surname in the case of representatives of different towns does *not* imply identity
of personality.

Godknave and John Lytfot together to five successive parliaments; Colchester returned Elias Fitzjohn to five parliaments, not successive; Cambridge, Ipswich, Stamford, Newcastle-on-Tyne, Shrewsbury, Guildford, Lewes, and Scarborough, respectively, re-elected one man to four different parliaments in the reign. Eighty-seven towns were, between them, responsible for 222 re-elections. For separate parliaments only minimum figures can be suggested, owing to the loss of many returns and the difficulty of identifying surnames. It can, however, be asserted with reasonable certainty that in the parliament of 1298 at least fifteen of the burgesses had been returned before; in the parliament of 1300 [1] at least fourteen; in the parliament of 1301 at least thirty-two; in the parliament of 1302 at least thirty-four; in the parliament of 1305 at least forty-two; in the parliament of 1306 at least forty; and in the parliament of 1307 at least thirty-eight. We have seen that the average number of towns returning representatives to Edward I's parliaments can hardly have been less than eighty-six. The average number of burgesses in any one parliament would therefore be 172, and about one-sixth of that number in any parliament after 1300 would probably not be new-comers. Moreover, the number of re-elections is sufficient to suggest that the unwillingness of the medieval burgess to attend parliament may have been considerably exaggerated. Re-election in the small towns was probably inevitable with only a limited number of substantial burgesses to draw upon; but if attendance was so heavy a burden it is hard to see why Andrew de Pyrie of Oxford allowed himself to be returned seven times in Edward I's reign, or why William Godknave and John Lytfot of Hereford allowed themselves to be returned five times in succession, or why in important towns like Bristol, Grimsby, Cambridge, Yarmouth, Newcastle, Shrewsbury, Salisbury, and York it was found necessary to impose the burden of attendance three or four times on the same individual. There may well have been some instances of bribery; but it is difficult to believe that it was so extensively practised as to account for the numerous instances of re-election in this reign.

[1] No original returns survive for this parliament except those for Yorkshire.

The reign of Edward I has been considered in some detail because it is essentially an experimental period, though it is unlikely that the authors of the medieval parliament thought of themselves as experimentalists. It is largely true that every period of English parliamentary history has been a period of experiment; but the reign of Edward I is so in a peculiar sense. By 1307 precedents had been formed which were to determine the composition and method of summons, though not the functions, of all subsequent parliaments. Parliaments were still being convened to which no representative commons were called; but the knights and burgesses had, by the end of the reign, been summoned with sufficient regularity to suggest that their presence was coming to be regarded as so desirable as often to be almost indispensable. During the troubled years of Edward II the value of a representative parliament as a factor in the struggle between Crown and baronage came to be more fully realized by both parties. This realization of their value ensured that such parliaments should at last become a permanent element in the constitution.

II

BOROUGH REPRESENTATION IN THE
FOURTEENTH CENTURY

THE material available for the parliamentary history of
the towns is naturally more abundant for the fourteenth century than for the thirteenth. The parliament rolls
increase in value and interest between the death of Edward I
and the death of Richard II, while the greater fullness of
the borough records makes it possible to solve some of the
problems for which there is no material in the earlier period.
Some of these problems call for separate treatment in later
chapters. The scope of this chapter is to follow a little
further some of the considerations already suggested.

From the beginning of Edward II's reign, representatives
of the commons are summoned to parliament with much
greater regularity than heretofore. Although they appear
at only three of the seven parliaments held in the first two
and a half years of the reign, yet between 1310 and 1327
there are only two occasions on which they are not summoned.[1] The burgesses are summoned to twenty-two parliaments in this reign, to fifty in the reign of Edward III,
and to twenty-four in the reign of Richard II. From about
1310 onwards, the presence of the knights and burgesses
is coming to be regarded as a matter of course, and, as a
consequence, we find few variations in the wording of the
writs of summons. The general uniformity of summons
was part of the gradual standardization of parliamentary
procedure which was taking place during the fourteenth
century. The wording of the writ rapidly became stereotyped, though attempts were made, from time to time, to
introduce alterations. It directed the sheriff to cause the
election, in his shire, of two knights girt with the sword,
specially suitable and discreet, and from every city two
citizens and from every borough two burgesses, from among
the more discreet and sufficient, and to cause them to come

---

[1] *Bulletin of the Institute of Historical Research*, vol. vi, no. 17, p. 76.

on the day and to the place appointed.[1] The alterations in
the form of the writ, once the experimental period of the
thirteenth century has been passed, are not of great importance, and most of them apply to the knights of the shire
rather than to the burgesses. From 1350 to 1355 the
sheriffs were enjoined to see that the knights, citizens, and
burgesses chosen 'be not pleaders, nor maintainers of quar-
rels nor such as live by pursuits of this kind, but responsible men of good faith, devoted to the general welfare'.[2]
In 1357 the writ directs that knights and burgesses be
chosen *de elegantioribus personis*.[3] In 1373, the citizens and
burgesses are to be chosen from those more discreet and
sufficient *qui in navigio ac in exercicio mercandisarum noticiam
habent meliorem*.[4] It is significant of the relative unimpor-
tance of the burgesses that the famous attempt of Richard II
and his Council to influence elections by the insertion of
the words *in debatis modernis magis indifferentes* in the writs
of 1387 applies only to the knights. These words are
omitted in the writs addressed to London, Bristol, and the
Cinque Ports.[5] It seems clear that no serious attempt was
made by the Crown during the fourteenth century to impose upon the burgesses any qualification for election to
parliament beyond the general necessity of sufficiency and
discretion.

Any calculation as to the number of towns making elections to the parliaments of Edward II must take into account
the loss of numerous returns. The only parliaments for
which the lists are complete are those of 1309, September
1313, 1315, May 1322, and 1324. The number of towns
making returns to these parliaments varies from eighty-two
in September 1313 to sixty-three in 1309, the average being
seventy. An average based on the eleven parliaments for
which not more than five sets of returns are missing (1307,
1309, August 1311, November 1311, September 1313,

---

[1] 'Tibi precipimus, firmiter iniungentes, quod de comitatu tuo duos milites,
gladiis cinctos, magis idoneos ac discretos comitatus predicti, et de qualibet
ciuitate comitatus illius duos ciues et de quolibet burgo duos burgenses de discrecioribus et magis sufficientibus eligi et eos ad dictos diem et locum uenire
facias.' *Rep. Dig. Peer.* iv. 684.

[2] Ibid. 590.   [3] Ibid. 616.
[4] Ibid. 661.   [5] Ibid. 725.

1315, 1318, 1319, May 1322, 1324, and 1325), gives the figure sixty-seven. Riess' calculation that the average number of towns returning representatives under Edward II was only sixty is again misleading because based on lists that are manifestly incomplete.[1] None the less, his main contention that fewer towns made returns under Edward II than under Edward I is incontrovertible. Instead of an average of eighty-six we have an average of seventy. The total number of towns making returns to the parliaments of Edward II was 110. These include eight towns—Bishop's Stortford, Farnham, Kingston-on-Thames, Dunstable, Bradninch, Chard, Berkhampsted, and Weymouth—which were not represented under Edward I. On the other hand fifty-nine of the towns electing representatives under Edward I disappear from the lists under Edward II. But of these fifty-nine only twenty-three made returns to more than one parliament of Edward I, and only three[2] appear in the lists at all regularly. With these three exceptions, none of the towns returning regularly in Edward I's reign ceased to do so under Edward II. A few important towns are noted as failing, on occasions, to make any reply. Of these, Southampton was the worst defaulter, making no return in 1307, 1309, 1311 (August), or 1321. The sheriff of Lincolnshire declared that he had received no reply from Grimsby in 1307, 1309, or 1313 (September), but a writ *de expensis* was issued to two Grimsby burgesses for attendance at this last parliament. Colchester failed to reply in 1312, Ipswich in 1313 (July), Scarborough in 1307, 1313 (September), and 1318, Chichester in 1307 and 1315, Portsmouth in 1309, 1318, and 1319, Rochester in 1315, Lynn in 1320, and there are several instances of failures to reply from the smaller towns. In January 1315, six months after Bannockburn, the sheriff of Northumberland endorsed the writ with a note explaining the failure of the shire to make any election.

'This writ', he wrote, 'was proclaimed in full county court (*in pleno comitatu*) and reply was there given me that all the knights

---

[1] Riess, op. cit., pp. 19-20.
[2] Weobley (Hereford), Milborne (Somerset), and Calne (Wilts.).

of my bailiwick would not suffice for the defence of the borders; and a mandate was sent to the bailiffs of the liberty of Newcastle-on-Tyne, who also replied that all the burgesses of the said town were scarcely sufficient for the defence of the town, and so nothing has been done to carry out this writ.'[1]

From the reign of Edward II comes the first definite instance of a burgess refusing to serve in parliament after election by his fellow-citizens. On 2 May 1322, the day on which parliament had been summoned to meet at York, the mayor and commonalty of Lincoln addressed a letter to the sheriff, stating that they had elected Henry of Hakethorn and Thomas Gamel, their fellow-citizens, to represent the city of Lincoln in parliament, and that now the said Thomas would not go, for anything they could do (*pur riens qe nous savons faire*), wherefore they had elected Alan of Hodelston in place of the said Thomas, and prayed that he might be received.[2] No reason is given for the refusal of Gamel to serve, but it is significant that the mayor and citizens were not content to seize the opportunity of evading the summons altogether, but thought it necessary to make a fresh election.

For ten of the parliaments of Edward III the returns appear to be fairly complete.[3] Calculations based on the returns to these ten show that the average number of towns making returns was seventy-five, the highest (1362) eighty-six and the lowest (1328) sixty-five. The later years of Edward III's reign show a marked increase in the number of towns which elected representatives. Seventy-eight appear in the returns for 1358, eighty in 1360, eighty-four in 1361, eighty-six in 1362, seventy-one in 1372,[4] eighty-one in 1373. The average for the last twenty years of the reign is much higher than for the reign of Edward II. There is a corresponding decrease in the number of towns noted as having failed to reply. Among the returns for the ten parliaments already referred to, only nineteen of

---

[1] *Names of Members of Parliament*, i, p. 49.

[2] Ibid. i, p. 65.

[3] 1328 (April), 1336;(March), 1341, 1346, 1358, 1360, 1361, 1362, 1372, 1373.

[4] The Cornwall returns are lost.

these notes appear, fourteen of which refer to the small Wiltshire boroughs. Cricklade, Devizes, Malmesbury, and Marlborough made no returns in 1358, 1360, and 1361, Bedwyn and Ludgershall made none in 1361. Dunwich and Ipswich made no return in April 1328, but writs *de expensis* were issued to two Ipswich burgesses for attendance at this parliament.[1] Dunwich again failed to reply in 1362, and Scarborough failed in 1341 and 1362. The whole reign shows only sixty-one failures to reply in fifty full parliaments. It was natural that this should be so. A tradition was growing up in each county as to which towns should be summoned to parliament and which should be exempt. Moreover, the development of the towns in the fourteenth century, the increase of trade, and the rise of a wealthy merchant class made it possible for the sheriffs to secure returns from towns which had been unable to sustain the burden at an earlier period. The new towns which appear on the parliamentary lists of Edward III's reign are few;[2] but the small towns which had so often avoided making returns under Edward II appear on the lists with far greater regularity under Edward III.

Circumstances necessitated a number of special claims for exemption from parliament in this reign, such claims coming chiefly from the northern counties. The sheriff of Northumberland, in 1327, endorsed the writ with the words:

'The community of the county of Northumberland reply that they are so far destroyed by their Scottish enemies that they have not wherewith to pay the expenses of sending two knights to the council to be held at Lincoln; and the bailiffs of the liberty of the town of Newcastle upon Tyne reply that they are so heavily burdened with the safe keeping of the town that they can spare no one from the said town. So the execution of this writ is not possible at present.'[3]

Again, in 1332, the writ to Northumberland was returned with the following endorsement:

---

[1] *Names of Members of Parliament*, i, p. 84.
[2] Richmond (Yorks), Maldon, Fremington, Newcastle-under-Lyme, Modbury, Stoke Courcy, Poole.
[3] *Names of Members of Parliament*, i, p. 79.

'William of Tyndale sheriff of Northumberland replies thus: because the men both of the county of Northumberland and of the town of Newcastle-upon-Tyne greatly fear that the peace between the kingdoms of England and Scotland may be broken by certain Scots they cannot conveniently go away at present; therefore the aforesaid men have not elected any knights or burgesses for the present parliament.'[1]

In 1327 the sheriff of Surrey and Sussex complained of lack of time to carry out the King's commands.

'This writ', he writes, 'was brought to me by a certain stranger, in the county of Sussex on Monday, the vigil of the nativity of the Blessed Virgin (7 September); and as no county-court was due to be held before the date named in the writ, the election of knights could not take place, nor could the writ be sent to the bailiffs of cities and boroughs, owing to lack of time; and so nothing has yet been done about the execution of the writ.'[2]

The figures for Richard II's reign show an even higher average than those of Edward III. Full, or nearly full, returns are extant for the parliaments of 1378, January 1380, February 1383, April 1384, November 1384, 1386, February 1388, September 1388, 1393, 1395, and January 1397. The average number of boroughs making elections to these eleven parliaments was eighty-three, the highest number being eighty-eight (April 1384), the lowest seventy-eight (1393). The total number of towns noted as having failed to reply is, for these eleven parliaments, twenty-one, for all the twenty-four parliaments of the reign, thirty-six. The experimental period is over and, with a very few exceptions, returns are now being made to parliament with unfailing regularity. The northern sheriffs were again forced occasionally to plead exemption. The sheriff of Westmorland noted, in September 1388, that the borough of Appleby had been destroyed by the Scots, 'so that there is no burgess, nor any other, dwelling there'.[3] The following year the Westmorland writ bears a similar endorsement: 'there are no burgesses within my bailiwick because the borough of Appleby has been totally destroyed by our enemies the

[1] Ibid., p. 99.
[2] *Names of Members of Parliament*, i, p. 79.   [3] Ibid., p. 236.

Scots.'[1] No boroughs hitherto unrepresented returned burgesses to the parliaments of Richard II.

The problem of the borough elections, though still obscure, is less obscure for the fourteenth century than for the thirteenth. In London the publication of the royal writ of summons in the Husting Court, when, as we have seen, the real business of election was done elsewhere, became a mere formality which the recording clerk passed over in silence. In the course of the fourteenth century this proclamation may even have lapsed from use until revived by the stringent measure of 1406. Certain phrases in the Letter Books suggest that this was so, that the sheriffs, on receiving the writ, handed it directly to the mayor and aldermen. Thus, the entry in *Letter Book E* is followed by a memorandum, 'Be it known that this writ was delivered by the Sheriffs to the Mayor and Aldermen'.[2] Evidence is scanty for the greater part of the fourteenth century, because so many of the entries concerning elections in the Letter Books are purely formal, 'A and B were elected by the Mayor, Aldermen, Sheriffs, and the whole commonalty', while the date is often lacking. It is significant, however, that when the date of election is given it was frequently a Monday, the day on which the Court of Husting met at the Guildhall. We are told that, in 1341, the writ was read in the Guildhall, on Monday after the Feast of St. Lawrence, in the presence of the mayor, certain aldermen, 'and other good men summoned from each ward to make the election'.[3] The elections of 1296, 1352, 1354, and October 1377 were likewise made on a Monday.[4] When pressure of business allowed, it was probably convenient to elect the parliamentary representatives on the day on which the Husting met and to notify the sheriffs immediately. That the Husting was regarded as the normal place for the proclamation of royal orders is shown by two writs issued in the middle of the fourteenth century, one in 1352, directing the sheriffs to read aloud in the Husting the statute recently made in

---

[1] *Names of Members of Parliament*, i, p. 239.
[2] *Cal. Letter Book E.*, p. 145. [3] Ibid., p. 30.
[4] *Letter Book C.*, fol. 226 ; *Cal. Letter Book F.*, p. 247 ; *Cal. Letter Book G.*, p. 20 ; *Cal. Letter Book H.*, p. 75.

parliament,[1] the other in 1360 directing them to cause the citizens to assemble 'in the Husting or at some early date' for the purpose of electing four of their number to attend the King's Council. This last election was made on Monday, 2 March 1360.[2]

In 1378 the election of the two aldermen representatives was made *per aldermannos*, that of the two commoners *per communitatem*.[3] It is unlikely that these words denote any fundamental change in practice, for the real power of nominating the aldermen for parliament must always have lain with their brethren in office. The first specific mention of the Common Council in connexion with a parliamentary election does not occur until 1383, when Brembre, More, Norbury, and Essex were elected 'in a Common Council held at the Guildhall' on Monday, 18 February.[4] It is significant that this election took place during the brief period (1376–83) when the old Common Assembly (lately reorganized as a definite Common Council) consisted of representatives, not of the wards, but of the misteries.[5] The stereotyped phrase, 'certain good men from every ward', which had hitherto been used to describe the electing body, was thus no longer applicable. London thus presents an example of a division of power which was probably not uncommon elsewhere. The Husting, as the County Court of the City, was the special province of the sheriffs to whom the writs were sent and by whom the returns were made. In theory, and from the point of view of the Crown, the election of parliamentary representatives in the Husting was the normal procedure. In practice, so early as the end of the thirteenth century, the Husting Court proved to be too cumbersome and too overworked a body to attend to this relatively insignificant business. The elections were therefore entrusted to the aldermen and a representative body of citizens chosen from the wards. This body may be identified with the experimental common assembly of the earlier fourteenth century and, by the reign

[1] *Cal. Letter Book F.*, p. 240.   [2] *Cal. Letter Book G.*, pp. 113–14.
[3] *Cal. Letter Book H.*, pp. 97–8.   [4] Ibid., p. 211.
[5] Cf. Dr. Tait's article on 'The Common Council of the Borough' in *English Historical Review*, xlvi, pp. 1–29.

of Richard II, with the newly organized Common Council. The formal proceedings in the Husting either lapsed or ceased to have any real significance until, as will be shown, they were revived by Act of Parliament early in the fifteenth century.

Only two other towns in the fourteenth century shared with London the privileges of county rank. Bristol became a county in 1373, York in 1398. Both these towns were thus exempt from the control of the sheriff of the counties in which they had formerly lain. They had their own sheriffs and their own shire courts and were responsible for the return of their own representatives to parliament. But, unlike London, the citizens of York and Bristol were not called upon to send four representatives apiece. The charter granted to Bristol in 1373 stated definitely that the burgesses elected to represent the town in parliament should not exceed the usual number of two, but they must be knights of the shire as well as burgesses.[1] That the representatives were acting in a double capacity was usually stated afresh each time a parliamentary return was made. For instance, the mayor of Bristol writes in 1421, in a letter of identification for the representatives:

'We, the Mayor and Community of the town of Bristol, have unanimously constituted as our representatives (*constituimus et in loco nostro posuimus*) Thomas Morton and Henry Gildeney, burgesses and merchants of the town of Bristol, to attend the parliament both as knights for the shire of Bristol and as burgesses for the vill and borough of Bristol . . .'[2]

Thus the charter of 1373 probably made little practical difference to the manner of conducting a parliamentary election. The two representatives who had formerly been elected at the borough court would, after 1373, be elected in a similar assembly calling itself the shire court.[3] The same was probably true of the city of York, which, with one or two exceptions in the fifteenth century, continued to return two representatives.

With regard to elections in the ordinary boroughs at this

---

[1] Latimer, *Bristol Charters*, p. 76 sq.
[2] P.R.O. Parliamentary Writs and Returns, Bundle 12.
[3] Latimer, op. cit., p. 103.

period perhaps only one point can be made with certainty. There was no uniformity of procedure between the towns of one county and the towns of the next, nor even between towns in the same county. The material available hardly allows of generalization, but at least it seems clear that each town followed its own custom without regard to the custom of its neighbours. The normal place in which to hold an election would be the borough court or assembly, and the character of the electorate would therefore depend upon the constitution of these assemblies. Although no attempt had yet been made to secure orderly and responsible elections by the introduction of a definite property qualification, there cannot have been many towns in which the mass of the inhabitants took part in the election. In the great majority of English towns control of municipal affairs either had fallen or was rapidly falling into the hands of an oligarchy of well-to-do merchants. It was from this class that the parliamentary burgesses were chosen, and, as a rule, it was their fellow-merchants who made the choice. Such high-sounding phrases as ' the mayor and all the burgesses ', ' the mayor, bailiffs, and whole community ' cannot be taken at their face-value. Mr. Salter has shown that in the Oxford records the words *communitas* and *burgenses* are used indifferently to denote the members of the gild, those who ' if they were not actually a majority in point of numbers represented all the wealth and stability of the town '.[1] What is true of Oxford is true of many other English towns. It was the *burgenses* or the *communitas* in this restricted sense that usually elected the parliamentary representatives of the borough.

The records of certain towns tell us something of the methods of election prevalent in the fourteenth century. That these methods were sometimes extremely complex is shown by a study of the material available at King's Lynn. The earliest description of a parliamentary election at Lynn belongs to the fifteenth century, but an entry in the *Red Register* shows that election by jury was customary in 1373,[2] and so early as 1334 we read of the appointment of a

---

[1] *Munimenta Civitatis Oxonie*, p. xxvii.
[2] *Red Register of Lynn*, ii. 113.

committee or jury of twelve 'for making provision in respect
of all business touching the community in the King's parliament and elsewhere'.[1] The method in use at Lynn was
as follows. On the day appointed for the election the mayor
summoned a general assembly of the more substantial burgesses to the Gildhall and there read aloud the sheriff's
precept. The mayor then nominated four burgesses, who
in their turn nominated four others ; these eight again
nominated four. The jury of twelve so constituted were
chosen from the *Jurati* or governing body of Twenty-four
and from the other *potentiores* of the Trinity Gild. After
their nomination the twelve withdrew from the main hall
to make their choice, returning later with a slip of parchment bearing the names of the parliamentary representatives.
This slip was handed to the town clerk, who was responsible
for its safe deposit in the Gildhall chest after the proclamation of the names. The two representatives chosen seem to
have been seldom members of the electing body, but almost
always of the Council of the *Jurati* and *ipso facto* of the
Trinity (Merchants') Gild.

At Ipswich, in 1474, it was ordained that all burgesses
resident should, 'according to ancient custom', have 'their
free election of burgesses of the parliament whensoever the
same shall be'.[2] The words seem to imply that traditionally
the franchise was vested in all the burgesses, but whether
it was so interpreted in the practice of the fourteenth century we do not know. Nathaniel Bacon, the seventeenth-
century author of the Ipswich *Annalls*, shows himself curiously
unaware of any parliamentary traditions in Ipswich before
the middle of the fifteenth century. In recording the names
of the burgesses elected in January 1447 he adds a note
that these were the first burgesses of parliament for the
borough.[3] An ordinance made by the corporation of Cambridge in 1452 contains a similar reference to the customary
method of election in the town.[4] The ordinance declares
that henceforth the parliamentary burgesses are to be chosen
by a majority of burgesses in the Gildhall, 'and not one for

---

[1] *Hist. MSS. Comm., 11th Rep.*, Appendix 3, p. 240.
[2] Bacon, *Annalls of Ipswche*, p. 135. [3] *Ibid.*, p. 104.
[4] Cooper, *Annals of Cambridge*, i. 205.

the bench by the mayor and his assistants and another by the commonalty, *as of old time hath been used*'.[1] Here we seem to find a reflection of the method employed in the London election of 1378, when the aldermen representatives were elected *per aldermannos*, the commoners *per communitatem*. The attempts to abolish this practice in Cambridge in the interests of greater purity of elections show that it was unpopular with the governing body of the town, probably because it gave too much power into the hands of the commonalty.

At Norwich, in the fourteenth century, elections to parliament were made in the assembly or *congregacio*. This body, which had possibly originated as a general assembly of all the burgesses, was gradually becoming more oligarchic in character. As in other growing towns, this tendency to concentrate power in the hands of a few was due partly to the increase of capital and its accumulation in the hands of a small number of merchants, partly to the legislation following the Black Death which required an upper-class magistracy to enforce it, and partly to the example set by London.[2] At the election to the first parliament of Richard II, held on 2 October 1377, there were present the four bailiffs of the city, fifteen citizens, mentioned by name, 'and others of the commonalty'.[3] In the following spring the citizens received a charter from Richard II, confirmatory of all previous charters. At the same time they petitioned the King to grant them the 'liberty' already granted to the citizens of London, namely, the right of vesting authority in the mayor and aldermen 'with the consent of the commonalty'. They asked that four bailiffs and twenty-four citizens, chosen each year by the community of the town, might have power to make such ordinances and remedies for good government as might seem necessary to them. This was granted by a charter of 1380, and henceforth the assembly of four bailiffs and twenty-four citizens 'seem to be seeking to draw away power from the rest of the community into their own

---

[1] The italics are mine.
[2] Hudson and Tingey, *Records of the City of Norwich,* I. lii sq.
[3] Norwich Assembly Roll, 3 (1377).

hands '.[1] It was this limited body that continued to elect the parliamentary burgesses.

At Salisbury the same process was at work and reacted inevitably upon the franchise, though the power of government was less narrowly concentrated than at Norwich. By the middle of the fourteenth century the rulers of Salisbury were the mayor, who was elected annually, two coroners chosen by virtue of the King's writ, two provosts, and a Council divided into two classes, the superior consisting of twenty-four citizens, the inferior of forty-eight.[2] Basing their conclusion on the wording of the official return, the authors of *Old and New Sarum* suggest that the parliamentary elections for Wiltshire were made 'by a deputation from each place in the county hall at the same time as the election of the Knights of the shire '.[3] But as we have seen, the wording of the returns is often ambiguous, and it is clear from the Salisbury records that, at least by the reign of Henry IV, the parliamentary representatives were being regularly elected by an assembly or *convocatio* consisting of the mayor and some thirty leading citizens drawn, one may infer with certainty, from the governing body.[4]

At Northampton the constitution of the electing body is less clearly indicated, but the intention of the leading burgesses to secure control of elections is as plain as at Norwich or Salisbury. The fact that from about the beginning of the fourteenth century the general assembly of the burgesses had to be held in St. Giles's Church instead of in the Gildhall, because there was more room in the former, shows that it must have been attended by a considerable number of burgesses.[5] Until 1489 the presence of all the burgesses was necessary for the passing of new by-laws or trade regulations, and the Act of Parliament which prohibited this refers to the confusion caused in times past at the election of 'mayors, bailiffs, and other officers' by the presence of a multitude of the inhabitants

---

[1] Hudson and Tingey, loc. cit.
[2] Hatcher and Benson, *Old and New Sarum*, i. 79.   [3] p. 68.
[4] Archives of the Corporation of Salisbury, Ledger A. 1, *passim*.
[5] Markham and Cox, *Records of Northampton*, ii. 13 sq.

'being of little substance and behaviour and of no sad-
ness, discretion, wisdom, nor reason'.[1] It may have been
on account of the unusually democratic nature of their
general assembly that the leading burgesses passed, in
1382, a regulation which, if observed, would have secured
them effective control of at least one of the parliamentary
representatives.

'At a congregation held in the Church aforesaid (St. Giles's) on
Tuesday in Easter week in the time of Lawrence Haddon, Mayor,
Simon Daventre and Richard Rawlyns were elected burgesses for
the parliament to be held at Westminster on the morrow of
St. John before the Latin Gate, then next ensuing, and further-
more *it was then ordained that everyone last holding the office of
mayor of Northampton should be hereafter elected burgess of Parliament* if he shall not have discharged the office of burgess before,
the office of the mayoralty aforesaid being no hindrance.'[2]

This attempt to restrict the choice of the assembly does
not, however, appear to have been successful. On one occasion only before 1489 do the records show the return
of the ex-mayor as one of the parliamentary burgesses.

A petition from the citizens of Rochester to Henry IV,
in 1410, reveals a curious custom which might occasionally do away with the necessity for an election. In reply
to a royal command to pay the wages of the parliamentary
representatives of the town, the bailiff replied that the citizens of Rochester had a custom, which was also a custom of
their ancestors from time immemorial (*a tempore cuius con-
trarii memoria non extitur*), that if any stranger, not born in the
city, should take up his residence there, become a freeman of
the city and enjoy its privileges and franchises, he should
serve once in parliament, as a representative of the town, at
his own expense.[3] With this may be compared the arrange-

---

[1] Ibid. i, p. 101.

[2] *Liber Custumarum*, ed. Markham, p. 56 (the italics are mine).

[3] P.R.O. Parliamentary Writs and Returns, C. 219, Bundle 10: '. . . si aliquis
ligius domini regis forinsecus et non de eadem ciuitate natus ueniat infra
ciuitatem predictam ad essendum liberum ciuem domini regis necnon ad gauden-
dum et utendum omnibus et singulis libertatibus et franchesiis ciuitatis predicte,
debet una uice . . . transire ad parliamentum domini regis quando summoneri
contigerit, et ibidem expectare durante eodem parliamento sumptibus suis propriis
et expensis pro communitate ciuitatis predicte.'

ment made at Ipswich in 1469, whereby John Alfray of
Hindley, elected to the York parliament which was subsequently prorogued *sine die*, agreed to serve without payment 'in consideration of his admission to be free burgess
of this town.'[1] It would be interesting to know the origin
of this Rochester custom, no trace of which has been
discovered in the records of the neighbouring town of Canterbury. As a device for saving the community the burden
of parliamentary wages it may well have been adopted
elsewhere by some of the smaller towns.

The evidence, incomplete though it is, is all in support
of the conclusion that during the fourteenth century the
election of parliamentary burgesses was in nearly all towns
the exclusive privilege of a few of the wealthier citizens.
The parliamentary franchise was only one, and by no
means the most important, of the many powers and privileges which were gradually falling into the hands of the
capitalist class. Yet it can hardly be maintained that, in
this matter of the franchise, the wealthier citizens were
combining to deprive their fellow-burgesses of their
rights. The municipal records of the fourteenth century
afford no single instance of a dispute over the right to
take part in an election to parliament. There is no evidence to suggest that the ordinary townsman showed any
reluctance to leave the choosing of parliamentary burgesses
to those responsible for the government of the town. If
the leaders in the great cities had by the end of the century
acquired some sense of the value of representation, it was,
so far as we can judge, a conception still foreign to the
mass of the urban population.

In an age when election to parliament was not widely
recognized as a privilege we shall not expect to find many
instances of outside interference with elections. With
some exceptions, it is not until the next century that
partisans are found seeking election for themselves or
their nominees in the towns. Yet many who were not
burgesses possessed the power of interference and doubtless exercised it when they wished. Towns lying within
the liberty of a great lord could hardly have withstood

[1] Bacon, *Annalls of Ipswche*, p. 129.

him had he wished to nominate a burgess for parliament.
There is no reason to suppose that the action of the
Bishop of Norwich in laying down rules for the conduct
of elections in Lynn, which is referred to in the records
of the fifteenth century, was without precedent in other
towns and in an earlier century. If the lord of the liberty
were interested he could interfere; but the relative insignificance of the burgesses in parliament made it unlikely
that he would often seek to exercise his powers. Hardly
less considerable were the powers of interference possessed
by the sheriff. The results of the borough elections were
communicated to him and the return drawn up by him
without witnesses. The statute of 1406, which sought to
remedy this defect, stated in plain terms that the sheriffs
had in the past been guilty of tampering with the election
of the knights of the shire.[1] That this interference was
not confined to the county elections is shown by two incidents in the reign of Richard II. In 1384 the mayor,
bailiffs, and commonalty of Shaftesbury petitioned parliament for redress against John Strecche, sheriff of Dorset,
who had falsified their return. They had elected Walter
Henle and Thomas Seward to represent them in parliament, but the sheriff, because he supposed that Thomas
Seward would work for the King's advantage in parliament,[2] had substituted the name of Thomas Camel, who
had been returned to the King's great loss and in opposition to their will, and had received his expenses from the
commonalty.[3] The following year (1385) a similar incident
occurred in Barnstaple.[4] In reply to royal writs ordering
them to pay the expenses of John Henrys, who had represented the town in parliament, the bailiffs replied that
they were unable to do so as Henrys was an inhabitant of
the county of Somerset, not of the county of Devon. They
added, further, that at the time of the election the sheriff

---

[1] . . . 'at the grievous complaint of the Commons of the undue election of the
Knights of counties for the Parliament which be sometime made of affection of
Sheriffs.' *Statutes*, 7 Henry IV, c. 15.

[2] '. . . suereit e moeveroit en le dit parlement pur le profit e avantage nostre
seigneur le roy.'

[3] *Names of Members of Parliament*, i, p. 220.

[4] Ibid., p. 225.

of Devon had returned Henrys without their assent or knowledge, at the instance of Henrys himself and his friends, for the sake of gain, and that they are therefore not responsible in the matter. Although the petitioners' motive in making these appeals may have been rather to secure reimbursement than to assert their electoral rights, yet the incidents show how great were the facilities for interference which the existing system offered to the sheriffs. It was possible for the sheriff to disregard the wishes of the townspeople to such an extent that he could substitute his own nominee on the return, secure his attendance in parliament, and even persuade or coerce the rightful electors to pay his wages. Such a system called for drastic reform; and there can be little doubt that the introduction of the electoral indentures in the fifteenth century was the sequel to a long story of abuse.

A study of the returns for this period makes it difficult, if not impossible, to maintain the thesis that re-election to parliament was rare. The London returns afford an illustration of this point. Re-election (in the sense of election to more than one parliament) was certainly not uncommon in the fourteenth century. From 1355 onwards London was required to send four representatives to every parliament, and, with the single exception of the parliament of 1371, four names are found on every return made between 1355 and 1500. A study of the returns for thirty-eight full parliaments held between 1354 and 1399 gives the following results.[1] One hundred and fifty-two elections were made, but only seventy-six separate persons were elected as a result. Of these seventy-six, one (John Hadle) was returned eleven times; Adam Karlill was returned seven times; Simon Bedyngton (or Benyngton), William Essex, and John Organ were each returned six times; Adam Fraunceys and John Philipot five times; Bartholomew Frestlyng, John Tornegold, and William More four times.

---

[1] No London returns are extant for the parliaments of May 1382 and January 1383. The parliament of June 1371 (to which the sheriffs were directed to send certain specified knights, citizens, and burgesses who were in the last parliament), being exceptional in its composition, has not been included in any of these calculations. See the list of London representatives in Beaven, *Aldermen of the City of London*, i, pp. 262–85.

Nine persons were returned three times, ten persons twice, and forty-seven once only. Thus it remains true that not to be re-elected was more usual than to be re-elected. On the other hand, when twenty-nine out of a total of seventy-six persons were returned to more than one parliament, it can hardly be maintained that re-election was a rarity. The facts suggest that the Londoners attached some value to parliamentary experience, for to one only of these thirty-eight parliaments were four untried men returned together.[1]

What was true of London was true of many other towns of relatively large population. Bristol, Norwich, and York, geographically remote from one another, may be taken as examples of important towns. Such complete returns as survive show that in the period 1307–99 Bristol made at least 138 elections, but the number of persons returned was only seventy-four, that is, just over half the number of elections. Of these seventy-four persons, three were returned six times to parliament, four were returned five times, one four times, nine three times, twelve twice, and forty-five once only. It is noteworthy that in Bristol re-election becomes much more common from the beginning of Edward III's reign. In the reign of Edward II twenty separate persons were elected as a result of twenty-six elections. Taking the period as a whole, we find that the majority of the representatives of Bristol were returned once only, but re-election is, none the less, very frequent. In Norwich it was almost as common for a man to be re-elected as not. A minimum total of 152 elections in this period resulted in the election of only sixty persons.[2] Of these sixty, one was returned fifteen times,[3] one twelve times,[4] two eight times, one seven times, two six times, two five times, three four times, seven three times, six twice, and thirty-five once. Norwich reflects nothing of the increasing frequency of re-election noticed at Bristol. Repeated election of the same representative was as com-

---

[1] Adam Stable, John Warde, John Birlyngham, and Adam Karlill were all returned for the first time to parliament in 1373.

[2] The names returned by the second writ have been accepted for the parliament of 1323-4.

[3] Walter Bixton.   [4] Thomas But.

mon under Edward II as under Richard II. At York, although 141 elections resulted in the choice of sixty-six persons, re-election was actually less common than at Bristol or Norwich. The small number of persons elected is to some degree accounted for by the fact that William Graa was returned fourteen times and his son Thomas twelve times. Of the remaining sixty-four representatives, one was returned seven times, three five times, four four times, seven three times, seven twice, and forty-two once only.

If the frequent return of the same individual was common in the greater towns, we shall naturally expect to find it even more common in the smaller towns, with only a limited number of suitable burgesses upon which to draw. Calne (Wilts.) returned only six different persons as a result of eighteen elections in the first ten years of Richard II's reign, and of these six, one (William Wychampton) was elected to eight parliaments. Shoreham (Sussex), another of the very small boroughs, chose twelve different persons as a result of forty elections between 1377 and 1399, and of these twelve, Richard Bernard was returned to ten parliaments, Simon Benefeld to seven. A large town, Yarmouth, elected twenty-seven persons as a result of sixty-two elections in the reign of Edward III, and of these twenty-seven, one (William de Gaysle) was returned eighteen times. Bedford, a town in which re-election was less common than in many, made forty-five elections in the reign of Richard II, as a result of which twenty-six persons were elected. Scarborough elected twelve persons as a result of twenty elections under Edward II. Reading elected nineteen persons as a result of thirty-two elections in the same period. Of the boroughs on the whole it may be affirmed with certainty that, while the majority of the elected representatives served once only, a very considerable number of them served with greater frequency. Thus in each of our fourteenth-century parliaments there was to be found a nucleus of burgesses with some degree of parliamentary experience, a nucleus which might include such parliamentary veterans as John Hadle of London, Thomas Graa of York, Walter Bixton of Norwich, and William de Gaysle of Yarmouth. Re-election was no rarity, and there cannot have been much opposition on the part of these persons who were thus elected eight, ten, twelve, or fifteen times.

For many of the parliamentary boroughs the fourteenth century was a time of great development. In spite of the Black Death and the drain of the French war, it was, for many English towns, an age of rapidly increasing municipal prosperity. It may be that only a few of the greater burgesses as yet carried much weight in parliament; but by the end of Richard II's reign, service in parliament had become traditional, and precedents had been formed as to methods of election, scales of parliamentary wages, and of parliamentary taxation. And if the majority of the towns were still unaware of, or indifferent to, the political influence which representation in parliament might ultimately enable them to wield, at least they had developed a very keen sense of the extent to which the parliamentary representative might be used to serve the local interests of his constituents.

III

BOROUGH REPRESENTATION IN THE FIFTEENTH CENTURY

BETWEEN the accession of Henry IV and the death of Henry VII only fifty-seven full parliaments were held in England. Under Henry IV and Henry V, parliaments met regularly, twenty-two being summoned during the twenty-three years covered by these two reigns. Under Henry VI there were several intervals of two or more years in which no parliament was held. None was summoned between 1439 and 1442, between 1442 and 1445, between 1450 and 1453, or between 1455 and 1459. Edward IV held only seven parliaments in the twenty-two years of his reign,[1] Richard III summoned one, Henry VII summoned five.[2] In attempting to calculate the number of towns making elections to fifteenth-century parliaments, we still have to allow for serious losses among the returns. No official returns and no enrolled expenses writs are preserved for any parliament later than 1478, although it has been possible to discover some of the names of borough members from local records and other sources. For four of the parliaments of Henry IV (1399, September 1402, 1406, 1407) and for six of the parliaments of Henry V (1413, November 1414, 1419, 1420, May 1421, and December 1421), the returns are almost complete. Fairly full returns have also been preserved for sixteen of the parliaments of Henry VI[3] and for three (1467, 1472, 1478) of the parliaments of Edward IV. Using these parliaments alone as a basis for calculation, we find that under Henry IV the highest number of towns returning representatives is eighty-one (1399), the lowest seventy-one (1407), the average seventy-five, as against an average of

---

[1] The parliament summoned in the name of Edward V in 1483 never met.

[2] The names for the parliament of 1491–2 are missing from the official list of members of parliament, but they have been supplied from another source. See *Bulletin of the Institute of Historical Research*, vol. iii, no. 9, pp. 168–75.

[3] 1422, 1423, 1425, 1426, 1427, 1429, 1431, 1432, 1435, 1437, 1442, 1447, February 1449, November 1449, 1450, and 1453.

eighty-three in the reign of Richard II.[1] Notice of a town's failure to make reply to the sheriff's summons is becoming altogether exceptional. The only defaulting town in this reign is Dunwich, which made no reply in 1406 or 1407. Under Henry V the highest number of towns making returns is eighty-seven (December 1421), the lowest seventy-four (1419), the average eighty. No towns are noted as having failed to make a return. Under Henry VI the highest number of towns making returns is ninety-six (1453), the lowest seventy-seven (1425), the average eighty-seven. The figures for Henry VI's reign are, therefore, higher than for any previous reign, a fact which is to be accounted for partly by the better preservation of the returns, partly by the addition of some new boroughs, and partly by a steadily increasing appreciation of the value of a seat in parliament. There are no failures to reply noted in this reign. Of the three parliaments of Edward IV for which returns are preserved, that of 1467 has returns from at least ninety-six boroughs, that of 1472 from at least ninety-seven, and that of 1478 from at least 101, the highest figure, so far as we know, for any medieval parliament since 1295.

No hitherto unrepresented towns appear on the lists of those making returns to the parliaments of Henry IV and Henry V, though Ashburton (Devon), which returned Walter Denys and Richard Horston to the parliament of 1407, had made no return since 1298. But towards the middle of the century the general attitude to parliament seems to be undergoing a change. Attendance is becoming less of a duty and more of a privilege. The right to be represented in parliament by burgesses who shall be ' admitted and incorporated in the said parliaments in the same way as other burgesses of other boroughs in the realm ' was granted by charter to Ludlow in 1462, and to Much Wenlock in 1468.[2] In Henry VI's reign a number of new towns begin to return representatives to parliament. Wootton

---

[1] These calculations include the additional returns discovered since the publication of the official list : see Appendix III. The Cinque Ports have not been included.
[2] *Cal. Charter Rolls,* vol. vi, pp. 160, 232. Much Wenlock was to return one burgess only.

Bassett elects for the first time in 1447, Hindon and Westbury in February 1449, Heytesbury in November 1449,
Gatton in 1453, Grantham in 1467, Ludlow and Much
Wenlock in 1472. We must not exaggerate the change, for,
so late as 1453, the charter to New Woodstock contains a
proviso that 'the mayor and commonalty shall not be com-
pelled to choose any burgess for the borough to come to the
King's parliaments',[1] and, earlier in the century, a town of
the importance of Colchester sought and obtained a twelve-
year exemption from sending a burgess to parliament.[2] Yet
it is significant that the number of boroughs returning
representatives increases just at the time when party-feeling
was beginning to run high in England. In view of the
impoverishment of the nation by foreign and civil wars,
it is perhaps unlikely that these small country boroughs
were themselves eager to secure representation in parliament. It was not from them, but from the squire and landlord class, with its concentrated interest in party feuds, that
the impetus came. 'There be a dozen towns in England
that choose no burgess which ought to do it', wrote John
Paston, in words which suggest that the creation of a
'pocket-borough' was a matter of no great difficulty.[3] It
was the influence of party-leaders among the aristocracy
and country gentry that caused the appearance of new
boroughs in parliament, and it was mainly by them or their
supporters that such seats were filled.[4] Representation in
parliament had a value for the discerning, and the Venetian
merchant who exclaimed in his wrath, 'I care nat for the
parlement of a strawe', was evidently speaking in a manner
calculated to wound the susceptibilities of Englishmen.[5]

The towns returning representatives to parliament in the
fifteenth century may be divided roughly into four groups.
(1) Towns which were shires incorporate, in which the
election took place in the county court of the city. (2)
Towns which, although not shires in themselves, yet elected
their representatives at the county court of the shire, held

[1] *Cal. Charter Rolls*, vol. vi, p. 127.　[2] *Cal. Patent Rolls*, 1413–16, p. 23.
[3] *Paston Letters*, iii, p. 55.　　　[4] *Infra*, ch. VII.
[5] Archives of the Corporation of London; Journal 4, fol. 107 dorso. This
incident occurred in 1445.

in the town. (3) Towns which elected their representatives in the borough court and notified the sheriff by messenger. (4) Towns which sent a fixed number of delegates to the county court, either to make election there or to report an election already made. As will be seen, it is not always easy to determine, in the absence of any precise statement, whether a town belongs to the second or third of these groups, but when the town in question is the county town it may probably be classed in the second group. It is hoped that an examination of these different groups may help to elucidate some of the obscurities surrounding the subject of medieval borough elections.

The fifteenth century saw one important alteration in the writs of summons affecting the towns, which arose as a consequence of a statute of 1406 regulating the conduct of elections. The writ of 1407 directs that the returns shall henceforth be made by indenture between the sheriff and the electors.

'We enjoin you,' it runs, ' that, having made proclamation of the day and place of parliament, in the next county court which shall be held after the delivery of this writ, you shall cause to be elected two suitable and discreet knights girt with the sword, and from every city in the shire two citizens and from every borough two of the more discreet and sufficient burgesses, freely and indifferently by those who are present at the time of the proclamation according to the form of the statute issued in the last parliament. And you shall cause the names of the knights, citizens and burgesses thus elected to be written in indentures between yourself and those taking part in the election . . .'[1]

By a statute of 1413, a residence qualification was required, though no mention of residence is found in the writs. The statute ordained ' that the Citizens and Burgesses of the Cities and Boroughs be chosen men, Citizens and Burgesses resiant, dwelling and free in the same Cities and Boroughs and no other in any wise '.[2] Legislation on such matters may have been partly the result of the apparent increase in the power of parliament under the Lancastrians.

---

[1] *Statutes*, 7 Henry IV, c. 15; *Rep. Dig. Peer.* iv. 802.
[2] *Statutes*, 1 Henry V, c. 1.

Although the burgesses were still of minor importance, the commons as a whole had, by the reign of Henry IV, proved themselves to be a vital member of the body politic, and it was natural that recognition of this fact should be accompanied by an awakened interest in the qualifications of both electors and elected, and that irregularities which had been the subject of complaint in an earlier period should now be prohibited by law. The indentures drawn up as a result of the Act of 1406 provide us with a new source of information of first-rate importance. Some of these indentures were printed by Prynne,[1] but the majority lie still in manuscript in the Public Record Office. As they are subscribed with the names of the electors they provide a valuable supplement to the local records, and together with them form the basis for the group classification of parliamentary boroughs suggested above.[2]

The first group—towns being shires incorporate in which the election took place in the county court of the city—includes the most important towns of England. By the end of the fifteenth century it consisted of eleven towns—London, Bristol, York, Norwich, Lincoln, Newcastle-on-Tyne, Kingston-on-Hull, Southampton, Nottingham, Coventry, and Canterbury—each of them sufficiently important to deserve separate treatment.

The statute of 1406 affected London no less than the other counties of England. If the formality of proclaiming parliamentary writs in the Husting Court had been allowed to lapse during the fourteenth century, this Act obliged the sheriffs to revive it. The writ of summons of the year 1407 enjoins that election be made 'in the King's next court in the city by those present at the time of the proclamation'.[3] That of 1410 is more explicit. Proclamation of the parliament is to be made in the next Husting, the election to take place in the Husting Court, and the return to be sent into Chancery under the seals of the sheriffs and those attending the election. The supplementary writ altering the meeting-place of this parliament from Bristol to London

---

[1] In his *Brief Register of Parliamentary Writs.*
[2] Some examples of indentures will be found in Appendix II.
[3] *Cal. Letter Book I.*, pp. 56–7.

directs that election shall be made in full county court (*in pleno comitatu vestro*).[1] Drastic as these orders sound, it was evidently not difficult to evade them. The aldermen and common councillors must naturally have been unwilling to allow the election of representatives to pass from them to the suitors of the Husting, and although the return of 1416 states duly that the four representatives were elected 'at a Husting for Common Pleas held on Monday, 10th February',[2] later entries in the records show that the real election continued to take place in the smaller bodies. In 1419, both aldermen and commoners for parliament were nominated in the Court of Aldermen.[3] In 1420, the election was made *in pleno hustengo et communi concilio*, and the presence of the mayor, the recorder, and eleven aldermen is noted.[4] The sheriffs stated, in the return of 1432, that the four representatives had been chosen 'at the Husting held before the Feast of St. Gregory', and again, in 1435, 'at the Husting for Common Pleas held before the Feast of St. Giles.'[5]

But in 1439 the two aldermen were elected in a Common Council held on Wednesday, 21 October, the two commoners in another Common Council held on the following Friday.[6] In 1445, and again in 1450, the aldermen were

---

[1] Ibid., pp. 81–3.　　　　[2] Ibid., p. 145.

[3] Journal 1, fol. 60 : ' Die iovis in festo Sancti Mathei Apostoli anno Henrici vti vij°, maior, Rec', Whit', Merlawe, Waldern, Crowmer, Wotton, H. Barton, Norton, Penne, T. Aleyn, Renwell, ambo uicecomites, W. Chichele, Gedney, Whitingham, R. Chichele, Fauconer . . . Concessum est quod H. Barton et N. Wotton, aldermanni, sunt milites ad parliamentum etc.' fol. 60 dors. ' Sabbati uicesimo ix° die Sept'. Maior, Rec', Crowmere, Wotton, Barton, Penne, Aleyn, Rounwell, Standelf, ambo uicecomites . . . Concessum est quod Ricardus Meryvale, vintner, et Simon Seebald sellarius sunt milites ad parliamentum etc. '

[4] *Letter Book I.*, fol. 258. ' Die martis duodecimo die Nouembris anno regni regis Henrici quinti post conquestum octauo in pleno hustengo et communi concilio, presentibus Willelmo Cauntebrigge Maiore, Iohanne Fray Recordatore, Thoma Knolles, Willelmo Waldern, Willelmo Crowmere, Thoma Fauconer, Willelmo Sevenok, Iohanne Penne, Iohanne Parveys, Iohanne Coventre, Iohanne Botiller, Roberto Whityngham, et Roberto Tatersall, ex assensu communi prefatorum Aldermannorum, nullo dissentiente Thomas Fauconer et Iohannes Michell aldermanni et Iohannes Higham et Salamon Oxney communarii electi sunt eundi ad parliamentum.'

[5] *Cal. Letter Book K.*, pp. 139, 190–1.

[6] Journal 3, fol. 25. ' Commune concilium tentum in die mercurii xxj^{mo} die octobris . . . Isto die electus est ad interessendum in parliamento proximo futuro

elected in the Court of Aldermen, the commoners in Common Council.[1] The Journal records a resolution by the Court of Aldermen in 1451 to summon a Common Council for the purpose of electing the parliamentary representatives and an under-sheriff.[2] In 1460, the writ of summons was read in the Husting for Common Pleas held on 22 September, and the election was made in Common Council the same day.[3] On 29 December, 1462, it was agreed at a Court of Aldermen that a 'Husting and Common Council' for the election of parliamentary representatives should be held on the following Tuesday.[4] On Monday, 7 February, 1463, the writ was read in a Husting for Common Pleas, and the election took place in Common Council the following day.[5] Further, it is perhaps significant that the record of elections in the Husting is found always in the Letter Books, while the unorthodox elections in the Courts of Aldermen and Common Council are entered only in the Journals. The latter, as is well known, served as rough memoranda-books for both these courts, selected extracts being copied from them into the official Letter Books. In the event of an enquiry it would be the Letter Books, not

dominus Willelmus Estfeld miles et aldermannus. Eodem die eciam electus est ad interessendum in parliamento proximo futuro Robertus Clopton aldermannus.

' Commune concilium tentum die ueneris xxiijo die octobris . . . In isto concilio elegerunt in ciues parliamenti pro communitate Galfridum Feldyng et Iohannem Carpenter nuper communem clericum ciuitatis.'

[1] Journal 4, fol. 60, 60 dors. ; Journal 5, fol. 4.

[2] Journal 5, fol. 47 dors. ' Iovis primo die Octobris anno supradicto, Maior, Recordator, Frowik, Pattesle, Catworth, Olney, Gregory, Norman, Wifold, Feldyng, Derby, Cantelowe, Habraham, Hulyn. . . . Isto die consideratum est quod habeatur commune concilium pro eleccione ciuium ciuitatis pro parliamento futuro facienda. Et eciam pro eleccione facienda unius sub uicecomitum uice Billyng.'

[3] Hustings Proceedings, vol. i, fol. 43 b. ' Communa Placita tenta in Husteng' London' die lune proximo post festum Sancti Mathei Apostoli, anno xxxixo Henrici vjti. Isto die facta proclamacione etc. legitur breue pro ciuibus parliamenti eligendis etc.

Journal 6, fol. 267. ' Commune concilium tentum die Lune xxijdo die Septembris anno xxxixo. Isto die electi sunt ciues pro parliamento Willelmus Marowe, Philippus Cook, aldermanni, Ricardus Nedeham, Robertus Basset, communarii.

[4] Journal 7, fol. 19. ' Iovis xxixo die Decembris, Maior, Recordator, Norman, Marowe, Scot, Hulyn, Lee, Wyche, Phelip, Josselyn, Tayllour, Oulegreve, Flemyng, Lambard, Irlond, Basset, Hampton. Isto die concordatum est quod proxima septimana in die martis erunt Husteng et commune consilium pro eleccione ciuium pro parliamento tenendo apud ciuitatem Ebor' vto die Februarii.'

[5] Hustings Proceedings, vol. i, fol. 48 b ; Journal 7, fol. 21.

the rough Journals, that would be produced for inspection.

The conclusions suggested as to parliamentary elections generally, in medieval London, may be briefly summarized. Although the Husting, as the county court of London, was the official and proper place for the holding of parliamentary elections, this business devolved, in the course of the fourteenth century, on the Courts of Aldermen and Common Council. The formal proceedings in the Husting either lapsed completely or ceased to have any real significance until revived by the statute of 1406, which was directed against unjust monopolies of the franchise. By this date, the election of representatives to parliament had become a valuable privilege. The aldermen and common councillors, in order to satisfy the requirements of the King's Chancery, revived the proclamation and formal election in the Husting, but themselves retained the real choice of representatives, which they made in either or both of their courts, at the Gildhall, generally during a session of the Husting. The names were probably submitted to the Husting for formal approbation before being entered on the return.

Bristol, as we have seen, returned two representatives only. Elections were held normally in the shire court of the city, but the sheriff was free to make his own arrangements for the election if no shire court was due to meet between his reception of the writ and the opening of parliament. In 1426, he added a note to his return in which he stated that, as no shire court was due to be held after the arrival of the writ, he had caused its contents to be publicly proclaimed and, with the assent of the mayor and many others who were present, he and 'the more discreet and sufficient of the burgesses of the town' had met in the Gildhall and elected Henry Gildney and John Langley, merchants and burgesses, to represent the town in the forthcoming parliament.[1] From 1432 onwards, the franchise in Bristol was restricted to forty-shilling freeholders in conformity with the statute of 1429. The statute applied only

---

[1] P.R.O., C. 219, Bundle 13. The case is an interesting illustration of the formality and publicity which must have accompanied a meeting of the shire court.

to the shires, but Bristol is the only one of the urban counties which makes specific statement in its returns of its adherence to the forty-shilling rule.[1]

The York indentures state that elections to parliament were made in full county court of the city by a body of citizens ranging in number from ten to forty-eight.[2] The indenture of 1419 shows the names of fifteen citizens as electors of the two representatives,[3] but the memorandum-book, which also records the election, notes the presence of the mayor, six members of the Council of Twelve, and seventeen members of the Council of Twenty-four, as well as the two sheriffs.[4] It is possible that we have here evidence of a double process—a real and a formal election—similar to the London custom. Contrary to all precedent, four citizens from York were summoned to the parliament of Edward V in 1483, which never met;[5] but with the accession of Richard III, the number of those summoned was again reduced to two.

Norwich became a county in 1404, and the 'composition' of 1415 decreed 'that burgesses that shul be chosen for Knyghtes of the Shyre of the Cite shuln be chosen by the comon semble and the persons so chosen her names shul be presented and publysshed in pleyn shire wit inne the Cite to the Meire, Shireves and to her counseil ther beande in the Gyld halle.'[6] It seems clear that we have here yet another instance of the double election. The burgesses are to be chosen in the common assembly; but the formal presentation of their names is to be made in full shire court and it is to the shire court only that the indentures refer. The latter regularly record the elections as taking place *in pleno comitatu ciuitatis Norwici*, but the local records show that, so late as 1488, the real election was still being held in the common assembly.

---

[1] The indenture of 1429 was drawn up between the sheriff, on the one hand, and, on the other, the mayor, fourteen citizens whose names are given, ' et alios probos homines uille predicte in eodem comitatu comorantes et residentes quorum quilibet habet liberum tenementum ad ualorem xls per annum et amplius in eadem uilla ', P.R.O., C. 219, Bundle 14.

[2] Ibid., Bundles 10–17.   [3] Ibid., Bundle 12.

[4] *York Memorandum Book*, ii, p. 87.   [5] Davies, *York Records*, p. 144.

[6] Hudson and Tingey, *Norwich Records*, i. 107.

Parliamentary elections at Lincoln were held ' in the full county court of the city, held in the Gildhall '. The electors were the mayor and about twenty-five of the more substantial burgesses, ' with the consent of other worthy citizens then being present.' [1] At Newcastle-on-Tyne, until about 1435 elections were made regularly in the Gildhall by twelve *probi homines* who, in the words of the return of 1433, ' appeared personally in full shire-court, with the assent of the whole community of the town '.[2] After 1435, the number of electors seems to have increased. The indenture of 1437 bears the names of twenty-two witnesses; that of 1447 of thirty-five, that of 1450 of fifty, that of 1459 of thirty-five, and those of 1467 and 1472 of twenty-four.[3] At Kingston-on-Hull, which became a county in 1440, the franchise was in the hands of about eighteen burgesses who made their election in the full shire court of the city. In 1478, these electors consisted of nine aldermen, nine other burgesses specially named, ' and some other burgesses of the town of Kingston, with the unanimous assent of other worthy men who were then present there.' [4] At Southampton, the elections which, before the town became a county, had been proclaimed by deputies in the shire court at Winchester, were, after 1447, made in the full county court of the town, and the indentures bear the names of the mayor and a limited number of burgesses, eighteen in 1449, thirteen in 1453, twelve in 1478.[5]

At Nottingham, the fifteenth century seems to have been a period of experiment. Between 1411 and 1425 the representatives of the town were elected by eight burgesses (named) ' and many others of the community of the borough '.[6] Between 1429 and 1447, the elections of the knights of the shire and the burgesses of the borough seem to have been made together at a shire court held in the town, the electors consisting of a number of *armigeri*, the mayor of Nottingham, and eight or nine burgesses. The returns were entered together on the same indenture, which was

---

[1] P.R.O., C. 219, Bundles 11–16.
[3] Ibid., Bundles 15, 16, 17.
[5] Ibid., Bundles 16, 17.
[2] Ibid., Bundle 14.
[4] Ibid., Bundle 17.
[6] Ibid., Bundles 11, 12, 13.

witnessed by the electors of both burgesses and knights.[1]
In 1449, and again in 1450, there were reversions to the
form of 1411, but the election was then made 'in the full
shire court of the town', Nottingham having become a
county in 1447. In 1467, although, according to the indenture, election was still made in the shire court of the town,
twenty-four electors chose, in that assembly, both the burgesses and the knights of the shire.[2]

Coventry, which became a county in 1451, had made
no elections to parliament for over a hundred years. Its
newly-acquired status made it imperative that it should be
represented, and the election indentures were henceforth
witnessed in full county court by a number of burgesses
varying from twenty to forty.[3] As the governing bodies of
the city consisted of a court of ten aldermen and a Common Council of twenty, it is clear that the electors must
sometimes have included burgesses who were not members
of either. At the time of the Reform Bill of 1832, the
parliamentary franchise of Coventry was found to be
vested in the freemen, that is, in those persons, not being
paupers, who had served seven years' apprenticeship to
one trade,[4] and it is possible that this custom dated from
the fifteenth century. At Canterbury, after the city became
a county in 1461, the franchise seems to have been more
narrowly limited. Indentures were witnessed 'in the full
shire court of the City, held in the Gildhall', by about
fifteen of the better citizens.[5]

The second group of boroughs, namely those (not being
shires themselves) which elected their representatives at
the shire court held in the town, may be held to include
with certainty the following: Appleby, Bedford, Cambridge, Canterbury (before 1461), Carlisle, Derby, Dorchester, Gloucester, Huntingdon, Leicester, Nottingham
(before 1447), Rochester, Warwick, Wilton, Winchester,
and Worcester. In all these towns, with more or less
regularity, the monthly shire court of the county was held
and the election (or it may have been merely the formal

---

[1] P.R.O., C. 219, Bundles 13, 14, 15.   [2] Ibid., Bundles 16, 17.
[3] Ibid.   [4] Poole, *Coventry*, p. 385.
[5] P.R.O., C. 219, Bundle 17.

presentation) of the representatives of the borough was made there. At this meeting the freeholders of the county as well as the burgesses would naturally be present; and sometimes the election of representatives for county and town alike seems to have been made by this mixed assembly. Instances of this may be seen in the returns for Appleby. The names of the knights for the county of Westmorland and of the burgesses for Appleby were returned on one indenture. The election was made 'in the full shire court of Westmorland at Appleby' and the witnesses to the indenture are a number of freeholders and burgesses (twenty-six in 1426, twenty-five in 1427, twenty-seven in 1429), who are described as *electores militum et burgensium*.[1] Very similar methods were adopted at Carlisle, Nottingham, Warwick, and Winchester. But the procedure was by no means invariable among these towns. In 1414, no knights are mentioned as consenting to the election of the Appleby burgesses, but the names of the burgess electors are given separately—the two bailiffs of the town and thirteen burgesses.[2] Again, in 1431 no burgess electors are named and the sheriff merely states on his return that he caused the two representatives of the borough to be elected.[3] These variations serve only to strengthen the supposition that what really happened was that the more influential burgesses agreed among themselves as to their choice of representatives and presented the names at the county court. As a formality, the sheriff would enter the names of certain burgesses present in court as being electors; sometimes this formality might be overlooked. It was not a matter of great importance, since the real election had already been made. At Cambridge, there was evidently a similar double process—a real and a formal election. Thus, the indentures reflect nothing of the change which was introduced into the method of election by the corporation ordinance of 1452 (see p. 56).[4] The formal electors in 1450 'in the full shire court at Cambridge' are the *maior balliui et communitas*, eight of whom are named. In 1455, they are the *maior balliui et burgenses*, in 1478, the *maior*

---

[1] Ibid., Bundles 13, 14.
[3] Ibid., Bundle 14.
[2] Ibid., Bundle 11.
[4] Cooper, *Annals of Cambridge*, i. 205.

balliui et communitas.[1] Yet we know that before 1452 it was customary for the mayor and his assistants (i.e. the bailiffs) to choose one representative and the commonalty the other and that, after 1452, in accordance with the ordinance, both were to be chosen 'by the most part of the burgesses in the Gildhall at the election'.[2]

At Canterbury, before the town was made a county, elections took place in full shire court, held sometimes at Canterbury, sometimes at Rochester. The electors named in the indenture were a number of freeholders and burgesses who elected the knights of the shire of Kent as well as the Canterbury and Rochester burgesses. Here again we have what is evidently a formal election of burgesses, the real election having been made previously. Between 1421 and 1432 the witnesses to the indenture were always twelve in number chosen 'from those who were present'.[3] But in 1432 there were thirty witnesses, in 1433, sixteen, in 1449, sixty-nine.[4] The sheriff of Kent had a double motive for caution in making his returns after 1429. The Act of that year had confined the county franchise to the forty-shilling freeholders; and his substitution of a nominee of the bishop of Rochester for one of the duly elected burgesses had been disputed by the citizens of Canterbury at some cost.[5] Subsequent returns contain the names of the full number of electors.

A study of the returns for the borough of Derby suggests that sometimes the real election, sometimes the formal, was entered on the indenture. Thus, in 1431, the only electors named for both knights and burgesses are thirteen *armigeri*; in 1433, ten *armigeri*, two bailiffs, and five burgesses; in 1435 seven *armigeri*, two bailiffs, and five burgesses; and in all these years the election was made *in pleno comitatu tento apud Derby*.[6] But in 1449 the names of two bailiffs and thirteen burgesses are recorded as electors of the borough representatives only; in 1459, two bailiffs and twenty-three burgesses; in 1478, the election was made by six burgesses (named) *et multos alios liberos et legales*

---

[1] P.R.O., C. 219, Bundles 16, 17.
[2] Cooper, loc. cit.
[3] P.R.O., C. 219, Bundles 13, 14.
[4] Ibid., Bundles 14, 15.
[5] *Infra*, p. 64.
[6] P.R.O., C. 219, Bundle 14.

homines, burgenses.[1] At Gloucester, the number of electors named is, in some years, so large that it suggests a roll-call of the whole county court. In 1427, for example, the names of one hundred and eighty-six electors of knights and burgesses are recorded, in 1433 there are one hundred and sixteen names.[2] In some other years the only electors named are the two bailiffs, notably in 1413, 1414, 1420, and 1450. In 1467 the election was made by the two bailiffs ' and all the other burgesses who were present at the election in the shire court, with the assent of the whole community of the town '.[3] It is possible that at Gloucester the mass of the burgesses took an active part in the election at the shire court, but it is more probable that the real power of choice lay with the bailiffs. At Huntingdon the regular elections in full county court by twelve burgesses[4] again suggest some previous arrangement, probably an actual election in the borough court, though no record of such an election is preserved.

The Leicester records provide us with an opportunity of checking the information afforded by the indenture. In 1478, according to the latter, the election took place in full county court at Leicester, the electors, who elected both knights and burgesses, being twenty-four in number.[5] But that this ' election ' was a pure formality is proved by an entry in the Leicester Hall Book to the effect that, at a Common Hall held at Leicester on 12 January, Peers Curteys (who was that same day raised to the Bench) was chosen by the Commons to be a burgess of parliament, while at the same time the mayor and his brethren chose John Wygston.[6]

There seems to have been an attempt at Worcester to apply the forty-shilling freehold rule to the electoral franchise of the borough. The electors of the burgesses at the county court of 1467 were the two bailiffs and twenty-eight others, being forty-shilling freeholders.[7] There is a suggestion of a similar attempt at Appleby.

In the third group of boroughs, consisting of those which

---

[1] Ibid., Bundles 16, 17.   [2] Ibid., Bundles 13, 14.
[3] Ibid., Bundle 17.   [4] Ibid., Bundles 10-17.   [5] Ibid., Bundle 17.
[6] *Records of the Borough of Leicester*, ii, p. 300.
[7] P.R.O., C. 219, Bundle 17.

made their elections locally and notified the sheriff subsequently, we must include a number of county towns
where the procedure was probably much the same as in
the county towns of the second group. Such are Hereford,
Ipswich, Northampton, Oxford, and Shrewsbury—towns
where the election is said to have been made in the
presence of a number of the burgesses, and where, as at
Leicester, formal confirmation in the shire court must
have taken place subsequently. At Hereford, elections
were always held in the Gildhall and the witnesses were
the mayor and about twelve citizens, 'with the assent of
their fellow-citizens.'   At Ipswich, the franchise seems to
have been narrowed in the course of the fifteenth century.
The electors in 1413 were the two bailiffs, two coroners,
thirteen burgesses, named, 'and the other burgesses of
the town'; but by 1453 the indenture was being witnessed
by the two bailiffs 'in the presence of "sixteen burgesses
named" and many others'.[1]   A protest against this monopoly was made in 1474, when it was ordained that 'all
burgesses resident should have their free election of burgesses of parliament'.[2]   At Northampton, the mayor and
bailiffs exercised the power of election 'with the assent of
the whole community'. At Oxford, the indentures were
witnessed by the mayor, two bailiffs, two or three aldermen,
and from ten to twenty members of the Gild.[3]   At Shrewsbury, as at Gloucester, there seems to have been a wider
franchise, for one hundred and five burgesses witnessed the
indenture of 1478.[4]

The towns of Berkshire, Norfolk, and Suffolk, at the
time when our indentures begin, were making their elections locally and notifying the sheriff by messenger. At
Reading, the mayor and the *communitas burgensium*, number-
ing about a dozen, gathered in the Gildhall to elect their
representatives ; at Wallingford, the mayor, two or three
aldermen, the bailiffs, and ten or twelve burgesses made
election, also in the Gildhall; at Windsor, the electors
were the mayor, the burgesses, and *probiores homines*. At
Lynn, as we have seen, there was an exceedingly complex

[1] P.R.O., C. 219, Bundles 10–17.   [2] Bacon, *Annalls of Ipswche*, p. 135.
[3] P.R.O., C. 219, Bundles 10–17.   [4] Ibid., Bundle 17.

method of election; at Yarmouth the elections were controlled by the four bailiffs; at Dunwich the electors were
the two bailiffs and some dozen burgesses.[1]

The last group consists of those towns which sent delegates or representatives to the county court to elect the
parliamentary burgesses there when that court was held
outside the town. The problem presented by this group
is obvious. Were the delegates really electors or did they
merely carry to the county court a report of the election
already made? Although very little direct information
bearing on the subject is available it seems almost certain
that the so-called 'electors' at the county court were
merely deputies. The necessary formalities—securing the
consent of the prospective candidates and finding sureties
for them—must have been performed before the meeting
of the county court. That this was so in Salisbury can be
proved from the town records. The indentures for the
years 1414–50 state that the representatives of all the Wiltshire boroughs were elected at the county court at Wilton
by a varying number of electors, usually about thirty.[2]
But the City Ledger records that in an assembly held in
1414 the parliamentary writ was read and the two burgesses were then elected. Similar entries occur in the ledgers
throughout the whole of the period in question.[3] Thus we
are led to ask why delegates were sent at all and why the
return was not taken by messenger as in Norfolk and
Berkshire. The answer would seem to be that it was the
most hardly-pressed sheriffs that resorted to this device of
summoning delegates. If we examine the list of counties
in which the practice was common we find that it includes
all those southern counties which contained a large number
of small boroughs—Cornwall, Devon, Dorset, Somerset,
Wiltshire, Sussex, Hampshire. It was obviously more satisfactory and less troublesome to summon delegates from
all the nine Wiltshire boroughs to the county court on a
certain day and to draw up one return for all of them than

---

[1] Ibid., Bundles 10–17.   [2] Ibid., Bundles 11–15.
[3] Salisbury Ledger A. 1, *passim*. Hatcher and Benson, in their *Old and New
Sarum*, give it as their opinion that parliamentary elections were made by deputation to the county court; but the evidence is all in favour of the opposite view.

to await the uncertain arrival of nine messengers, each with a separate return. On the other hand, this practice gave the sheriff ample opportunity to omit any name unpleasing to himself, and it is consequently forbidden by the statute of 1445 which directs the sheriff to send a precept to every town to make election locally.[1] The common indenture for all the towns of one county is thus gradually abandoned after the middle of the fifteenth century, though in some counties it lingered on long after the passing of the Act.

From the local records we may glean some information as to the incidental expenses of a parliamentary election in the fifteenth century. The messenger bringing the writ had to be suitably rewarded. He received 6s. 8d. at Norwich in 1418,[2] but only sixpence at Exeter in 1361.[3] Six shillings was spent at Hull 'in a treat when the writs came down to chuse the Parliament men' in 1453.[4] The citizens of Exeter spent a shilling on wine at the mayor's house on the day of the election of burgesses in 1407.[5] A dinner was given to the burgesses of parliament 'at Master Smith's' by their fellow-townsmen in Reading in 1497.[6] The drawing-up of the return and its dispatch to the sheriff or to Chancery was an additional expense which fell on the community. Parchment, wax, paper, and a box to hold the indenture cost a shilling in Reading in 1485.[7] The clerk who drew up the return had to receive a fee. At Leicester, in 1332, he received two shillings.[8] The clerk's work, being skilled, was paid at a high rate; but the messenger who carried the return from Reading to Oxford in 1432 received only twopence.[9] In 1429, the Reading return was sent back because it did not bear the mayor's name (*quia nomina maioris non fuerunt infra*),[10] an oversight which cost the town fourpence.

There is decisive evidence that, by the fifteenth century, outsiders, other than the sheriffs, were succeeding in exert-

---

[1] *Statutes*, 23 Henry VI, c. 14.
[2] Archives of the Corporation of Norwich, Chamberlains' Account Book I.
[3] Archives of the Corporation of Exeter, Receivers' Accounts, 33–4, Edward III.
[4] Hadley, *Hull*, p. 442.
[5] Exeter Receivers' Accounts, 8–9, Henry IV.
[6] *Historical Manuscripts Commission, 11th Rep.*, Appendix 7, p. 176.
[7] Ibid., p. 175.   [8] *Leicester Records*, ii, p. 11.
[9] *Historical Manuscripts Commission, 11th Rep.*, Appendix, p. 173.
[10] Archives of the Corporation of Reading, Account Roll, 8 Henry VI.

ing an influence on borough elections to parliament. So early as 1413 it was, as we have seen, found necessary to ordain 'that citizens and burgesses of cities and boroughs be chosen men, citizens and burgesses resiant, dwelling and free in the same cities and boroughs and no other in any wise '.[1] Local ordinances reflect the same tendency to interference with both electors and elected. At Salisbury, in 1448, a resolution was taken to elect none as members of parliament who were not citizens and resident in the city. About 1450 it was decreed that ' as well in the election of the mayor as of the citizens to be sent to Parliament and other ministers, every person shall be at liberty to nominate whom he pleases so that no one be elected by the nomination of a single person definitely '.[2] About ten years later the Corporation of Cambridge ordered ' that no one for the future shall be elected a burgess for parliament unless he be inhabitant and resident within the town aforesaid, upon pain of forfeiture of one hundred shillings '.[3] At Ipswich, in 1474, the following ordinance was passed :

' that all burgesses resident and no others shall have their free votes in election of bailiffs and other officers of the Town according to ancient custom upon the nativity of the Blessed Virgin Mary ; and their free election of Burgesses of the parliament whensoever the same shall be. If any person shall prosecute or bring any letter or message from or of two knights or two esquires to the bailiffs or burgesses of the town to be Burgess of parliament for the town or for the office of Common Clerk . . . such shall thereby be disabled for ever from holding such place or office.' [4]

Yet in spite of such ordinances, outsiders continued to interest themselves in borough elections. In 1450, a messenger was sent from Exeter with a letter from the Duke of Exeter to the Earl of Devon relating to the election of citizens for the coming parliament.[5]

[1] *Statutes*, 1 Henry V, c. 1.   [2] Hatcher and Benson, op. cit., i. 122.
[3] Cooper, op. cit., i. 211.   [4] *Annalls of Ipswche*, p. 135.
[5] Archives of Exeter Corporation, Receivers' Accounts, 29–30, Henry VI. The entry (which is crossed through in the manuscript) is as follows : ' Item, in argento dato Johanni Lange equitando de Exon' usque Stoke under Hameldon cum una littera domini ducis Exon' ad communicandum cum domino Comite Devon' pro ciuibus eligendis pro ciuitate predicta existentibus ad parliamentum domini regis pro eadem ciuitate—xxd.'

'Sir,' wrote William Wayte to John Paston between 1451 and 1456, 'thynk on Yernemouth that ʒe ordeyne that John Jenney or Limnor or sum good man be burgeys for Yernemouth; ordeyne ʒe that Jenneys mown ben in the Parlement for they kun seye well.'[1]

'I sent to Yermouthe and they have promysyed also to Doctor Aleyn and John Russe to be (burgesses) mor then iij wekys goo,' wrote John Paston to his brother Sir John in 1472, 'James Arblaster hathe wreten a lettyr to the Bayle of Maldon in Essex to have yow a burgeys ther. If ye mysse to be burgeys of Maldon, and my lord Chamberlain will, ye may be in a nother place.'[2]

About 1459, John, Viscount Beaumont, wrote to the mayor and burgesses of Grimsby:

'Right trusty and wel beloved I grete you well. And forasmuch as it is supposed that there shall now hastily ben a Parliament which if it so shall be I pray you right heretely consider that my right trusty and welbeloved servant Rauff Chaundeler is like newely to ben maund in y^{or} town at Grymesby wherfor of reson he shud rather shewe his diligence in suche as shall be thought spedefull for the wele of y^{or} said town thanne sum other straung persone, y^t may like you for my sake in y^{or} eleccion for ye burgesses of y^r said town to graunte y^r goodwill and voys to my said servaunt to th' entent that he myght be oon of y^r burgesis to apere for y^{or} said town in the said Parlement. And such as I may do for you I shall at all tymes the rather perfourme to my power as knoweth God which have you ever in keping.'[3]

About 1470, the mayor and burgesses of Grimsby were again approached, this time by Ralph, Earl of Westmorland:

'Right welbeloved,' he writes, 'I recommaunde me unto yowe. And whereas I understonde that youre towne of Grymesbye must send up to the Parliament two Burgessis of the same, wheche if ye do so will be to you no littil charge in susteanyng ther costis and expensis; wherefor as well for the welle of youre seide towne as other speciall causys I advise and hartely requyre you to send unto my hondes youre wrytte directed for the electioune of the seid Burgessis wheche I shall cause to be substauncially retourned and appoynt ij of my Counsale to be Burgessis for youre seid towne, who shall not only regarde and set forward the welle of the same in suche causis, if ye have any, as ye shall advertise me and theym

---

[1] Paston Letters (ed. Gairdner), i, p. 152.   [2] Ibid., iii, pp. 53–5.
[3] *Historical Manuscripts Commission, 14th Report*, Appendix 8, p. 250.

upon, but also dymynysshe y^{or} chargis of olde tyme conswete and used for the sustentacioune of these seid costes. And in this doyng ye shall shewe unto me a singular pleasure, and unto y^{or} selffis convenient profit: whereof I eftsoons hartely require yowe not to faile as ye intend to have my goode wylle and favor in lyke maner shewed accordingly. Thus hartely fare ye welle.'[1]

About 1452, William Wayte was urging John Paston to procure the return of another member of the Jenney family for the city of Norwich:

'Sir, labour ye to the meyer that John Dam or William Jenney be burgeys for the cetye of Norwych, telle them that he may be yt as well as Yonge is of Brystowe[2] and as the Recordour of Coventre is for the cite of Coventre, and it so in many places in Ingland.'[3]

The mingling of blandishment and threats in these letters was by no means always successful in attaining its object. Wayte's letter to John Paston failed to secure the election of either Jenney or Limnor at Yarmouth, and in spite of James Arblaster's letter to the Bailiff, Sir John Paston was not returned for Maldon nor for any other borough in 1472. The burgesses of Yarmouth kept their promise to John Paston and elected Aleyn and Russe; but Viscount Beaumont was unsuccessful in procuring the return of his 'trusty and welbeloved' Chaundeler for Grimsby. John Jenney was returned for Norwich in 1453, but failed to obtain re-election in 1455, though it is evident from his letter to John Paston that strenuous efforts were being made on his behalf. He writes, on 24 June:[4]

'As for this writ of the parliament of Norwich, I thank you that ye will labour therein; as for my friends there, I trust right well all the aldermen except Brown and such as be in his danger; I pray you speak to Walter Jeffrey and Harry Wilton and make them to labour to your intent. I pray you that, if ye think that it will not be, that it like you to say that you move it of yourself and not by my desire.'

The uneasiness betrayed in the last phrase proves that the game of borough-mongering was still attended with danger.

---

[1] Ibid., p. 252.
[2] Thomas Yonge represented Bristol in the parliament of 1450.
[3] *Paston Letters*, ii, p. 176.   [4] Ibid.

On the other hand, the disputed election at Canterbury referred to above affords a striking example how successful high-handed methods could sometimes be. In 1430, John Langedon, bishop of Rochester, persuaded the sheriff of Kent to over-ride the election made at Canterbury and to declare one John Bonnington, a servant of his own, duly elected to represent the city in parliament. The bailiffs and citizens declared that they had not elected Bonnington and disputed the return at some cost; but the bishop supported his servant. Bonnington served in parliament, and finally the citizens 'ad specialem rogatum predicti episcopi et eius instanciam' accepted Bonnington's claim and even handed over his wages, amounting to £2 13s. 4d., to Thomas Langedon, the bishop's brother.[1] Sometimes a borough elected a country gentleman on its own initiative. In 1483, the citizens of Salisbury elected the mayor and John Musgrove, esquire, 'provided always that, if the said John is not willing to accept this duty, then they elect John Hampton.'[2]

In the fifteenth century, as in the fourteenth, re-election in the boroughs was common. The London returns show a slight decrease in the number of those elected more than once. Two hundred and thirty-five elections were made, 126 persons elected.[3] The longest record was that of John Michell, alderman of Bridge Ward, who was returned seven times. Nicholas Wotton, Thomas Fauconer, and John Welles, were returned six times; Henry Frowyk, William Marowe, Thomas Fitz-William, and John Pekeryng, five times; Richard Merlawe, John Reinwell, Walter Gawtron, Thomas Catteworth and Thomas Urswyk four times; sixteen persons were returned three times; twenty-five twice; and seventy-two once only. As the value of a seat in parliament came to be more clearly appreciated it was natural that the number of citizens willing, if not eager, to be elected should increase in proportion, while the growing bitterness of party-feeling made frequent changes inevitable. Yet,

---

[1] Archives of Canterbury Corporation; Chamberlains' Account, 8–9 Henry VI.
[2] Archives of Salisbury Corporation; Ledger B. 2, 1 Richard III.
[3] London returns are missing for several parliaments, but the names can be supplied from the Letter Books for all except the parliament of 1401–2. See Beaven, *Aldermen of the City of London*, i, pp. 262–85.

even when allowance is made for these factors, it cannot be maintained that re-election was rare. The number of elected persons is still just over half the number of elections.

At Bristol, the proportion of re-elections is higher. Thirty-five persons were elected as a result of seventy-six elections. One was elected nine times,[1] one eight times,[2] one five times, one four times, five three times, nine twice, and seventeen once. At Norwich, the proportion is about the same. Forty-eight persons were elected as a result of ninety-seven elections. Two were elected seven times, three five times, three four times, three three times, ten twice, and twenty-seven once. At York, re-election was much rarer. Fifty-five persons were elected as a result of eighty elections. Four were returned four times, three three times, seven twice, and forty-one once only. Norwich and York alike have ceased to produce the parliamentary veterans of the previous century. A study of the returns as a whole suggests a slight decrease in the number of re-elections throughout the country, but the decrease is not sufficiently marked to give any support to the argument that re-election was a rarity.

By the end of the fifteenth century the constitution of the electorate had, in many of the boroughs, achieved the form which was to characterize it for several centuries to come. Political necessity, the indifference of public opinion, and, above all, the economic development of the later Middle Ages had ensured that, taken generally, the borough franchises should not be democratic. The great men in city and borough retained the power of nomination and inevitably chose the parliamentary representatives from among their own ranks. This concentration of power in the hands of a few made interference from without much easier of accomplishment in the towns than in the shires. Thus by the beginning of the Tudor period those conditions were already in existence which were to make possible that aristocratic control of the borough members of the House of Commons which reached its height in the eighteenth century.

---

[1] Thomas Yonge, the Recorder.   [2] Thomas Norton, merchant.

IV

THE PROBLEM OF ATTENDANCE

IN the foregoing chapters an attempt has been made to summarize what is known of the election of parliamentary burgesses in medieval England. Closely connected with the subject of elections is the problem which we have called the problem of attendance. It has recently been suggested that the number of citizens and burgesses who actually attended our medieval parliaments bore very little relation to the number elected and returned.[1] Supporters of this hypothesis argue that only a very small proportion of those elected troubled to put in an appearance, and that the figures shown by the returns afford a misleading picture of the real size of the medieval ' house ' of commons. The whole question is of primary importance. If this contention is justified, it must necessarily alter our whole view of the medieval parliament. It shows us the rulers of England acquiescing in a regular and flagrant breach of their own express commands, either because they were helpless to prevent it or because they were too indifferent to try to do so. Modern scholarship has dispelled the illusion of the wise Plantagenet, eager to take his people into partnership, ready to provide the nation with a ' balanced constitution '. But however we may differ as to their motives, the fact remains that the Plantagenet kings were in a very real sense the creators of parliament. Edward I and Edward III were strong kings, tenacious of their own interests. They showed on many occasions that they knew how to bend recalcitrant subjects to their will. If they had any interest in securing the regular attendance of an adequate complement of burgesses in their parliaments, it is hard to believe that they submitted without complaint to regular and persistent evasion on a large scale. If, on the other hand, they and their subjects were alike indifferent as to whether or not the burgesses attended, it is difficult to understand why the

---

[1] Notably by Dr. Pollard in *Evolution of Parliament*, 2nd edition, 1926, pp. 316-19 and Appendix ii.

boroughs continued to make their empty elections and the sheriffs their meaningless returns. If it be true that, with some few exceptions, only those burgesses for whom writs *de expensis* are enrolled attended parliament, then the medieval 'house' of commons shrinks to half its former size, and reveals itself as a body consisting only of the knights of the shires and of some score of merchants. We must banish from the picture the two industrious and reputable burgesses from each of the smaller towns, whose voice was seldom heard in parliament, but who represented a fair proportion of the wealth and solidity of the country. In short, the 'Mother of Parliaments' is revealed as something of a fraud; and this long-famous application of the representative principle is well on its way towards the limbo of unworkable medieval theories. It is therefore clear that the matter calls for closer examination, and it is proposed to consider in this chapter some of the relevant evidence.[1]

The possibility that many of the burgesses failed to attend was suggested by what has justly been described as the 'startling discrepancy' between the official election returns and the enrolment of the writs *de expensis* issued to members who did attend, to enable them to recover their wages and expenses. Dr. Pollard writes:

'The number of members "returned" to fourteenth-century parliaments was sometimes nearly three hundred; the number of those who actually attended, according to the enrolled writs *de expensis*, was seldom a hundred and never more than a hundred and fifty. To these the shires contributed their regular seventy-four—two knights for each of the thirty-seven shires; but the cities and boroughs whose names occur during the fourteenth century vary in number from three to thirty-eight.'[2]

As the enrolment of the writs *de expensis* issued to the knights is almost complete[3] for the fourteenth century, it is hardly possible to suppose that defective enrolment was

---

[1] For discussions relevant to the subject, see Tout, *Chapters in Administrative History*, iii. 291, n. 1.; J. G. Edwards, 'Personnel of the Commons in Parliament under Edward I and Edward II' in *Essays in Medieval History presented to Thomas Frederick Tout*, pp. 197–214; and my two articles in the *English Historical Review*, xxxix, pp. 511–25 and xlii, pp. 583–9.

[2] *Evolution of Parliament*, p. 317.

[3] There are some gaps; see J. G. Edwards, op. cit., p. 211.

the cause of the discrepancy. These and other considerations have led to the conclusion that, with a few important exceptions, when no writ *de expensis* was enrolled as having been issued to the representatives of a town, it was because those representatives had not been present in parliament. They had, indeed, been duly elected and returned, but 'there was a considerable hiatus between a member's return in the sheriff's writ and his bodily presence in parliament'.[1] The flaw in this argument appears, at first sight, to lie in the fact that for certain of the chief towns of England, notably London, York, Bristol, Norwich, Winchester, Salisbury, Southampton, and Yarmouth, writs *de expensis* were seldom or never enrolled, and it can hardly be supposed that these cities were seldom or never represented. Dr. Pollard meets this difficulty by suggesting that such towns 'made their own arrangements for feeing their members without recourse to these writs', and that, 'save for these exceptions, the writs may be taken as a fairly accurate indication of the size of the house of commons.'

If we could accept this hypothesis, our problem would be readily solved; if we reject it, we are still far from a satisfactory solution ; for it must be realized that we have no evidence to enable us to state decisively how many, if any, of the elected burgesses, unaccounted for in the enrolled writs *de expensis*, were present in any one of our medieval parliaments. But scanty though the evidence is, it is sufficient to prove that such an hypothesis does not solve our problem. If our material cannot supply us with a complete list of the burgesses present in any given parliament, it does at least show that 'the number of expenses writs issued[2] is no evidence at all as to the number of burgesses who sat in any particular parliament'.[3] There is only one source, other than the writs, from which we can hope to obtain definite proof of the attendance or non-attendance of burgesses, namely, the borough records. Where we find a record, in the borough accounts, of the payment of the members' wages, we need look for no further proof of attendance. But unfortunately for our purpose the great majority of

---

[1] *Evolution of Parliament*, p. 317.
[2] i.e. issued *and enrolled*.   [3] Tout, op. cit., p. 293.

the towns returning members to parliament have preserved
no early accounts. If the records of such towns as Yarmouth, Hereford, and Newcastle-on-Tyne have no help to
give us, little is to be expected from the small towns of
Somerset and Cornwall. The nature of the evidence makes
it impossible to be dogmatic, and any conclusions drawn
must necessarily be tentative. We can, as yet, hardly go
beyond negative assertions. It is still impossible to prove
that the attendance of the burgesses was as regular or as
complete as the attendance of the knights.

Evidence from the local records undoubtedly tends to
support the suggestion that the greater towns, which are
said to be exceptional, made their own arrangements for
feeing their members, and that the absence of an enrolled
expenses writ does not mean absence from parliament.
Winchester provides us with a good instance. Writs *de
expensis* were issued to its representatives, and duly enrolled,
for eighteen parliaments between 1300 and 1407.[1] The
account rolls of Winchester, known as the Compotus Rolls,
begin in the twenty-seventh year of Edward III, but are
by no means continuous. Ten rolls, each roll representing
a year's accounts, are preserved for the remaining twenty-
four years of Edward III; five are extant for the reign of
Richard II, and three for the reign of Henry IV. Yet these
eighteen rolls alone supply us with proof of the attendance
of Winchester citizens at ten parliaments other than those
shown in the writs, the payment of members present in each
being recorded.[2] Again, no writs *de expensis* are enrolled
for Norwich after 1343, but Norwich citizens certainly did
not cease to attend parliament. Norwich is fortunate in pos-
sessing an almost unbroken series of her City Chamberlains'

---

[1] 1300 (*Names of Members of Parliament*, i, pp. 10–12); Jan. 1307 (*Parl. Writs*,
i, p. 191); August 1311 (ibid., ii. 1, p. 73); Sept. 1313 (ibid., p. 108); 1315
(ibid., p. 138); 1316 (ibid., p. 172); 1318 (ibid., p. 219); Jan. 1327 (ibid.,
p. 458); Feb. 1328 (*C.C.R.* 1327–30, p. 374); April 1328 (ibid., p. 388); March
1330 (*C.C.R.*, 1330–3, pp. 137–8); 1331 (ibid., p. 412); Feb. 1334 (*C.C.R.*,
1333–7, p. 304); Jan. 1340 (*C.C.R.*, 1339–41, p. 447); 1343 (*C.C.R.*, 1343–6,
pp. 136–7); 1371 (*C.C.R.*, 1369–74, pp. 316–17); 1406 (*Rot. Claus.*, 8 Henry IV,
m. 7 d.); 1407 (ibid., 9 Henry IV. m. 8 d.)
[2] 1353, 1354, 1357, 1360, Oct. 1377, 1378, 1379, 1395, Sept. 1397, Feb.
1413. Transcripts of the Compotus Rolls by Mr. J. S. Furley are in the
Winchester Public Library.

F

Rolls, covering the years 1375–1420. These rolls afford
proof of the presence of Norwich citizens in twenty-four
parliaments between 1375 and 1415.[1] The records of Salisbury provide us with an even more striking example of the
unreliability of the enrolled writs as proof of attendance in
parliament. Unfortunately we have no accounts earlier than
the year 1398, when the City Ledgers begin. The Ledgers
tell us that, between 1398 and 1415, Salisbury citizens
were paid for attendance at six parliaments, namely those
of 1399, 1404, 1407, 1410, February 1413, and January
1414.[2] Writs *de expensis* were enrolled for the parliaments
of 1399, 1400–1, 1402, 1403–4, and 1406.[3] Thus we know
that Salisbury was represented in ten out of the fourteen
parliaments held between 1398 and 1415, but only in one
instance does the enrolment of the writ coincide with the
record of payment in the City Ledgers. London citizens
very seldom had writs *de expensis* enrolled. They are known
to have done so on five occasions only, in 1300, 1318, April
1328, March 1336, and September 1336.[4] Notices of the
payment of wages for service in parliament are scanty enough
in the London records of the fourteenth century. Payment
was made for the York parliament of 1314, the Lincoln parliament of 1315, the York parliament of 1319, the Lincoln
parliament of 1327, the York parliament of 1328, the York
parliament of 1335, the Gloucester parliament of 1378, and
the Cambridge parliament of 1388,[5] a list which gives support to Dr. Tout's suggestion that London paid its representatives only when parliament met at a distance from the
city,[6] It is clear that neither the enrolled writs nor the
recorded payments afford any clue as to the number of

---

[1] 1376, 1378, 1381, May 1382, Oct. 1382, Oct. 1383, Nov. 1384, 1385,
1386, Feb. 1388, Sept. 1388, Jan. 1390, 1391, 1393, 1395, Jan. 1397, Sept.
1397, 1402, 1406, 1407, 1410, 1411, Feb. 1413, May 1413. City Chamberlains'
Rolls, *passim*; Hudson and Tingey, *Norwich Records*, ii. 44, 48, 51.

[2] Archives of Salisbury Corporation, Ledgers A. 1 and B. 2.

[3] *C.C.R.* 1399–1402, pp. 109, 331; *C.C.R.* 1402–04, p. 367; *Names of
Members of Parliament*, i, p. 266; *Rot. Claus.* 8 Henry iv, m. 17 d.

[4] *Names of Members of Parliament*, i, pp. 10–12; *Parl. Writs*, ii. 1, p. 219;
C.C.R., 1327–30, p. 388; ibid., 1333–7, pp. 662, 707.

[5] *Cal. Letter Book E.*, pp. 33, 71; *Cal. Letter Book D.*, p. 20; *Cal. Plea and
Memoranda Rolls*, i, p. 30; *Cal. Letter Book E.*, pp. 225, 281; *Cal. Letter Book
H.*, pp. 108, 346.

[6] Tout, op. cit., iii. 291–3; *infra*, p. 84.

times that London's representatives appeared in parliament. London is, admittedly, exceptional; but, perhaps, in this matter less exceptional than has sometimes been supposed.

It has been shown that London, Norwich, Winchester, and Salisbury, for one reason or another, paid their representatives without having writs *de expensis* enrolled. These towns, with the others already referred to, are said to be exceptions. But there are a number of towns, not included in the list of exceptions, which can be proved to have done likewise. The preservation of valuable records at Exeter makes it possible to draw some conclusions as to the practice there. Between 1295 and 1414, the representatives of Exeter had thirty-two writs *de expensis* enrolled.[1] But, just as at Salisbury, local records of payments to members seldom coincide with the enrolment of writs. The Receivers' Accounts, which run in a fairly continuous series from 1331 onwards,[2] contain notes of the payment of citizens for attendance at thirty-six parliaments, only five of which coincide with those for which writs are enrolled.[3] Thus the total of known attendances for Exeter is raised from the thirty-two shown by the writs to sixty-three in all.

At Canterbury, though the ancient accounts are much less full than at Exeter, we find traces of a similar state of affairs. The first volume of Chamberlains' Accounts opens

[1] 1305 (*C.C.R.*, 1302–7, p. 330); 1307 (*Parl. Writs*, i, p. 191); Aug. 1311 (ibid., ii. 1, p. 73); Sept. 1313 (ibid., p. 108); 1314 (ibid., p. 126); 1318 (ibid., p. 219); 1319 (*C.C.R.*, 1318–23, p. 139); 1321 (ibid., p. 487); Feb. 1328 (*C.C.R.*, 1327–30, p. 374); April 1328 (ibid., p. 388); Dec. 1332 (*C.C.R.*, 1333–7, p. 95); 1335 (ibid., p. 500); Jan. 1337 (*C.C.R.*, 1337–9, p. 114); Feb. 1338 (ibid., pp. 388–9); Jan. 1340 (*C.C.R.*, 1339–41, p. 447); March 1340 (ibid., p. 468); July 1340 (ibid., p. 493); Jan. 1348 (*C.C.R.*, 1346–9, p. 495); March 1348 (ibid., pp. 511–12); 1351 (*C.C.R.*, 1349–54, p. 358); 1352 (ibid., pp. 468–9); 1353 (ibid., p. 620); 1354 (*C.C.R.*, 1354–60, p. 72); 1362 (*C.C.R.*, 1360–4, pp. 440–1); 1366 (*C.C.R.*, 1364–8, p. 169); Nov. 1380 (*C.C.R.*, 1377–81, p. 498); May 1382 (*C.C.R.*, 1381–5, p. 134); April 1384 (ibid., p. 454); 1386 (*C.C.R.*, 1385–9, p. 300); Jan. 1390 (*C.C.R.*, 1389–92, p. 180); 1400–1 (*Names of Members of Parliament*, i, p. 260); April 1414 (ibid., p. 281).

[2] *Hist. MSS. Comm., Report on the Records of the City of Exeter* (1916), p. 409.

[3] Archives of Exeter Corporation, Receivers' Accounts, *passim*. The parliaments are those of 1343, Jan. 1348, March 1348, 1351, 1352, 1355, 1358, 1368, 1369, Feb. 1371, 1372, 1373, 1376, Jan. 1377, 1379, 1381, Nov. 1384, 1385, 1386, Feb. 1388, Sept. 1388, Jan. 1390, 1391, 1393, 1394, 1395, Sept. 1397, 1399, Sept. 1402, 1403–4, Oct. 1404, 1406, 1407, 1410, Feb. 1413 and May 1413.

with the year 1393. These accounts record the payment of citizens for attendance at fourteen parliaments between 1393 and 1415.[1] The enrolled writs *de expensis* prove the attendance of Canterbury citizens at twenty-two parliaments before 1393, and at six after 1393.[2] Four of these last six coincide with the entries of payments in the Account Books, thus leaving ten parliaments for which no writs were enrolled, but which were undoubtedly attended by Canterbury's representatives, the total of proved attendances for the city being thus brought up to thirty-eight.

The remarkable series of records preserved at King's Lynn affords similar evidence. Thirty-four of the annual Chamberlains' Rolls for the reign of Edward III have been preserved, the earliest belonging to the year 1327; six are extant for the reign of Richard II, and one for the reign of Henry IV. Supplementing these with the Assembly or Gild Hall Rolls, one of which has been preserved for Richard II's reign, and four for Henry IV's reign, we obtain definite proof of the attendance of Lynn burgesses at thirty-four parliaments between 1327 and 1413.[3] But, according to the enrolments, writs *de expensis* were issued to Lynn burgesses nine times only in the whole of the fourteenth century, and only twice does the local record of payment coincide with the enrolment of a writ.[4] Thus, we have proof that the

---

[1] 1393, 1395, Jan. 1397, 1399, 1401, Sept. 1402, 1403–4, 1406, 1407, 1410, 1411, Feb. 1413, May 1413, April 1414.

[2] 1305 (*C.C.R.*, 1302–7, p. 330); Aug. 1311 (*Parl. Writs*, ii. 1, p. 73); Sept. 1313 (ibid., p. 108); 1315 (ibid., p. 138); 1318 (ibid., p. 219); 1320 (*C.C.R.*, 1318–23, p. 338); Jan. 1327 (*Parl. Writs*, ii. 1, p. 458); Feb. 1328 (*C.C.R.*, 1327–30, p. 374); April 1328 (ibid., p. 388); Nov. 1330 (*C.C.R.*, 1330–3, p. 177); Feb. 1334 (*C.C.R.*, 1333–7, p. 304); Oct. 1339 (*C.C.R.*, 1339–41, p. 275); 1344 (*C.C.R.*, 1343–6, p. 44); 1351 (*C.C.R.*, 1349–54, p. 358); 1352 (ibid., p. 468); 1353 (ibid., p. 620); June 1371 (*C.C.R.*, 1369–74, p. 316); 1373 (ibid., p. 612); Jan. 1380 (*C.C.R.*, 1377–81, p. 357); 1386 (*C.C.R.*, 1385–9, p. 300); Feb. 1388 (ibid., p. 496); 1394 (*C.C.R.*, 1392–6, p. 278); Sept. 1397 (*C.C.R.*, 1396–9, p. 304); 1403–4 (*Names of Members of Parliament*, i, p. 265); 1406 (*Rot. Claus.* 8 Henry iv, m. 17 d.); 1407 (ibid., 9 Henry iv, m. 8 d.); May 1413 (*C.C.R.*, 1 Henry v, p. 103).

[3] Feb. 1328, March 1332, Sept. 1332, Feb. 1334, March 1336, Sept. 1336, Jan. 1337, Feb. 1338, 1346, 1354, 1355, 1357, 1358, 1360, 1362, 1365, 1366, 1371, 1372, 1373, 1376, Jan. 1377, Oct. 1377, Jan. 1380, Nov. 1380, 1381, Nov. 1384, 1402, 1403–4, 1404, 1407, 1410, Feb. 1413, May 1413. *Hist. MSS. Comm.*, *11th Report*, Appendix 3, pp. 213–16; Archives of the Corporation of King's Lynn, Chamberlains' Rolls and Gild Hall Rolls, *passim*.

[4] The parliaments are those of 1318, 1319, April 1328, Nov. 1330, Sept. 1331,

borough was represented in at least forty-one parliaments between 1295 and 1413.

Attention has been drawn by Mr. J. G. Edwards to the valuable evidence of the Leicester records.[1] Writs *de expensis* to Leicester are enrolled for twenty-two parliaments in this period.[2] But local records prove that at least thirty-six parliaments were attended by Leicester burgesses.[3] Writs were enrolled for only eight of these thirty-six, so that the attendance of Leicester burgesses on fifty different occasions must be regarded as proved ; and this is a minimum estimate for, as Mr. Edwards has pointed out, even among the Leicester records there are several gaps of one or more years.

It is hardly necessary to dwell again on the example of Reading, where the records show the presence of representatives in nine parliaments between April 1354 and September 1388, for none of which writs to Reading are enrolled,[4] or of Shrewsbury, whose accounts record the payment of expenses to members of five parliaments between August 1311 and

Feb. 1334, 1335, Sept. 1336, March 1340. *Parl. Writs*, ii. 1, p. 219 ; *C.C.R.*, 1318–23, p. 139; *C.C.R.*, 1327–30, p. 388 ; *C.C.R.*, 1330–3, pp. 177, 412 ; *C.C.R.*, 1333–7, pp. 304, 500, 707 ; *C.C.R.*, 1339–41, p. 468.

[1] Op. cit., p. 209.

[2] 1305 (*C.C.R.*, 1302–07, p. 330) ; 1314 (*Parl. Writs*, ii. 1, p. 126); 1315 (ibid., p. 138); 1316 (ibid., p. 172) ; Sept. 1327 (*C.C.R.*, 1327–30, p. 226) ; Feb. 1328 (ibid., p. 374) ; April 1328 (ibid., p. 388) ; Nov. 1330 (*C.C.R.*, 1330–3, p. 177) ; Dec. 1332 (*C.C.R.*, 1333–7, p. 95) ; Feb. 1334 (ibid., p. 304) ; 1351 (*C.C.R.*, 1349–54, p. 358) ; 1354 (*C.C.R.*, 1354–60, p. 72) ; Feb. 1371 (*C.C.R.*, 1369–74, p. 290) ; 1376 (*C.C.R.*, 1374–7, p. 430) ; 1378 (*C.C.R.*, 1377–81, p. 222) ; Nov. 1380 (ibid., p. 498) ; Oct. 1383 (*C.C.R.*, 1381–5, p. 415) ; Feb. 1388 (*C.C.R.*, 1385–9, p. 496) ; Sept. 1388 (ibid., p. 658) ; 1399 (*C.C.R.*, 1399–1402, p. 109) ; 1400 (*Names of Members of Parliament*, i, p. 261) ; 1406 (*Rot. Claus.* 8 Henry IV, m. 17 d.)

[3] 1301, 1306, 1309, Nov. 1311, 1314, 1315, 1316, 1318, 1319, 1320, 1321, May 1322, 1324, Sept. 1332, Dec. 1332, Feb. 1334, Sept. 1334, 1335, March 1336, Feb. 1338, Feb. 1339, Oct. 1339, ? Jan. 1340, 1341, 1344, 1351, 1352, 1353, 1354, 1358, 1360, 1369, Feb. 1371, 1372, 1373, Jan. 1377.   Bateson, *Records of the Borough of Leicester*, i, pp. 235, 246, 248, 267, 278, 296, 300, 320, 324, 328, 333, 339, 344, 347 ; ii, pp. 11, 14, 17, 26, 41, 45, 46, 47, 48, 60, 75, 77, 80, 91, 108, 110, 144, 147, 148, 158.   The entries on ii, p. 141 appear to refer to the parliaments of 1361, 1362, or 1363, which have not, however, been included in the above list.

[4] Mr. Edwards quotes eight : 1354, 1368, Jan. 1380, Nov. 1380, April 1384, Nov. 1384, 1385, and Sept. 1388. *Hist. MSS. Comm.*, *11th Report*, Appendix 7, pp. 171–2.   The ninth instance (1372) is taken from the Account Roll of William Catour, mayor 1373–4, in the Archives of Reading Corporation.

September 1336, for only one of which a writ is enrolled,[1] and to two burgesses for attendance at the parliament of October 1407, for which there is likewise no writ.[2] Few of the lesser towns have records which supply direct evidence; but we know that Wallingford sent at least one representative to the parliament at Bury St. Edmund's in November 1296, for which no writs at all are enrolled.[3] We know, too, that, despite the absence of a writ, Barnstaple sent at least one member to the parliament of January 1395.[4]

It may well be argued that the great majority of the towns already mentioned were of sufficient size and importance to be regarded as exceptional, and that no generalization as to the boroughs at large may fairly be deduced from the evidence they afford. Every student of English municipal history learns to be chary of generalization; and it is the absence of records for the smaller towns, such as the little boroughs of Cornwall, Yorkshire, and Wiltshire, that makes any final solution of this problem of attendance impossible at present. We have only the writs as evidence, and arguments based on a study of the writs tend to be negative or hypothetical or both. Yet it is worth while to notice some of the difficulties which arise if we assume that, with the smaller towns at least, the absence of an enrolled writ *de expensis* proves non-attendance in parliament. Why, for instance, should the representatives of Lostwithiel, a borough which made frequent returns throughout the fourteenth century, have appeared in the parliaments of 1311[5] and 1327[6], absented themselves for nearly fifty years, appeared again in 1371 and 1373,[7] and then ceased altogether to attend? Is it credible that five Devon boroughs

---

[1] Mr. Edwards quotes four: Aug. 1311, March (or. Nov.) 1330, Sept. 1331, and March (or Sept.) 1336. *Hist. MSS. Comm.*, *15th Report*, Appendix 10, p. 27; Owen and Blakeway, *History of Shrewsbury*, i, p. 546. The fifth instance (Dec. 1332) is drawn from a bailiff's account in the Archives of Shrewsbury Corporation. A writ *de expensis* is enrolled for the parliament of March 1330 (*C.C.R.*, 1330-3, pp. 137-8).

[2] *Hist. MSS. Comm.*, *15th Report*, Appendix 10, p. 27.

[3] *Hist. MSS. Comm.*, *6th Report*, Appendix, p. 591.

[4] Chanter and Wainwright, *Barnstaple Records*, ii. 103.

[5] *Parl. Writs*, ii, 1, p. 73.   [6] Ibid., p. 458.

[7] *C.C.R.*, 1369-74, pp. 290, 612.

sent two representatives apiece to the parliament of 1351,[1]
while Somerset, Surrey, and Sussex sent none at all,
although they had made returns as usual? Or that only
Horsham (a town which, according to the writs, had sent no
burgesses to parliament since 1300) should have appeared
with Chichester as representative of the Sussex boroughs
in the parliament of 1368 ?[2] The writs afford innumerable
instances of this kind, and we are driven thereby to ask
again if the gulf between theory and practice was really
so wide, if the organization of parliament was indeed so
chaotic that the king's commands could be openly and
repeatedly defied, even by those counties lying closest to
London, in the most populous and prosperous part of the
country.

Sources other than the writs and the local records help
us only too seldom. The monastic chroniclers, in their
brief descriptions of the various parliaments of the fourteenth century, say nothing of any failure to attend on the
part of the burgesses, but such a matter might well have
been outside the scope of their knowledge. Once only
does a chronicler hazard precise figures. The author of
the *Anonimalle Chronicle of St. Mary's York*, describing the
Good Parliament of 1376, says that there were present
'toutz les barones et baneretes de valew de la terre et cciiij^{xx}
[280] chivalers et esquiers et citisayns et burgeis pur la com-
munealte de diuerses cites et burghes et countees'.[3] Now,
of the seventy-four knights returned, we know from the
enrolled writs *de expensis* that seventy-three were present; [4]
so that, if the figures are exact, there must have been 207
citizens and burgesses, representing some 100 cities and
boroughs. Yet only twenty-two towns had writs enrolled
at the conclusion of this parliament.[5] It is, of course, possible
that the chronicler took his figures from the sheriffs' returns,

---

[1] Exeter, Tavistock, Barnstaple, Torrington and Dartmouth: *C.C.R.*, 1349–54,
p. 358.
[2] Ibid., 1364–68, p. 481.   [3] *Anonimalle Chronicle*, pp. 79–80.
[4] *C.C.R.*, 1374–7, pp. 428–9.
[5] Ibid. The towns were Bedford, Reading, Wallingford, Wycombe, Cambridge, Colchester, Gloucester, Hereford, Leominster, Hertford, Huntingdon,
Leicester, Grimsby, Lincoln, Northampton, Newcastle-on-Tyne, Oxford, Bridgnorth, Shrewsbury, Stafford, Guildford, and Southwark.

to which he may have had access. As these returns are lost we have no means of comparing his figures with theirs. But had there been such a great discrepancy between the returns and the actual attendances, it seems highly unlikely that so shrewd an observer as the York chronicler or his informant should not have noted it. Moreover, we know from local sources that Lynn, Exeter, and Norwich were all represented in this parliament, without having enrolled writs.

The Rolls of Parliament, from which so much might be expected, take us very little further towards the solution of this problem. Mr. Edwards[1] has drawn attention to the appointment, in the parliament of March 1340, of a committee of knights, citizens, and burgesses to hear petitions. All the knights chosen were duly-elected members of parliament; of the six burgesses, five can be assigned, almost certainly, to the five constituencies of Nottingham, Cambridge, Colchester, Wycombe, and Norwich respectively. Only one of the six names does not appear in the returns for this parliament, but none of them appear in the enrolled writs *de expensis*.[2] We know that by the time of Richard II a 'roll-call' had been instituted which must, presumably, have been based on the sheriffs' returns,[3] and though the existence of such a roll does not prove anything about attendance, it does at least suggest that the government had some interest in trying to ensure that elected representatives should attend.

It is clear, then, that persons might actually attend parliament without having a writ *de expensis* enrolled, whether or not they received such a writ. But it is also clear that they might sometimes attend and receive a writ which was never enrolled. When, in 1308, William de Boyton, one of the representatives of Suffolk in the parliament of 1306, brought an action against the under-sheriff of Suffolk for payment of his parliamentary wages, the latter admitted that he had received the writ *de expensis*, but no writ for Suffolk is enrolled for the parliament of 1306.[4] Again, the Salisbury Ledger Book contains a number of writs *de*

---

[1] Op. cit., p. 208. [2] *Rot. Parl.*, ii, p. 113.
[3] Ibid., iii, p. 132.
[4] Madox, *Firma Burgi*, p. 100, note *u*; *Parl. Writs*, i, pp 177–8.

expensis sewn to the folio, for which there is no corresponding enrolment on the Close Roll.[1]

The argument, put forward by some writers, that it was to the interest of the boroughs to avoid representation in parliament so that they might be taxed with the shires at the rate of a fifteenth, instead of with the boroughs at the higher rate of a tenth, will not bear examination. Whatever may have been the test by which a community was reckoned as a borough for purposes of taxation, it was certainly not that of representation in parliament. For purposes of taxation, the term ' borough ' seems to have been interpreted in the widest possible sense, and many small towns which seldom or never returned members to parliament paid at the rate of a tenth. For instance, in 1334, fifteen Somerset boroughs (Bath, Bridgwater, Wells, Langport, Taunton, Axbridge, Weare, Stoke Courcy, Nether Stowey, Milverton, Dunster, Chard, Milborne Port, Montacute, and Ilchester) paid a tenth, although the surviving returns for the decade 1330–40 show that five was the maximum of Somerset boroughs then making returns.[2] The same year, twenty Devon boroughs (Barnstaple, Exeter, Plympton, Tavistock, Torrington, Totnes, Totton, Dartmouth, Dodbrooke, Kingsbridge, Ashburton, Sutton Prior, Lydford, Okehampton, Bideford, South Molton, Crediton, Tiverton, Bradninch, Honiton, and Modbury) contributed the tenth, but the maximum number making returns to parliament at this period was six.[3] The Surrey taxation return of 1332 shows that the tenth of that year was paid by Guildford, Kingston, Reigate, Southwark, Bletchingley, Sheen, Banstead, Byfleet, Gatton, and Witley, although only Guildford and Southwark made returns to parliament.[4] These and many other instances show that the obligations entailed by residence in a borough were not to be lessened by evasion of representation in parliament. On the contrary, it was through the co-operation of the borough representatives with the knights of the shire that control of taxation might best be maintained. It was to the interest of the burgesses to send their

---

[1] In the period 1399–1414.   [2] Exchequer Lay Subsidies, 169/6.
[3] Exchequer Lay Subsidies, 95/8.
[4] *Surrey Taxation Returns*, pp. 1–7.

representatives to Westminster equipped with full powers
to resist all taxes which the general opinion of the commons
held to be excessive.

Finally, mention must be made of those claims to exemption from service in parliament which have often been quoted
to prove the unpopularity of such service. There are not
many of them, but why were they made at all? Why should
little towns, like Torrington and Maldon, have gone to the
trouble and expense of securing royal exemptions (which,
in the case of Maldon, had to be more than once renewed),
when they could have attained the same result simply by
failing to attend?[1] Do not these petitions suggest that
evasion was not so easy after all, that the king's commands
could not be disregarded with impunity? Doubtless the
exemption in law was a safeguard; but if we are taking
the enrolled writs as evidence of attendance, we know that
a great many of the smaller towns were very successful in
evading their duties, without the expense of a parliamentary
petition.

The conclusion suggested by these reflections is negative.
Even allowing for exceptions, we must not take the enrolled expenses writs as our guide in trying to estimate
the number of burgesses present in parliament. Burgesses
attended repeatedly without obtaining such writs, or at all
events without having them enrolled. But neither are the
local records infallible, even in those few towns where they
have been preserved without a break over a considerable
number of years. We find many records of payment where
there is apparently no writ; but we find an almost equal
number of writs for which we have no corresponding records
of payment in the borough accounts. In fact, as we have
seen, it is the exception rather than the rule to find a local
record of the payment sanctioned by the writ. This may
have been because no payment was made; if so, the writ
cannot have carried much weight. Or it may have been
simply that the accounts were kept in a haphazard fashion
and that many items of expenditure escaped notice. We can
only guess at the reason, but the facts are a striking reminder
of the insufficient nature of the evidence at our disposal.

[1] Pollard, *Evolution of Parliament*, p. 394.

It is hard to find any satisfactory general explanation for the paucity and irregularity of the expenses writs. There may have been failure to enrol. We know that writs were issued after the cessation of all enrolments in 1414,[1] and it is quite possible that the clerk responsible for the entries on the Close Rolls was not always conscientious in the performance of his duties. Yet, as Dr. Pollard remarks, ' Official negligence is a somewhat facile solution of archivistic problems,' and though it may account for some of the gaps, it cannot possibly account for them all. A petition presented by the commons in the parliament of 1429 suggests that the clerks found the issue of writs for the boroughs not worth the trouble it involved. The petitioners state that, whereas ' wise and notable persons ' used to represent the cities and boroughs in parliament, now, owing to the non-payment of wages in certain towns, such persons will not consent to serve, and only the ' poor, feeble and impotent ' are returned, to their own great loss. Wherefore the petitioners ask that every one of the citizens and burgesses may have his proper wage, and that, at the end of every parliament, writs may be issued for them, as well as for the knights, as was done in former times.[2] The fact that the

---

[1] See the references in *Evolution of Parliament*, p. 388, n. 1.

[2] *Rot. Parl.*, iv, p. 350. ' Item priont les Communes de cest present Parleament que la ou Citezeins et Burgeis eslus de venir a votre Parleament, par les elections des Gentz des Citees et Burghs deinz votre Roialme, ount ewe, et d'aunciene temps accustume de droit devoient avoir, pur lour gages et expenses, chescun jour durant votre Parleament, ii *s*; c'est assavoir, chescun d'ieux ii *s*, pur chescun jour durant votre dit Parleament ; des queux gages, les ditz Citezeins et Burgeis, et chescun d'eux, d'aunc'ien temps ount ewe, et de droit dusent avoir, lour Br' al Vic' del Countee, ou tiell Citees et Burghs sont, pur lour ditz gages lever et a eux deliverer, come les Chivalers des Countees veignnauntz a votre Parleament ount ewe et use ; les queux gages en diverses Citees et Burghs a maveis ensample sont ore de novell sustretes, par issint que la ou divers notables persones et sages, devaunt till' sustrete des gages, veignent a votre dit Parleament, pur le bien de vous, et tout la Roialme, ore ne sont eslus ne veignont, si noun les gentz pluis febleez, pluis poverez et impotentes, et la duraunt votre dit Parleament gisont a lour propre costages, a lour perpetuell anientisment, si noun que due remedie soit purveu en cest cas. Que please a votre Roial Mageste le dit matere de considerer et grauntier par auctorite de cest present Parleament, que les ditz Citezeins et Burgeis et chescun d'eux, aient lour gages de ii *s* come devaunt est dit, pur chescun jour duraunt votre Parlement et a fyne de chescun Parleament, eient lour Br' a Vic' pur lever les ditz deniers, si come les ditz Chivalers des Countees ount, et d'aunciene temps ount ewe ; nient contristeant ascun usage, custume ou ordinaunce, usurpation ou sustrete des gagez, fait a contrarie. Purveu toutz foitz que cest Estatuit

petition was refused shows plainly not only that the suggestion was regarded as impracticable by the government, but also that the habit of serving in parliament without wages was, by this date, widespread. Nor can we reach any general solution, even for an earlier period, by reference to the rates of payment prevalent in the boroughs. The whole question of wages is discussed in the following chapter; it is sufficient to notice here that, of those boroughs which apparently failed to obtain writs, some paid the statutory rate, some paid more, and some less. It seems possible that many burgesses found the writ superfluous, or at least not worth the delay and expense which obtaining it must often have involved. If circumstances were favourable to securing the writ speedily, or if they anticipated difficulty in securing their money when they returned home, then they might apply for the writ. Otherwise, it must often have been an unnecessary formality; for we know that many towns paid their representatives regularly, with or without the writ, and that others devised means of persuading certain persons to serve for little or no reward. In a town like Oxford, which sued regularly for expenses writs, a custom of ' no writ, no wages' may easily have grown up, for in this, as in most other matters concerning the towns, local custom prevailed against central regulation. It mattered little to the king and his ministers whether or not the knights and burgesses took advantage of the concessions offered them by the writs, and so the scanty issues and scantier enrolments went on, unchecked, until, perhaps, it was no longer thought worth while to enrol the writs at all. It seems useless to try to find a simple cause to explain a complex situation. The suggestion put forward here is, merely, that the evidence before us justifies the assumption that, if the numbers present in any medieval parliament did not reach the imposing total indicated by the returns, at least they were greatly in excess of the total indicated by the enrolled expenses writs. If we have escaped from the error of crediting any medieval ruler

teigne lieu, si bien pur les Citezeins et Burgeis deinz cest present Parleament ore assemblez et venuz, come des Citezeins et Burgeis a venir a voz Parleamentz, ou voz heirs, en temps a venir.

' Responsio. Le Roi s'advisera.'

with the political wisdom of the nineteenth century, and the sovereign power of the sixteenth, we must still beware lest we fall into the equal error of regarding our early kings as incapable of foresight, and powerless to exact obedience even from the humbler of their subjects.

V

THE PAYMENT OF THE PARLIAMENTARY BURGESSES

THE payment of representatives of the shires and towns summoned to parliament under the king's writ is as old as parliament itself. It was wisely assumed that the representatives would be unable to defray their own expenses, and the obvious alternative was to make the communities which elected them responsible for the payment of their wages. The customary rate of payment came to be four shillings a day for the knights and two shillings a day for the burgesses, to be paid for each day of the journey there and back as well as for the duration of parliament. Payments on this basis are regularly enjoined in all the expenses writs from the beginning of Edward III's reign, but the practice followed was by no means so regular. Some towns held the regulation wage to be inadequate; others found the raising of it beyond their powers. Various schemes were devised in order to raise the wages or to avoid paying them in full. The theory that the burgesses were paid at the rate of two shillings a day remained a theory for many of the boroughs. Instances drawn from the municipal records show how often the rate of payment was determined, not by government regulation, but by local custom.

The normal rate of payment for service in parliament was never adopted in London. So early as 1296, the body which elected the two aldermen to represent the city in parliament agreed at the time of the election that they should be paid at the rate of twenty shillings a day.[1] Possibly this rate proved excessive, for two years later each of the representatives received instead a round sum of 100 shillings to cover all his expenses at the York parliament. This payment, like that of 1296, was made before and not after the meeting of parliament.[2] In 1314, John de Gisors and William

---

[1] '. . . concesserunt eisdem unanimi assensu singulis diebus pro expensis suis eundo et redeundo xxs.' *Parl. Writs*, i. 49.
[2] *Cal. Letter Book B.*, pp. 214-15.

de Leyre received twenty and fifteen marks respectively for their services in the parliament at York, which entailed an absence of twenty-seven days from London.[1] On the whole, the city treated its representatives with extraordinary liberality. For the Lincoln parliament of 1327, which lasted only nine days, Robert de Keleseye received £10 ; the other representative, Benet de Fulsham, generously paid his own expenses.[2] In 1389, the four representatives of London at the Cambridge parliament of the previous year presented the chamberlains with a bill for £112 7s. 0d. for purely personal expenses. These included the purchase of special clothing for the representatives and their servants, lodgings in a house which seems to have been refurnished and partly rebuilt for the purpose, gifts to minstrels, laundry, and an expenditure on wine amounting to £9 2s. 0d.[3] This habit of extravagance reached such lengths that in 1425 and again in 1429 the Court of Aldermen was driven to protest. A mild sumptuary measure limited any alderman representing the city of London in parliament, who had already passed the chair, to ten yards of cloth at fifteen shillings the yard for his gown and cloak, and fur worth 100 shillings, other aldermen to the same amount of cloth and fur worth five marks. A commoner was allowed five marks' worth of fur and five yards of cloth. Each alderman was allowed eight yards of cloth at twenty-eight pence the yard for two attendants, each commoner four yards for one, unless parliament met 'in some remote place', when the commoners' allowance was increased to equal that of the aldermen.[4] These provisions were confirmed in Common Council, but it may well be doubted whether any real economy was achieved. William de Estfeld, elected to parliament in 1439, was allowed double the amount paid to his fellows because his knighthood was said to entail additional expense.[5] In April 1450, before the meeting of parliament at Leicester, the Common Council considered the question of allowances to representatives and passed a

---

[1] *Cal. Letter Book E.*, p. 30.   [2] *Cal. of Plea and Memoranda Rolls,* i, p. 30.
[3] Riley, *Memorials of London,* pp. 511-12.
[4] Journal 2, fol. 41 ; Sharpe, *London and the Kingdom,* i. 273-4.
[5] Journal 3, fol. 25.

resolution that for the future the rate of payment should be forty shillings a day, payable from the date of leaving London to the date of return, for any parliament held *in aliquo loco regni remoto a civitate*.[1] In 1459, when parliament was about to meet at Coventry, this resolution was reaffirmed, but nullified, for all practical purposes, by a saving clause that allowance should be made for extra expenses incurred *pro proficuo et honore civitatis*.[2] A similar resolution was passed in 1463, and a week later a proviso was added that should the elected representatives incur any expenses in connexion with a parliament which afterwards failed to meet, they should be reimbursed by the community.[3]

In the prodigality with which she treated her parliamentary representatives London differed signally from the other constituencies. Although, as will be seen, some of the wealthier towns paid their representatives at a higher than the statutory rate, there is no known instance of a figure approaching even ten shillings a day, while the difficulty of raising the minimum wage required for the knights of the shire was more than once the subject of a parliamentary petition. Yet it has to be remembered that these London payments were occasional. Although the clothing allowance seems to have been granted for every parliament, all those entries of money payments to representatives which have been found among the records of the city refer to parliaments held at a distance, and all general ordinances regulating expenses contain some such qualifying clause as *in aliquo loco remoto a civitate*. Since they had to pay so seldom, it may well have seemed to the Londoners that they could afford to pay generously, and the pride of purse for which they were noted probably led them to desire that their representatives should rival the nobility in the magnificence of their appearance in parliament. None the less, the payment of parliamentary expenses, even at rare intervals, proved a heavy drain on the resources of the city, and in spite of London's wealth the chamberlains seldom found it easy to meet the accounts presented to them. Benet de Fulsham's act of generosity in 1327 neither followed nor .

---

[1] Journal 5, fol. 32.　　　　　[2] Journal 6, fol. 166 b.
[3] Journal 7, fol. 52.

created a precedent. In 1314, it was proposed to pay the expenses of the representatives by a levy of one penny in the pound on the chief chattel of every one assessed for the last fifteenth.[1] In 1327, the expenses of Robert de Keleseye, amounting to £10, were paid out of the sum of £100 received by the mayor from the sheriff on account of a prisoner who had escaped through his negligence.[2] In 1328, Richard de Bettoyne felt so uneasy about the payment of his wages that he put in a claim for a coverlet furred with minever, which had been forfeited to the chamberlains during the recent disturbances in the city. It was valued at eight marks and delivered to him in part payment.[3] After the parliament held at York in 1334, the commonalty borrowed £10 from a fishmonger named Richard Gubbe in order to pay the wages of the representatives.[4] In 1378, a committee of aldermen and commons under the chairmanship of the mayor (John Philipot) was formed to consider, *inter alia*, the expenses of those elected to the parliament at Gloucester. The committee's recommendation 'that an enquiry be made as to some better method of raising money to defray the City's expenses than a tax on victuals' was not immediately helpful.[5] In 1389, the chamberlains had nothing in hand for paying the representatives, and their expenses had to be made chargeable on the Gildhall revenue.[6] Again, in 1439, a meeting of Common Council had to be summoned to provide for the expenses of the citizens at the Reading parliament, since the chamberlains confessed that they had nothing wherewith to defray them.[7] The surplus of an allowance made in parliament for the defence of the City was applied to the payment of members' wages in 1447.[8] Three years later an ordinance of Common Council, which must have fallen heavily on all classes, directed that fees for enrolments of apprentices, admissions to the Freedom, and enrolments of deeds and wills should be doubled from 1 April until the end of May and thenceforward for one whole year, in order to meet the parlia-

[1] *Cal. Letter Book E.*, p. 33.   [2] *Cal. Plea and Memoranda Rolls*, i, p. 30.
[3] *Cal. Letter Book E.*, p. 225.   [4] Ibid., p. 281.
[5] *Cal. Letter Book H.*, p. 108.   [6] Ibid., p. 332.
[7] Journal 3, fol. 33 b.   [8] Journal 4, fol. 158.

mentary expenses of the representatives.[1] In 1454, possibly
because of the unpopularity of this ordinance, the Common
Council tried to throw the whole responsibility for payment
of members on the chamberlains ;[2] but ten years later they
were again faced with the problem what was to be done
when the chamberlains had insufficient money in hand to
meet their obligations.[3] The obvious solution of this problem—drastic limitation of the wages—was never adopted,
lest it should seem to reflect on the 'honour and profit' of
the city of London, but the necessity of finding such wages
must have lent an added bitterness to the protests of the
citizens when parliaments were held in the provinces.

The city of York, which ranked as a county from the
end of the fourteenth century, treated its representatives
as knights, and paid them at the rate of four shillings a day.
Thus Thomas Rideley and William Girlington received
£20 between them for fifty days' service, including the
journey, in the parliament of January 1442,[4] and Thomas
Crathorn and William Stokton received £12 16s. for thirty-
two days' service in the Bury parliament of 1447.[5] The
regulation payment was supplemented if the representatives
incurred any additional expenses on behalf of the city while
parliament was sitting. John Thrisk and Richard Buksey
were paid a supplementary wage of £1 8s. 4d. in 1445,[6]
Richard York and Robert Hancok received £2 18s. extra in
1485.[7] When parliament met at Westminster, twelve days
were usually allowed for the journey there and back ; but in
1483 the Council agreed that, whereas the coronation of
Edward V was to take place before parliament opened, the
representatives of York should be paid for eight days before-
hand instead of six so that they might be at the coronation
'to commune with soch lords as shall be there for the wele
of the Cite'.[8] In 1486, when York was expecting the visit of

---

[1] *Cal. Letter Book K.*, pp. 330–1.　　　[2] Journal 5, fol. 129 b.
[3] Journal 7, fol. 199.
[4] Archives of York Corporation, Chamberlains' Account Roll, 20 Henry VI.
[5] (York) Chamberlains' Account Book, vol. i, fol. 72.
[6] 'In diuersis expensis factis London' per dictos Iohannem et Ricardum pro
causis et negotiis ciuitatis.' (York) Chamberlains' Account Roll, 23 Hen. VI.
[7] 'pro diuersis custagiis et expensis.' Ibid., 1 and 2 Hen. VII.
[8] Davies, *York Records*, p. 145.

Henry VII, it was suggested that, in view of the complaints of poverty which had been made to the king on the town's behalf by the Archbishop of York, the representatives should forgo their wages for the last parliament.[1] Possibly the representatives themselves refused to agree to this suggestion, for wages amounting to £22 18s. were paid to them in spite of it.[2] Lengthy sessions meant a large outlay on wages. John Thrisk and Richard Buksey were paid £59 for 148 days' service in the long parliament which sat, with several prorogations, from 25 February 1445 until 9 April 1446.[3] This is the largest single expenditure on parliamentary wages which has been found among the York records.

The records of Norwich reveal a curious fluctuation in the rate of parliamentary wages. From February 1351, when Richard de Bytteryng and Robert de Bumpsted received £7 6s. 8d. for a parliament which lasted only twenty-one days,[4] to December 1417, when Robert Brasier and Robert Dunston received £12 13s. 4d. for thirty-eight days' parliamentary service, the representatives of Norwich were paid at the rate of 3s. 4d. per head per day.[5] But the record of the payment to Richard Monesle and Robert Dunston for service in the parliament of 1422 (£9 8s. for forty-seven days) shows that they are paid at the rate of two shillings, and the representatives in the parliaments of 1423, 1425, and 1426 were all paid at the lower rate. In 1429, there is a reversion to the former custom, Thomas Wetherby and Thomas Ingham receiving £42 13s. 4d. for an absence of eighteen weeks and two days.[6] For the remainder of Henry VI's reign, 3s. 4d. was paid, but for the parliament of 1463, Thomas Elys, to whom the description *miles*

---

[1] York Corporation House Books, vol. vi, fol. 12 '. . . Also that in consideracion of that at the Kinge Highnesse remembering the povertie, decay and ruyn of this cite showed unto hym by the moost Reverend fader in God Tharchbishop of York, Richard York and Robert Hancok late being at his parliament and other be content to have no money of the same Citie . . .'

[2] (York) Chamberlains' Account Roll, 1 and 2 Henry VII.

[3] Ibid., 23 Henry VI.

[4] Hudson and Tingey, *Norwich Records*, ii, p. 39.

[5] Archives of Norwich Corporation, Chamberlains' Account Book, 1384–1448.

[6] Ibid., 1384–1448; 1423, John Gerard and Richard Monesle, £23 5s. for 117 days; 1425, Walter Eton and John Gerard, £16 8s. for 82 days; 1426, Simon Cook, £8 8s. for 80 days.

parliamenti is applied for the first time in place of *civis par-liamenti*, had to be content with two shillings.[1] Possibly it was thought that the more dignified title would compensate for the lower wage. It seems probable that 3*s*. 4*d*. was the payment sanctioned by local usage, but that in difficult years a man might be asked to accept the normal rate current in the towns.

Norwich, like other towns, found the raising of parlia-mentary wages no easy matter. It is significant that the executors of Thomas Ingham, who represented Norwich in the parliament of 1445, had to put in a claim for his par-liamentary wages after his death in 1453.[2] In 1454, John Chittok, alderman, was allowed to nominate six or eight persons for admission to the Freedom of the City in com-pensation for an unpaid debt of £6 owing to him for parlia-mentary wages from the time he was sheriff.[3] In 1461, the Assembly passed a resolution to the effect that one of the chamberlains should be responsible for the payment of wages to the two representatives in the last parliament, and that this should be done as quickly as possible (*tam cito quam commode poterit fieri*).[4] In 1474, the late Mayor of Norwich offered to cancel a debt of twenty marks owing to himself from the city, if John Aubry and Thomas Bekenham, who then represented the city in parliament, would give up their wages and if all other aldermen would cancel any debts owing to them from the city.[5] Four years later, Henry Wilton, who represented Norwich in the parliament of 1478, also struck a bargain with the Assembly, but from a less disinterested motive. He offered to give up his claim to the sum of £4 16*s*., owing to him as parliamentary wages, in return for perpetual exemption from the offices of coroner, sheriff, or constable

---

[1] (Norwich) City Chamberlains' Roll, 1463–4.   [2] Ibid., 1453.

[3] Norwich Assembly Book I, 27 Nov. 1454, 'Dicto die concessum est Iohanni Chittok aldermanno sex uel octo personas ex sua provisione in ciues recipiendos pro illis sex libris qui debentur ei et pro quibus districciones cepit dum fuit in officio uicecomitis pro feodo ciuium pro parliamento electorum. . . .'

[4] Ibid. 1461.

[5] Ibid., 27 Oct. 1474, 'Et ad hanc congregacionem Ricardus Ferror maior anno ultimo profert relaxare xx^{ti} marcas prius sibi concessas si Iohannes Awbry et Thomas Bekenham nunc ciues ciuitatis ad parliamentum domini regis relaxent eorum uadia sibi accrescentia pro dicto parliamento et si omnes alii nunc alder-manni qui petunt aliquod debitum de communitate relaxent illud.'

of the city (*si eadem communitas ad hanc congregacionem con-donare dignaretur eum in perpetuum ab officiis coronatoris, uice-comitis et constabularii dicte ciuitatis fore exoneratum*). The Assembly, after careful consideration of the good deeds of Henry in the past (*integra congregacio intime ponderans plura beneficia que temporibus retroactis dictus Henricus . . . ad utile et commodum ciuitatis perpetrauit*), accepted his suggestion.[1] In 1486 it was agreed to raise £10 from the community in part payment of the £16 owing to John Paston and Philip Curson, the city's representatives in the first parliament of Henry VII, but a few weeks later the mayor and two other citizens were deputed to speak with the representatives, evidently in the hope that they would be found willing to forgo all or part of the debt (*ad intelligendam eorum disposicionem et quantum uel totum de xvj li. pro eorum expensis habere de communitate uoluerint*).[2]

Possibly it was in emulation of Norwich that the burgesses of King's Lynn arranged to pay their representatives at the high rate of 3s. 4d. per head per day, from about the year 1350. Earlier in the century the rate of payment seems to have been higher still.[3] The two representatives in the York parliament of February 1334 received between them £6 15s. 9d., and the two representatives in March 1336 £8 11s. 8d., though each of these parliaments sat for ten days only.[4] Thomas de Melcheburne received £2 in 1336 for attending a parliament at Nottingham which met on 23 September and was dissolved on 26 September.[5] £5 2s. 10d. was paid to the representatives in February 1339 when parliament sat for fifteen days,[6] but only £5 in 1354 when the session lasted for twenty-three days.[7] In 1358, the payment of £17 6s. 8d. to Geoffrey Drewe and John de Cokesford for a parliament which lasted only twenty-three days seems to suggest that the 3s. 4d. rate was then being

---

[1] Ibid., 1478.   [2] Ibid., 1486.

[3] So early as 1341 complaint was made to the King that bailiffs of cities and boroughs had levied excessive sums for the expenses of citizens and burgesses going to various parliaments, councils, and conferences, beyond the sums assigned in Chancery for such expenses. *Cal. Close Rolls*, 1341–3, p. 109.

[4] *Hist. MSS. Comm.*, *11th Report*, Appendix 3, p. 213.   [5] Ibid.

[6] Archives of the Corporation of King's Lynn. Chamberlains' Accounts, 12–13 Edw. III.

[7] Ibid., 28–9 Edw. III.

paid,[1] though in 1361 John Lamb and Nicholas Swerdeston received only £3 6s. 8d. for a parliament which sat from 24 January to 18 February.[2] In 1366, £9 18s. 2d. was paid for a parliament lasting eight days, exclusive of the journey. The roll for the first year of Richard II states definitely that the rate of payment is 3s. 4d.[3] That this wage was arranged by local ordinance seems to be implied in the entry of the payment, in 1380, of £8 16s. 8d. to John de Brunham for fifty-three days' parliamentary service ' *capiens per diem uadia per communitatem ordinata* '.[4] It was not until 1442 that the 3s. 4d. rate was abandoned and an agreement reached in the assembly of the burgesses that two shillings a day should henceforth be paid.[5]

This reduction of wages was the outcome of bitter experience. For years past the burgesses had found the utmost difficulty in raising the large sums demanded by their representatives in parliament. The records afford abundant illustration of the strain to which the town was subjected as a result of these too liberal payments. Again and again, the four chamberlains, on whom the responsibility for raising the wages was laid, found it impossible to pay more than a part of the amount owed; the remainder had to be written up as a debt against the town.[6] In 1423, the sum of forty shillings, paid by one William Waynfleet for admission to the freedom of the borough, was allotted to the parliamentary burgesses *pro arreragiis expensarum burgensium parliamenti*.[7] The next year, the Assembly agreed to a proposal to levy a tax of £50 on the town, to be assessed by constabularies, the collectors being chosen in the Assembly. Two years later, the sum of £43 for wages was raised in

---

[1] Archives of the Corporation of King's Lynn. Chamberlains' Accounts, 31–2 Edw. III.

[2] Ibid., 34 Edw. III.

[3] Ibid., 1–2 Ric. III, 'xix*li*. xiij*s*. iiij*d*. . . . pro uadiis Iohannis Dockyngge et Thome Morton euntium uersus parliamentum . . . per lix dies, quilibet capiens per diem iij*s*. iiij*d*.'

[4] Ibid., 3–4 Ric. II.   [5] Assembly Book II, 20 Henry VI.

[6] e.g. Gild Hall Roll, 1 Henry V, ' Burgenses parliamenti petunt pro uadiis et expensis suis secundum consuetudinem per tempus parliamenti pro lviij diebus . . xxiij*li*. vj*s*. viij*d*. Et inde solutum est eis x*li*. xv*s*. Et sic debentur eisdem xij*li*. xj*s*. viij*d*.'

[7] Assembly Book II, 2 Henry VI.

the same way.[1] Sometimes the representatives wisely insisted on part payment in advance. In 1460, Simon Pygott and William Pilton took £5 before they set out, and claimed only £3 4s. on their return.[2] They were fortunate if the whole sum was ever paid to them, for nearly every entry of payment in the fifteenth century is a confession of inability to pay more than a fraction of the sum demanded.

If Norwich and Lynn were extravagant in their payments, Exeter was parsimonious. It is difficult to discover any system underlying the payments to representatives in Edward III's reign, but it is at least clear that they fell very far short of the prescribed rate. Nicholas Wyting and Robert Cranthorne received forty shillings between them for the parliament of January 1348, which lasted for thirty days.[3] In 1351, Nicholas Wyting and Robert Bymster received sixty shillings between them for a parliament of twenty-one days;[4] in 1352, Simon atte Pytte and Thomas Spycere received forty shillings between them for a parliament of thirty days;[5] in 1368, Roger Plente and John Prestcote received £1 6s. 8d. for a parliament of twenty-one days.[6] These and similar entries suggest that the payments seldom exceeded one shilling a day and were often considerably below that rate. Yet a note on the roll referring to the fifth year of Richard II informs us that the rate was then 2s. 6d. a day, and records a payment accordingly.[7] From this time onwards the payments seem to have been quite haphazard. £6 0s. 6d. was paid to Peter Hadlegh and his fellow for the parliament of November 1384, which sat for forty-three days;[8] but in 1397 William Wilford and William Frye received £10 for the Westminster and Shrewsbury sessions, which together lasted for only eighteen days—a sum which, even with a generous allow-

---

[1] Assembly Book II, 3 and 4 Henry VI.
[2] *Hist. MSS. Comm., 11th Report*, Appendix 3, p. 167.
[3] Archives of Exeter Corporation. Receivers' Accounts, 22–3 Edward III.
[4] Ibid., 24–5 Edward III.   [5] Ibid., 25–6 Edward III.
[6] Ibid., 41–2 Edward III.
[7] Ibid., 1–2 Richard II. Note on dorse, 'Et postea allocatur eidem [Roberto Wylford] iiij*li*. pro expensis suis ad parliamentum tentum apud Westmonasterium in crastino Sancti Iohannis ante portam Latinam anno regni regis Ricardi secundi quinto pro triginta duobus diebus capienti pro quolibet die . . . ij*s*. vj*d*.'
[8] Ibid., 8–9 Richard II.

ance of time for the journeys involved, means a rate of payment per head of, roughly, four shillings.[1] A similar rate seems to have been paid in 1403, when the two representatives received £30 for a parliament lasting for sixty-six days.[2] In October 1404, for no reason stated, one of the representatives received £5 3s., the other only £2 13s. 4d.[3] At the beginning of Henry V's reign we are told that the rate of payment is 1s. 4d. a day.[4] In 1422, the representatives received £8 for a parliament of forty days, a payment which suggests the normal two-shilling rate.[5] But the following year John Salter received £8 3s., John Shaplegh only £5 for service in the same parliament.[6] The same men, representing the city in 1426, were paid approximately 2s. 6d. each per day.[7] The fluctuation continues throughout the fifteenth century. By 1461 the rate of 1s. 4d. was again being paid,[8] but in 1487 it has risen to two shillings.[9] The complete absence of any consistency in these payments suggests that Exeter simply paid her representatives whatever could be afforded at the time. Under such a system an expenses writ would have been of little use, and the facts disclosed by the Receivers' Accounts may perhaps help to explain the frequent absences of the city's name from the enrolled lists of towns receiving such writs. The records tell us little of how the parliamentary wages were raised, but it is clear that in Exeter, as elsewhere, payment was not always prompt. In 1379, the sum of twenty shillings was paid to the second husband of a woman, on his becoming a freeman of the city, to cover all that had been owing to the first husband for his service in several parliaments.[10]

---

[1] Archives of Exeter Corporation. Receivers' Accounts, 21–2 Richard II.

[2] Ibid., 2–3 Henry IV.   [3] Ibid., 3–4 Henry IV.

[4] Ibid., 3–4 Henry V. ' Item solutum Rogero Golde et Roberto Veysey pro uadiis suis burgensibus existentibus ad parliamentum domini regis scilicet pro lxxvj diebus eundo et redeundo—x *li*. ij*s*. viij*d*. capiens uterque per diem xvj*d*.'

[5] Ibid., 1–2 Henry VI.   [6] Ibid., 2–3 Henry VI.

[7] £17 16s. between them for a parliament of 66 days. Ibid., 4–5 Henry VI.

[8] Ibid., 1–2 Edward IV, dorse.   [9] Ibid., 3–4 Henry VII,

[10] Ibid., 3–4 Richard II, ' Et xxs. pro ingressu Ricardi Smalecombe, nunc uiri Sibille Bozoun, in libertatem Exon' de fine suo, loco omnium debitorum in quibus maior et communitas tenebantur Iohanni Bozoun quondam uiro de Sibille pro expensis dicti Iohannis existentis ad diuersa parliamenta pro communitate ciuitatis predicte.' John Bozoun represented Exeter in 1365, 1369, 1371, 1372, 1373, 1376, and Jan. 1377, but some payments had already been made to him.

The payments are usually made *per preceptum maioris*, but nothing is said about the means employed by the mayor to raise the money.

At Canterbury, from 1393, when the Chamberlains' Accounts begin, to 1445, the burgesses were regularly paid at the normal two-shilling rate. The representatives in the parliament of February 1445 accepted payment at the rate of one shilling a day *ad specialem requisitionem ciuium ciuitatis Cantuar'*,[1] but after the next parliament (1447) the customary rate was again paid.[2] In 1449, Thomas Walter received one shilling a day *ex permissione sua propria*. His companion, William Bold, was paid at the same rate, with or without his permission, but was given twenty shillings in addition to his wages *pro diuersis factis in eodem parliamento nomine communitatis ciuitatis*.[3] In 1459, the representatives at the Coventry parliament were paid two shillings for each day of the journey there and back, and one shilling and fourpence for each day of attendance at parliament,[4] and this became the customary method of payment until the end of the fifteenth century. An exception was made in 1491, when one of the representatives, Edward Bolney, was paid two shillings a day for the whole period, the other, William Atwode, presumably at his own request, receiving only one shilling for the time of his actual attendance at parliament.[5]

The public spirit of her parliamentary representatives helped, more than once, to relieve Canterbury of the whole or part of the burden of wages. In 1406, Edward Horn gave 6s. 8d. from his wages *ad empcionem tenementi uocati Le Lyon ad usum communitatis*,[6] and the next year John Sextayn gave 13s. 4d. and Richard Water 10s., also from their wages, for the same purpose.[7] In 1467, John Fogge gave up the whole of the wages due to him.[8] In 1483, George Browne 'on account of the peculiar affection and love which he had and

---

[1] Archives of Canterbury Corporation. Chamberlains' Accounts, vol. ii, 24–25 Henry VI.

[2] Ibid., 25–6 Henry VI.   [3] Ibid., 29–30 Henry VI.

[4] Books of Accounts, vol. ii, 38 Henry VI.

[5] Ibid., vol. v, 7–8 Henry VII.

[6] Chamberlains' Accounts, vol. i, 8 Henry IV.   [7] Ibid., 9 Henry IV.

[8] Ibid., vol. ii, 7–8 Edward IV, ' Et Iohanni Fogge militi alteri burgensi pro tot diebus nichil eo quod relaxauit uadia sua in eodem parliamento.'

hopes to have for the city of Canterbury, and because of the many gracious words and deeds shown him by his fellow-citizens on many occasions, freely and gratefully remitted his wages in the aforesaid parliament'.[1] The city had reason to be grateful to him, for in Canterbury, as elsewhere, payment of parliamentary wages was a serious matter. It was common for a proportion of the wages to be handed to the representatives in advance, at the time of their departure, and for the remainder to be paid in instalments over a period of one or more years.[2] In 1399, forty shillings of rent due from him for his tenement of Kingsmead was remitted to Thomas Lane, one of the parliamentary burgesses, in lieu of wages.[3] Such instances show that these payments were a real burden. Yet Canterbury paid more regularly and more consistently than many other towns and, so far as we know, never made the mistake of attempting to pay more than the statutory rate.

Salisbury likewise showed no tendency to over-pay. In the first half of the fifteenth century, the representatives seem to have received the regulation two-shilling wage,[4] but in 1447 the record of payment for the parliament at Bury St. Edmunds states that the rate is one shilling a day.[5] In 1463, there was a return to the two-shilling rate,[6] but in 1485 it was laid down by the mayor and his brethren,

---

[1] Chamberlains' Accounts, vol. ii, 22–3 Edward IV, ' Georgius Browne miles, alter burgensis parliamenti predicti propter admirabilem affeccionem et dileccionem quas habuit et habere intendit erga ciuitatem Cantuar' ac propter multarum graciarum dicciones et multiplices gratitudines sibi per conciues eiusdem ciuitatis frequenter ostentas, igitur feoda sua et expensas suas factas in eodem parliamento causis predictis beneuole et gratanter remisit.'

[2] e.g. Book of Accounts, vol. ii, 19 Richard II, ' Roberto Ferthyng in partem solucionem uadii pro parliamento xl*s*. Et idem Robertus recepit in principio dicti parliamenti xxx*s*.' Ferthyng sat in the parliament of Jan. 1394, so payment was long overdue.

[3] *Hist. MSS. Comm.*, *9th Report*, Appendix 1, p. 137.

[4] Hatcher and Benson, *Old and New Sarum*, i, p. 117, state that the first specific entries of parliamentary wages in the city's accounts begin about 1429, but payments are recorded from the first year of Henry IV.

[5] Archives of Salisbury Corporation. Ledger A. 1, 25 Henry VI, '. . . suprascripti ad conuocacionem predictam concesserunt Thome Temple et Iohanni More existentibus in parliamento tento apud Bury iiij*li*. viz. capiendis per diem unus eorum xij*d*.'

[6] Ledger B. 2, 2 Edward IV.

'that such citezeyns as shalbe chosen for this citee to be at the Kyng's parlement at Westminster to be holde the vij^{th} day of Novembre next comyng shall take eche of them xijd a day as ther wage and no more';[1]

and four years later the Assembly passed a similar resolution. But in 1495 they were overawed by the receipt of an expenses writ, and on 2 March,

'at this present convocacio it is agreid accordyng to the write of o^r soverayn lord the Kyng for the payment of the wages of Richard Eliott and John Hampton cetezens chosen for the cyte of Sar' for the parliament holden at Westmester as it aperith the xiiij^{th} day of Octobr the yer above wreten for lxvj dais takyng by the day ijs sum' xiij*li*. iiijs.'[2]

The records of Salisbury seem to echo a conflict, more persistent here than elsewhere, between the elected representatives and the governing body of the town on the matter of payment of wages. The representatives sued fairly regularly for expenses writs, and these writs were often sewn to the folio of the ledger on which the payment was recorded. It appears that the representatives looked upon the writ as a safeguard against attempts to reduce their wages, and that they were even prepared to resort to legal measures to obtain their just reward. In 1470, the Assembly promised John Aport and Thomas Pyrie, who were still unpaid for their services in the parliament of 1467, that they should receive their wages *absque ullo breue inde prosequendo seu alia quacumque secta pro eisdem facienda*.[3] The promise was not kept. In 1474 an expenses writ had to be issued in favour of Aport and Pyrie ordering the payment to them of £12 12s. od.,[4] but even this proved unavailing. In 1476, the two representatives began an action against the mayor, who resisted their claim and secured their expulsion from the Assembly. Eventually, however, they won their case, payment was made, and the town was obliged to indemnify the mayor for the costs of the suit, amounting to £6 17s. 8d.[5] This experience, so far from teaching them wisdom, led the mayor and his brethren to try a new means of curtailing wages. At the time of the election of citizens for the parlia-

---

[1] Ibid., 1 Henry VII. [2] Ibid., 11 Henry VII.
[3] Ibid., 10 Edward IV. [4] Ibid., 14 Edward IV.
[5] Hatcher and Benson, op. cit., i, pp. 196–7.

ment of January 1478, John Hampton and Roger Holes appeared on behalf of Edward Hardgyll, one of the representatives elected, and undertook that he would not ask more than forty shillings in wages, no matter how long the parliament should last.[1] If this promise was made with Hardgyll's knowledge, he found it convenient to forget it. At the conclusion of the parliament he and his fellow representative appeared in the Assembly and presented a writ enjoining that they be paid the sum of £9 8s. for forty-seven days' service. The writ was not disputed, and arrangements were at once made for the collection of the money by the usual method of a tax on movables, for which assessors and collectors were named in the Assembly.[2]

At Winchester, the two-shilling rate was normally paid, at least from the beginning of Richard II's reign.[3] Earlier in the century the representatives were often asked to accept a lower wage, and on the few occasions when parliament met at Winchester nothing was paid. On the other hand, wages were frequently supplemented when the representatives undertook special duties for the town.[4] At Plymouth, in 1495, the two representatives received only forty shillings between them.[5] The corporation of Cambridge, in 1427, ordained ' that for the future the burgesses elected to parliament shall have only twelve pence a day during the parliament', and though two shillings had been paid in 1424, there is no instance of a subsequent departure from the one-shilling rule.[6] Two shillings a day was paid at Hull in 1453, the expenditure on parliamentary wages for that year amounting to £21 8s. 0d.[7] One shilling a day was paid at Reading

---

[1] Ledger B. 2, 17 Edward IV.

[2] Ibid., 18 Edward IV. Cf. the proceedings in the Assembly of 1453: ' Electi sunt ad assidendum homines in ciuitate predicta commorantes de bonis mobilibus pro communitate eiusdem ciuitatis ad parliamentum domini regis pro expensis Willelmi Hore et Iohannis Hall burgensium ciuitatis predicte ut in breue domini regis plenius apparet.' The names of eight assessors and four collectors follow. Ibid., 32 Henry VI.

[3] One shilling a day was paid in 1421. *Hist. MSS. Comm., 6th Report*, p. 602.

[4] Furley, *Winchester Records*, pp. 111–12.

[5] Worth, *History of Plymouth*, p. 169.

[6] Cooper, *Annals of Cambridge*, pp. 172, 176, 178, 179, 184, 185, 186, 230, 236, 239.

[7] Hadley, *Hull*, p. 442.

for service in the parliament of 1372,[1] but the presentation of an expenses writ by the representatives in 1476 suggests that by this time they were at least claiming, if not obtaining, the regulation rate.[2] Southampton in the fifteenth century adhered to the two-shilling rate, though payment was often made by instalments. The steward recorded the payment of £5 19s. to Walter Clerk in part payment of his parliamentary wages for 1455, but subsequently the entry was crossed through and a note added, 'takyng but half wages accordyng to his promys'.[3] In 1450, the mayor and William Stone drank ale together at the town's expense before Stone set out for parliament.[4] One shilling a day was paid at Shrewsbury in the fifteenth century;[5] but Barnstaple, in 1395, paid £3 to one of its representatives for service in a parliament which sat for only twenty days.[6] Colchester seems to have raised its parliamentary wages in most haphazard fashion. Richard Heynes, for his service in the parliaments of 1487 and 1491, was granted all the moneys payable 'in the King's court of the town by warrants and records assigned' until the sum of £11 4s. owing to him should be made up. Thomas Jopson was allowed certain rents in part payment for his services in 1491. An annuity of £1 6s. 8d., being the rent from two mills 'at the New Hythe', was set aside for Thomas Christemasse, who served as a burgess in the parliaments of 1488 and 1489.[7] In 1465, one of the Dunwich burgesses agreed to serve for 'a cade of full herring'.[8] Rochester, as we have seen, obliged each 'foreign' burgess to serve once in parliament without wages in consideration of his admission to the Freedom.[9] In 1296, the mayor, aldermen, and whole community of Walling-

---

[1] Archives of Reading Corporation. Mayors' Accounts, Parcel xlv, 47–8 Edward III.

[2] Guilding, *Reading Records*, i. 72.

[3] Archives of Southampton Corporation. Stewards' Accounts, 1458.

[4] Ibid., 1450: 'Item, paide for good ale to the meyr and to William Stone for Stone is ben awy to Londonward to the parlement . . . ijd.'

[5] *Hist. MSS. Comm., 15th Report*, Appendix 10, p. 27. Archives of Shrewsbury Corporation. Bailiffs' Accounts, *passim*.

[6] Chanter and Wainwright, *Barnstaple Records*, ii. 103.

[7] *Red Paper Book*, pp. 124–7.

[8] Porritt, *Unreformed House of Commons*, i, p. 155.

[9] *Supra*, p. 37.

ford granted to Osbert de Nottlee and Agnes his wife 'for the great labour which the said Osbert has undertaken to sustain for us in the parliament of the Lord King to be holden at St. Edmund's on the morrow of All Souls'' a certain lane without the door of their hall in exchange for another and also 'a little corner place' at the east end of their place of Canecrofte.[1] In the twenty-eighth year of Henry VIII, Thomas Denton, one of the Wallingford burgesses, signed a contract with the mayor and burgesses by which he undertook to serve in parliament without wages 'as hath been of old custom used',[2] and it is possible that many of the smaller boroughs were able to make a similar arrangement, especially by the fifteenth century, when canvassing by outsiders had become general.

The facts relating to parliamentary wages afford yet another instance of the absence of uniformity in the organization of the English boroughs. Since the payment of such wages was a matter of no urgent interest to the Crown, local custom prevailed against government regulation. London might be munificent in its payments, Norwich and Lynn too liberal, Exeter and Cambridge parsimonious, Winchester and Canterbury reasonably just, but the chancery would not concern itself unless a direct complaint were made. The same indifference was shown with regard to the methods of raising wages. It was left to the governing body of each town to decide whether they would levy a systematic tax on movables, set aside a part of the town's rents, or bribe the representatives with powers and privileges; whether they would pay in advance, or by instalments, or not at all. Further, though the records make it

---

[1] *Hist. MSS. Comm., 6th Report*, p. 591.

[2] From a manuscript fragment in the archives of Wallingford Corporation: 'Thys byll made the fyrst day of June witnesseth that I, Thomas Denton gent, elected and chosyn burges in the king's parliament by the Mayour of Wallyngford hys brethrene and burgeys of the said borough . . . for the discharge of the said mayer and the comynaltye of the seid borough *according to the olde customes of the kyng's parliament in tymes paste* . . . refuse all maner of fees as hath byn of olde custom usyd, but clerelye to answere for the seid borowe the tyme of the parliament contynewyng withoute any fee. In witnesse wherof I the seid Thomas hath [*sic*] delyuered and sealed thys byll at myne owne hande the fyrst day of June in the xxviij yere of oure sovereyne lorde kyng Henry the viij[th]. Per me Thomam Denton.'

clear that the payment of parliamentary wages was a burden, they show too that, by the fifteenth century, most towns had reached some working compromise. Under-payment was common, but so far as can be gathered from the records examined, most of the towns seem not to have questioned the necessity of electing representatives and of offering them some reward for labours which were often enough both manifold and arduous.

VI

THE BURGESS PERSONNEL OF THE MEDIEVAL PARLIAMENT

THE parliamentary burgesses of medieval times produced no great political leader. Owing to such adverse conditions as the subordination of the Commons to the Lords throughout the Middle Ages, and the short duration of the average parliamentary session, the rise of a great politician was almost an impossibility. Yet it is a serious error to imagine that the 'estate' of the burgesses in our medieval parliaments consisted merely of a number of insignificant townsfolk. Among them were to be found men of wealth and experience, leaders of local politics in London and the great cities of England, some of whom held positions of national importance. Moreover, apart from their common election as representatives of towns, the parliamentary burgesses were not a homogeneous body, and their diversity of type increases with the passage of time. Two distinct groups may be discerned in all our medieval parliaments, the smaller consisting of wealthy merchants, members of the capitalist class, drawn mainly from London and such great cities as Bristol and York, the larger consisting of representatives of the lesser towns, men who had, perhaps, risen to positions of importance in their borough council or merchant gild, but who lacked the wealth and experience of the great capitalists. These were the normal and persistent types. But, by the fifteenth century, and more especially in the reign of Edward IV, the estate of the knights begins to overflow into the estate of the burgesses. We find the smaller boroughs beginning to return country gentlemen, knights, and esquires, usually though not invariably resident in the county, and (despite the fact that some of them had taken the trouble to become technically burgesses) utterly removed by upbringing and occupation from the normal dweller in a small town. Very significant are the charters granted to Ludlow and Much Wenlock in the reign of Edward IV, which allow that the burgesses shall choose *from themselves or others* burgesses to come to the king's parliaments.[1] Some of these 'others' were members of ancient families; some were retainers or dependants, either of the Crown or of influential magnates, for whom borough constituencies were found in order that they might support the interests of their masters. Some were, perhaps, beginning to use parliament as a stepping-stone to an official career, others may have valued the social and professional contacts which it afforded. Whatever the motives which drew them, it is clear that, at least by the middle of the century and probably very much earlier, membership of parliament had a definite value, and the habit of canvassing the small boroughs was well established before the days of the Tudors. The 'estate' of the burgesses at the end of the Middle Ages included a mixed company of wealthy merchants, small traders, country squires, officials, and lawyers. Thus it is as a number of groups, not as a single whole, that the burgess element in parliament may most profitably be studied.

A constant factor in the medieval parliament was the group of wealthy merchants drawn from the greater towns and united by their common interest in trade and national finance. From the earliest days of parliament the lists of London's representatives contain the names of such men. The first list of all—that of 1283—includes the names of the Gascon merchant Henry le Galeys, then mayor of London and destined to be mayor of Bordeaux in the following year, and of Gregory de Rokesle, goldsmith, wool-merchant, and Master of the Exchange.[2] Richard de Bettoyne, goldsmith, who sat in the parliaments of February and April 1328, played a conspicuous part in the political crises of Edward II's latter years. He with others enabled Mortimer to escape from the Tower in August 1323,[3] and after the triumph of Isabella in 1326 he was appointed joint warden of the Tower and elected mayor of the city.[4] As mayor, he accompanied the elected representatives to the Lincoln parliament of 1327, bearing letters from the commonalty to the King, the Queen,

---

[1] *Cal. Charter Rolls*, vol. vi, pp. 160, 232.   The italics are mine.
[2] Sharpe, *London and the Kingdom*, i. 116.
[3] *Chronicles of Edward I and II*, i. 301.   [4] Ibid., i. 318.

and members of the Council, praying that the Courts of Exchequer and King's Bench should not be removed from Westminster to York.[1] Richard de la Pole, who represented London in the parliament of September 1332, combined the offices of alderman of Bishopsgate and king's butler.[2] John de Grantham, who sat in the parliaments of February 1328, November 1330, and February 1338, owned property in eight London parishes and in the town of St. Omer.[3] Other wealthy and important citizens who represented London in the parliaments of the fourteenth century were John de Causton, who owned a brewery and houses in the parish of St. Mary-at-Hill and shops in the parish of All Hallows, and, at his death, left money for the maintenance of several chantries in the city;[4] John de Stodeye, king's butler, mayor of London, and escheator there;[5] John de Northampton, the famous puritan mayor and leader of the victuallers' party in the city; his rival, Nicholas Brembre, goldsmith; and the great financier, Sir John Philipot, who acted as paymaster to Edward III. Among Philipot's acts of munificence were the equipping of a squadron of 1,000 armed men in 1377, and the defrayal, during his mayoralty, of the cost of one of the two stone towers built below London Bridge. In the summer of 1379, he provided ships for Buckingham's expedition to Brittany, and a few years later undertook the transport arrangements for Despenser's 'crusade'. On his death in the summer of 1384 he bequeathed lands to the city for the relief of three poor people for ever.[6] Philipot and his contemporary Walworth earned reputations as financiers which were unsurpassed by any other merchants of the period. In the fifteenth century, London was represented by such well-known citizens as Drew Barantyn, the mayor who had taken the initiative in welcoming Henry of Lancaster to London in 1399; Richard Whittington, a great part of whose fabulous wealth was devoted to promoting the welfare of his fellow citizens;[7] Ralph Josselyn, draper,

---

[1] *Calendar of Plea and Memoranda Rolls of the City of London*, i, pp. 57–8.
[2] Beaven, *Aldermen of London*, i. 33.
[3] *Calendar of Wills in the Court of Husting*, i. 476.
[4] Ibid., i. 672.   [5] *Cal. Close Rolls*, 1354–60, pp. 458, 598.
[6] See the article in *Dictionary of National Biography*.
[7] *Calendar of Wills in the Court of Husting*, ii. 432.

who twice filled the office of mayor and was created a Knight
of the Bath by Edward IV;[1] and Thomas Urswyk, recorder
of the city, who showed conspicuous valour in the Faucon-
berg rising of 1471, and subsequently became a Baron of
the Exchequer.[2]

Men of this type were frequently returned by the great
cities of England throughout the fourteenth and fifteenth
centuries. Thomas Graa, sometime mayor of York, who
sat in at least twelve of Richard II's parliaments, was a man
of great position and influence. In March 1388, he, with
three others, was summoned before the King's Council to
treat of matters of national importance, and two months
later he was appointed ambassador to Prussia.[3] In 1400,
Graa was appointed, together with the archbishop of York,
the mayor of York, and the abbot of St. Mary's, to receive
the loans to the King which were to be sent to York, and
to make arrangements for their repayment.[4] Henry Goldbetere, who represented York in 1336, 1340, and 1341,
was one of the leading English merchants. He had been
a member of the wool syndicate of 1337, and subsequently
undertook much government business.[5] William de la Pole,
who was returned to parliament by Hull in the reign of
Edward III, was head of the great merchant family of de
la Pole, ancestors of the Earls of Suffolk. He was mayor
of Hull, king's butler, and Baron of the Exchequer, and
on more than one occasion advanced money to the Crown.[6]
Among the representatives of Bristol were the great William
Canynges, benefactor of the church of St. Mary Redclyffe,
and one of the richest men in fourteenth-century England;
Walter de Derby, to whom, with Henry Derneford, the town
was let to farm for a rent of £100 by Edward III in 1371,
and who owned the ship known as the *Gracedieu* of Bristol;[7]
John Bagot, a merchant of wide trading connexions, who
at the time of his first election to parliament in 1467 had

---

[1] *Short English Chronicle*, p. 80.
[2] Sharpe, *London and the Kingdom*, i. 317.
[3] *Cal. Close Rolls*, 1385-9, pp. 388, 403.
[4] *Cal. Patent Rolls*, 1399-1401, p. 356.
[5] Unwin, *Finance and Trade under Edward III*, p. 207.
[6] See the article in *Dictionary of National Biography*.
[7] Madox, *Firma Burgi*, p. 262; Seyer, *Bristol*, ii, p. 153.

already received the King's pardon for conducting an illicit trade with Scandinavia;[1] Philip Meade, mayor of the town in 1461, and connected by marriage with the Berkeleys;[2] and John Shipward, merchant, who built the tower of St. Stephen's.[3] Norwich returned such wealthy burgesses as Walter de Bixton, bailiff of the city in 1392, who, in 1385, together with another citizen, advanced the sum of 300 marks to the King on the town's behalf;[4] Thomas Spynk and Henry Lomynour, who in 1392 assigned to the bailiffs and commonalty three messuages, eighteen shops, forty-two stalls, and fifty-four shillings of rent with appurtenances, which they, with another citizen, held in burgage.[5] William Henstede, a fifteenth-century representative, was mayor of Norwich in 1442, and justice in the city ten years later.[6]

Until the intrusion of other elements in the fifteenth century, such wealthy merchants as these, almost all of whom had at one time or another filled the chief official positions in the great cities of England, must have been predominant among the parliamentary burgesses. Behind them we may discern our second group, the lesser townsfolk, men akin to the great merchants in the nature of their interests, but restricted by smaller resources and a narrower environment. Like the great merchants, these lesser men had filled responsible posts in their native towns, and most of them, if not comparable in wealth to a Philipot or a Canynges, were none the less solid and prosperous citizens. Such a man was Andrew de Pyrie, who represented Oxford thirteen times in the reigns of Edward I and Edward II, and held the office of constable of the town;[7] or Simon Cullebere, who sat in parliament for Bedford in 1327 and was mayor of the town in 1329;[8] or John Lombe of Lynn, who, in 1355, received the King's licence to load 200 quarters of wheat, 200 quarters

---

[1] *Cal. Patent Rolls*, 1461–7, p. 286.
[2] Seyer, *Bristol*, ii. 194.   His daughter married Maurice Berkeley, brother of William, Lord Berkeley.
[3] Seyer, loc. cit.
[4] Hudson and Tingey, *Norwich Records*, ii. 49.
[5] Ibid., ii. 252–3.   [6] Ibid., ii. 71; i. 305.
[7] *Oxford City Documents*, 1268–1665, p. 176.
[8] *Cal. Patent Rolls*, 1327–30, p. 428.

of oats, 100 quarters of beans and peas, and sixty tuns
of ale in ships not arrested for the King's service, and to
have them taken to any foreign parts not at enmity with
the King, to make his profit thereof.[1] The type persists
in the fifteenth century. Reading, in 1449, was represented by Simon Kent, mercer, and Thomas Clerk, draper;[2]
Dartmouth, in 1478, by Thomas Gale, shipowner and
burgess;[3] Exeter, in 1491, by John Atwylle, sometime
mayor of the city.[4] There is little to be said of them as
individuals, for most of them have left no memorial save a
few sparse references in the annals of their native towns;
but they formed a large proportion of the Commons'
'house' and represented a considerable body of public
opinion. Not all, however, were of unimpeachable re-
spectability. The violence and lawlessness of medieval
society had their representatives even among the members
of parliament. Ralph de Fauld, who was returned by Stafford in 1332, had been outlawed as a murderer five years
before.[5] John Mynors, who represented Newcastle-under-
Lyme in 1419 and 1422, was a 'notorious robber and de-
predator', the eldest of three brothers who devoted much
of their time to the organization of criminal escapades.
He was found guilty of several murders between 1407 and
1412, and was more than once convicted of rioting and
mill-breaking.[6] John Hawley, who represented Exeter in
1459,[7] and was himself Admiral of the West and collector
of customs, 'brought to a fine art piracy on a large scale'.[8]
Robert Acclom, member for Scarborough in 1401 and
1404, was guilty, as bailiff, of accepting bribes in order to
release convicted law-breakers. At the time of his return
to parliament he was carrying on a flourishing piracy business, and in October 1405 he and another parliamentary

---

[1] *Cal. Patent Rolls*, 1354–8, p. 285.
[2] *Names of Members of Parliament*, i. 341.
[3] *Cal. Patent Rolls*, 1467–77, p. 543.
[4] *Bulletin of the Institute of Historical Research*, iii. 9, pp. 168–75 ; *Cal. Patent Rolls*, 1476–85, p. 493.
[5] *Staffordshire Parliamentary History*, 1, p. 61.
[6] Ibid., i, pp. 194–6.
[7] Archives of the Corporation of Exeter. Receivers' Accounts, 39 Henry VI.
[8] *Transactions of the Royal Historical Society*, 4th Series, vol. viii, p. 115.

representative—William Harum—stole from a Hamburg ship an enormous cargo of beer, linen cloth, and 'wayn-scots'. After this incident he seems to have taken to flight, for his goods had to be distrained for non-appearance.[1] Richard Stury, who represented Shrewsbury in 1295, 1301, and 1313, one of the leading merchants of England, was described by Edward II in 1313 as 'maior mercatorum de regno nostro', and later in the same year as 'mayor of the wool-staple'. Yet in 1303 he was accused of breaking into a barn at Shrewsbury, and in 1320 he was defendant in an action of novel disseisin.[2]

The merchant, whether great capitalist or small trader, is the original type of parliamentary burgess, and there can be little doubt that it is men of this kind whose attendance is presupposed in the early writs of summons. The returning to parliament of such men as may be included in our first two groups suggests no problems, for they are the men who ought to be there. But a scrutiny of the returns to many of our fifteenth-century parliaments reveals the presence among the burgesses of a number of men who are not, properly speaking, burgesses at all. Their presence suggests a remarkable change in the personnel of parliament since the days of Edward II and Edward III, and gives rise to many important questions as to the identity of these men and the reasons for their election.

The parliament of 1478, as the last of our fifteenth-century parliaments for which the official returns are extant, forms a convenient starting-point for inquiry.[3] The number of burgesses returned was 202, representing 100 cities and boroughs. London returned four representatives, all the other towns two apiece, except Much Wenlock (Salop) which returned one, and Calne (Wilts.) which returned three. Of these 202 members, three bear the title of knight (*miles*), thirty-two that of esquire (*armiger*), two that of gentleman (*gentylman*). With the exception of

---

[1] *Cal. Patent Rolls*, 1402–5, pp. 147, 151, 353.   I am indebted to Miss Jean Rowntree for these references.

[2] Tout, *Place of Edward II*, p. 274, note 1.

[3] *Names of Members of Parliament*, i, pp. 363, 365.

Sir William Hampton, alderman of Vintry ward, and William Eland, esquire, a wealthy freeman of Hull, all these knights, esquires, and gentlemen were, as their titles indicate, of a different social class from the ordinary burgess. The names of the boroughs which returned them are in themselves very significant. The small boroughs of Surrey and Sussex—Gatton, Southwark, East Grinstead, Horsham, Midhurst, Shoreham, and Steyning—are responsible for eight of the esquires; the small boroughs of Wiltshire—Bedwyn, Calne, Chippenham, Cricklade, Malmesbury, Wilton, and Wootton Bassett—for another eight. Canterbury, Stafford, Salisbury, and Dunwich returned two esquires apiece; Portsmouth, Ipswich, Bridgnorth, Ludlow, and Maldon, one; Yarmouth and Bletchingley each returned a knight; and Wallingford two 'gentylmen'. Few of them could claim to be typical burgesses of the towns which they represented. Of the two knights, one was John Paston, who had secured election at Yarmouth; the other, Sir William Knyvet, though returned for Bletchingley, was also a Norfolk man who had sat in parliament for that county in 1467, served as justice of the peace in Norfolk, and was later to become steward of Castle Rising.[1] The Surrey and Sussex esquires included Ralph Wolseley (Gatton), a native of Staffordshire who had held the office of justice of the peace there, as well as those of Victualler of Calais and fourth Baron of the Exchequer;[2] Nicholas Gaynesford (Southwark), sheriff of Surrey and Sussex under Henry VI, an usher of Edward IV, and owner of certain manors in Surrey;[3] Richard Leukenore (East Grinstead), who had served as sheriff and justice in Surrey and Sussex,[4] and represented Horsham in the parliament of 1459, and Shoreham in that of 1467; Thomas Hoo (Horsham), a commissioner of array and justice of the peace in Sussex;[5] William Pestell (Midhurst), who had served as escheator both in Surrey and

[1] *Cal. Patent Rolls*, 1476–85, p. 362.
[2] Ibid., 1467–77, p. 31; ibid., 1476–85, p. 94.
[3] *Victoria County History of Surrey*, iii. 109; iv. 183–4.
[4] *Cal. Patent Rolls*, 1467–77, p. 326.
[5] Ibid., 1467–77, pp. 199, 633.

Sussex, and in Norfolk and Suffolk, and had represented Maldon in the parliament of 1472;[1] and John Apsle (Steyning), late sheriff, parliamentary representative of Arundel in 1459, and of Sussex in 1472. The Wiltshire esquires were men of the same type. They included William Paston (Bedwyn); Roger Hopton (Chippenham), yeoman of the Crown and usher of the King's Chamber;[2] Thomas Whityngton (Malmesbury), many times commissioner and justice of the peace in Gloucestershire;[3] and Edward Hardgill (Salisbury), yeoman of the Crown, usher of the Chamber, and ranger of certain royal forests in Hampshire and Oxfordshire.[4] Richard Haute, who was returned by Canterbury, was a nephew of the first Earl Rivers. At the marriage festivities of the little Duchess of York in 1477, he had been awarded the E of gold set with a ruby as being ' the best runner in hosting harness '.[5] William Clerk (Bridgnorth), Marshal of the King's Hall, had represented Much Wenlock in the parliament of 1472, and had been for many years Constable of Bridgnorth Castle.[6] Of the Dunwich representatives, Edmund Jenney was a member of the well-known family which so many times provided candidates for the shires and boroughs of East Anglia; Robert Brews had been Constable of Winchester Castle, and in 1484 received an annuity of £10 from Richard III ' for his good service to the King's father and the King '.[7] John Tymperley, junior (Ipswich), was a member of the Tymperley family, who were retainers of the Duke of Norfolk,[8] and sat in Parliament for Steyning in 1467, and for Bramber in 1472. Thomas Uvedale (Portsmouth) was the head of the great Hampshire family of Uvedale, and had represented the county in the parliament of 1455.

Further investigation of the returns for 1478 reveals

---

[1] *Cal. Patent Rolls*, 1461–7, p. 292 ; ibid., 1467–77, p. 387.
[2] Ibid., 1467–77, pp. 162, 592.
[3] Ibid., 1476–85, pp. 50, 322, 355, 560.
[4] Ibid., 1461–7, p. 24 ; ibid., 1467–77, pp. 90, 586.
[5] Scofield, *Life and Reign of Edward IV*, ii, p. 205.
[6] *Cal. Patent Rolls*, 1476–85, p. 34 ; ibid., 1461–7, p. 16.
[7] Ibid., 1476–85, pp. 35, 379.
[8] *Victoria County History of Surrey*, iii, p. 198.

the fact that this parliament included many other burgesses who, though not so designated on the returns, were undoubtedly members of the same class as the esquires and knights already mentioned. The six Cornish boroughs afford a good instance. Bodmin was represented by John Fyneux, a Kentish justice of the peace, and by Henry Chichele, a Cambridgeshire justice;[1] Helston by William Milford, a Somerset landowner, who had already sat for Tavistock in 1449, for Wareham in 1460, and for Barnstaple in 1467; and by John Bam or Bain, who may be identical with the John Bamme, 'gentilman', who sat for Rochester in 1467. Launceston was represented by John Fogge, probably son of Sir John Fogge, Treasurer of the Household, who sat for Kent in this parliament, and by Thomas Tresawell, a Cornish justice of the peace;[2] Liskeard by Richard Sheldon, afterwards an Exchequer auditor,[3] and by John Sheldewyche; Lostwithiel by Thomas Kebill, a Leicestershire justice, and by Thomas Powtrell, afterwards commissioner of array and justice of the peace in Derbyshire;[4] and Truro by Robert Cinte and Henry Frowyk, the latter a Middlesex landowner and justice.[5] The same conditions prevailed in many other towns. Alfred Cornburgh, who represented Plymouth in 1478, had been returned for Cornwall in 1467, served as sheriff and escheator in the Duchy and held other offices including that of usher of the King's Chamber.[6] His fellow member, Richard Page, was the King's solicitor and steward of Eltham Manor.[7] Richard Waget (Totnes) was a servant of the King's sister, Anne, Duchess of Exeter.[8] Ralph Ayssheton and Richard Hattefeld (Dorchester) were both King's servants, the former being custodian of the royal park of Windsor.[9] In short, it would seem that at least one-half of the borough representatives in this parliament were not true burgesses but either were country

---

[1] *Cal. Patent Rolls*, 1476–85, p. 563 ; ibid., 1467–77, p. 609.
[2] Ibid., 1476–85, p. 556.   [3] Ibid., 1476–85, p. 341.
[4] Ibid., 1476–85, pp. 563, 400, 557.
[5] Ibid., 1467–77, p. 622 ; ibid., 1476–85, p. 8.
[6] Ibid., 1476–85, p. 41.   [7] Ibid., 1467–77, pp. 180, 544.
[8] Ibid., 1467–77, p. 303.
[9] Ibid., 1467–77, p. 515 ; ibid., 1476–85, p. 499.

gentlemen who had persuaded the electors to return them, or else were members of the household-retainer, official, or civil-servant class for whom seats had been found by their masters.

With the returns for 1478 may be compared those for the long parliament of 1472–5.[1] Here we have official returns from ninety-seven boroughs, giving a total burgess attendance of 195, London returning four of these, and Much Wenlock again availing itself of its special privilege to return one member only. Of the total number of borough representatives, five were knights, and ten were esquires. London returned Sir Ralph Verney and Sir George Irlonde, Tavistock returned Sir John Gay, Guildford Sir George Browne and Appleby Sir John Scot. The ten esquires were John Prout (Reading), John Hords (Bridgnorth), William Worsop (Ipswich), Nicholas Gaynesford (Guildford), Laurence Lenthorp and John Tymperley, junior (Bramber), Richard Leukenore (East Grinstead), Thomas Hoo (Horsham), Christopher Furnes (Lewes), and William Merston (Midhurst). Thus the number of esquires, so designated, is much smaller than in 1478. Yet it may be doubted whether, in fact, the personnel of the two parliaments was very different in quality. The Cornish returns are lost, and it is therefore impossible to compare them with those of 1478, but the Wiltshire returns are interesting. Calne returns Roger Townsend, a Norfolk justice,[2] and in 1467 representative of Bramber, and John Hamond, who sat for Exeter in 1453 and had been justice of the peace in Hampshire;[3] Cricklade returned John Whittokesmede, whose remarkable parliamentary career can have had few parallels even in more modern times. He had already sat in seven parliaments and in each had represented a different constituency— Devizes in 1433, Downton in 1442, Salisbury in February 1449, Bath in November 1449, the county of Wilts in 1450, Calne in 1455, and Wilton in 1467, and in addition

---

[1] *Names of Members of Parliament*, i, pp. 360–2.
[2] *Cal. Patent Rolls*, 1467–77, p. 622.
[3] Ibid., 1467–77, p. 629.

had many times served the county as justice of the peace.[1]
Devizes returns Robert Nevyle, described both as 'gentilman' and 'king's servant',[2] and John Uffenham, who had
already sat once for Old Sarum and four times for Wilton.
Downton returns two Hampshire justices of the peace,[3]
Thomas Davers and Richard Jay, the latter having been
already four times returned by Shoreham. Heytesbury
returns Richard Erley, former member for Chippenham,
and Roger Uffenham. Hindon returns John Suliard, who
sat for Dunwich in 1459 and subsequently became tutor
to the Prince of Wales,[4] and Henry Spilman, a Norfolk
justice,[5] who sat for Norwich in 1467. Ludgershall returns
Robert Sheffield, who had been member for Lincolnshire
in 1442, and for Bedwyn in 1467, and justice of the peace
in Lincolnshire and the East Riding of Yorkshire.[6] Old
Sarum returns Giles Dacres, who had already represented
Shaftesbury, Wilton, and Wareham. Westbury returns
Philip Morgan, formerly member for Marlborough and for
Salisbury, a Wiltshire justice. Wilton returns John Pole,
a former representative of Shaftesbury and of Marlborough.
It seems clear that most of these 'burgesses' were outsiders who found in the numerous small boroughs of
Wiltshire a convenient stepping-stone to parliament. The
returns for 1472 afford many other like instances. Thus,
Thomas Jenney, who has to go as far as Devonshire to
find a seat, is returned by Tavistock, William Paston by
Newcastle-under-Lyme; William Knyvet transfers himself
from Norfolk to Melcombe Regis, and William Pestell
sits for Maldon. Thomas Fowler, who represents Wycombe, and was to represent Buckinghamshire in 1478,
was formerly a London fishmonger who had acquired
property and position in Buckinghamshire and by 1475
was usher of the King's Chamber.[7] John Tymperley,
senior, sits for Gatton; Peter Veske for Shoreham; John
Aleyn, Receiver-General to the Queen,[8] for Yarmouth.

---

[1] *Cal. Patent Rolls*, 1467–77, p. 635.   [2] Ibid., 1467–77, pp. 77, 588.
[3] Ibid., 1467–77, p. 629.   [4] Ibid., 1467–77, p. 366.
[5] Ibid., 1467–77, p. 622.   [6] Ibid., 1467–77, pp. 621, 636.
[7] Ibid., 1467–77, pp. 96, 550. Cf. *Victoria County History of Buckingham*,
iii. 484, iv. 301.
[8] Scofield, *Life and Reign of Edward IV*, i. 378.

The parliament of 1472 is thus a body essentially similar in composition to that of 1478.

Returns are extant for only one other of Edward IV's parliaments—that of 1467.[1] Out of a total of 193 names of burgesses, two bear the title of knight, fifteen that of esquire, three that of 'gentylman'. The knights are returned respectively by London and Canterbury; the esquires by Tavistock, Totnes, Shaftesbury, Grimsby, Yarmouth, Portsmouth, Dunwich, Ipswich, Reigate, Lewes, Shoreham (two), Cricklade (two), and Marlborough; the 'gentylmen' by Canterbury, Rochester, and Ipswich. Besides these, the returns reveal many familiar names, including those of Aleyn, Hardgill, Tymperley, Pastell, and Whittokesmede. They reveal also some interesting new names, such as that of Thomas Mauncell or Mansel (Wycombe), member of a family settled at Chicheley, Buckinghamshire, from the thirteenth to the seventeenth centuries;[2] of Nicholas Morley (East Grinstead), justice of the peace and commissioner of array in Sussex;[3] and of Peter Curteys (Appleby), King's servant, chief serjeant of Meath, and custodian of the King's wardrobe.[4] The parliament of 1467 is not noticeably different from the two which follow it, and it is clear that the process of substituting members of the knightly class for burgesses proper is at work all through the reign of Edward IV.

The process is little less obvious in the reign of Henry VI, for while the parliament of 1459 contains the names of ten esquires[5] out of a total of eighty-eight names surviving, that of 1453 contains only five,[6] that of 1450 only four,[7] that of November 1449 only three,[8] that of February 1449 only two,[9] that of 1447 none, that of 1442 one,[10] that of 1437 one,[11] and the earlier parliaments of the reign none

[1] Names of Members of Parliament, i, pp. 357–9.
[2] Victoria County History of Buckingham, iv. 314.
[3] Cal. Patent Rolls, 1467–77, p. 633.   [4] Ibid., pp. 273, 295.
[5] From Hereford (two), Ipswich, Bletchingley, Guildford, Southwark, Horsham (two), Downton, and Hindon.
[6] From Wallingford, Yarmouth (two), and Hindon (two).
[7] From Exeter, Lincoln, Ipswich, and Hindon.
[8] From Exeter, Lewes, and Appleby.
[9] From Rochester and Reigate.   [10] From Salisbury.   [11] From Wycombe.

at all. During the last decade of Henry's reign, we have parliaments very similar in type to those of Edward IV's reign. The parliament of 1453, for instance, includes among its burgesses such names as Leukenore, Morley, Tymperley, Gaynsford, and Hardgill. The number of such men diminishes perceptibly as we trace the returns back to the earlier years of the reign, though examples of them could certainly be found on the burgess-roll of every fifteenth-century parliament. At least from the beginning of Henry VI's reign, the tendency is noticeable to substitute country gentlemen or officials for burgesses; but it is not until the middle of the century that the tendency becomes so marked as to amount to a revolution in the personnel of parliament.

Certain obvious reasons for the change at once suggest themselves. The great influx of country gentry into parliament coincides with the beginnings of civil strife in England. With two sharply-divided factions struggling for control of the government, it was only natural that the magnates on either side should try to fill parliament with their supporters. Nor were the obstacles likely to be serious; for although attempts to interfere with elections in great cities like Norwich or Canterbury might lead to trouble, it was hardly probable that the inhabitants of the numerous small boroughs of Surrey or Wiltshire would raise any objection to the return of a gentleman who was, in nine cases out of ten, prepared to pay his own expenses. Some of the small boroughs had been, from the time of their inception, completely under the influence of the lords who had enfranchised them or of their successors, and could not, even if they so wished, offer opposition to a seignorial nominee. The advantages to the Crown of finding seats in parliament for royal servants in a period of dynastic strife were no less obvious. Further, the change in the personnel of the burgess element is indicative of a changed attitude towards parliament. Attendance is fast changing from a duty to a privilege, and it was the educated classes, the country gentry and the leading citizens of the great towns, who were the first to apprehend the change. By the latter half of the fifteenth century a

seat in parliament might mark a stage in an official career,
or might help to bring its holder to the notice of an influential patron. Ambition and policy made it alike desirable for the younger sons of great houses, for able civil
servants, and for the trusted retainers of magnates of all
parties. Thus the selfish motives actuating the landlord
class may have helped to save the House of Commons at
a period when there was, admittedly, little recognition of
its constitutional value.

Some of the results of this change of attitude have been
already noticed. We find that some of the smaller towns
are rapidly acquiring a reputation for accessibility among
seat-hunters. John Paston speaks of Maldon as such a
one, and Dunwich appears to have been another. Many
of the Surrey, Sussex, and Wiltshire boroughs seem to
have been freely canvassed by outsiders. A town like
Gatton, which first sent representatives to parliament in
1450, must have been a 'pocket-borough' from the beginning. Fourth from the bottom in the list of 'rotten
boroughs' in 1832, Gatton was never a place of any size
or importance. The Duke of Norfolk named it, in 1536,
as a town 'for which in times past he could have made
burgesses', and the history of the town bears out the
assertion. Some four years before the borough began to
return representatives to parliament, it was granted by
John, Duke of Norfolk to his retainer, John Tymperley,
who had licence to enclose the manor.[1] Tymperley
himself sat in parliament for the borough in 1472,
and in other years doubtless controlled the elections in
accordance with the wishes of his master. As we have
seen, Gatton in 1478 returned a Staffordshire gentleman,
Ralph Wolseley, who can hardly have obtained the seat
except by favour. Reigate is another example of a Surrey
borough which, by the fifteenth century, was completely
under the influence of the house of Norfolk. Reigate,
having first returned burgesses in 1295, has a much longer
parliamentary history than Gatton, and one of the most
interesting aspects of that history is the rise within its
walls of what can only be described as a parliamentary

[1] *Victoria County History of Surrey*, iii, p. 198.

family. Members of this family—the Skinners—represented Reigate in numerous parliaments between 1350 and 1572.[1] Although of bourgeois origin, as their name denotes, the Skinners had by the fifteenth century acquired property and position. About 1450, John Skinner married Joan Calcote, heiress of Chipstead. His son, Richard Skinner, who represented Reigate, in the parliaments of 1467, 1472, and 1478, inherited that property, together with a moiety of the manor of Cold Harbour and a third of the manor of Woodmansterne.[2] He is possibly to be identified with the Richard Skinner who was presented at a hundred court in Godalming in 1483 on a suspicion of Lollardy.[3] The rise of a family like the Skinners in a tiny borough like Reigate is a significant example of how a parliamentary career might link itself with increasing prosperity and improved social position. Yet the control of the Duke of Norfolk over elections is manifest. In 1419, 1420, and 1421 the borough returned John Pope, a bondsman of the Duke.[4] In 1453 and 1460 John Tymperley of Gatton was returned, and in 1478 Thomas Leukenore. At Newcastle-under-Lyme, elections were regularly controlled from the beginning of the fifteenth century. Newcastle was a borough of the Duchy of Lancaster and after the possessions of the Duchy merged with those of the Crown, at least one of the members was usually a nominee, and elections were controlled from the Staffordshire headquarters of the Duchy at Tutbury Castle.[5]

Yet another result of the rise in value of a seat in parliament is the frequent interchange of constituencies between those seeking election. Sometimes, though not always, these interchanges are limited to an area of one, two, or three counties. The career of John Whittokesmede, to which reference has been made, is merely a striking example of a phenomenon that is becoming more and more common.

---

[1] Smith, *Parliamentary Representation of Surrey*, pp. 30–1.
[2] *Victoria County History of Surrey*, iii, p. 192 ; iv. pp. 32, 249.
[3] '. . . non uenit ad missam in festialibus diebus, sed uiuit suspiciose.' Ibid., iii, p. 10.
[4] Ibid., iii, p. 249.
[5] Pape, *Medieval Newcastle-under-Lyme*, pp. 91–2. Wedgwood, *Staffordshire Parliamentary History*, i, pp. 184–8.

In the fourteenth century, it is possible to find scattered instances of the same man representing different constituencies in turn,[1] but such instances are rare. By the time of Edward IV, however, we are confronted with an overwhelming number of examples. Richard Leukenore sits, in turn, for Bramber, East Grinstead, Horsham, and Shoreham; Nicholas Gaynesford for Bletchingley, Guildford, Southwark, and the county of Surrey; John Apsle for Arundel, Steyning, and the county of Sussex; William Twynyo for Shaftesbury, Hindon, Weymouth, and Dorset; William Clerk for Bridgnorth, and Much Wenlock; Thomas Uvedale for Portsmouth, and the county of Southampton; William Milford for Tavistock, Wareham, Barnstaple, and Helston. Sometimes, the range of the seat-hunter is even wider. The Tymperleys, father and son, between them represented the towns of Bramber, Gatton, Ipswich, Reigate, Steyning, and Yarmouth; the Jenney family represented Dunwich, Norwich, Tavistock, and the county of Suffolk; William Paston sat for Bedwyn and Newcastle-under-Lyme; William Knyvet for Melcombe Regis, Bletchingley, and the county of Norfolk; Ralph Wolseley for Gatton and Newcastle-under-Lyme.

The position of these men in parliament was very different from that of the duly-elected burgess representatives of such a town as Lynn. Although most of them had some local associations with the town which they claimed to represent, such as the ownership of land or the tenure of office in the county, and though some of them may even have taken out burgage rights in the town, yet they could not feel the same responsibility for its welfare as if they had been resident burgesses. They were in parliament to serve, not their constituents, but their patrons or themselves. As many of them probably paid their own expenses, it would not be to the advantage of the burgesses to attempt either to control their actions or to ask for an account of their services. Unhampered by the burden of local business, these gentlemen-burgesses held a position closely akin to that of the knights

---

[1] e.g. William Heyberare represented both the town and the county of Gloucester in Richard II's reign; John Kene sat for Newcastle-under-Lyme in 1380 and 1388 and for Bridgnorth in 1384.

of the shire. As the majority of them were of the knightly class, and as many of them had been or were to be returned by their counties, the practical effect of their presence in parliament was to swell the ranks of the knightly class at the expense of the *bourgeoisie*, to lower the barriers between knight and burgess, and to prepare the way for the further consolidation of the House of Commons as an undivided whole.

In spite of the medieval suspicion against lawyers, and the prohibitions against electing them to parliament, lawyers were frequently returned for the towns. William Wayte, writing in 1450 to John Paston, urges him to procure the election of John Dam or William Jenney at Norwich, and adds, ' Telle them that he may be yt as well as Yonge is of Brystowe, or the Recorder is of London, and as the Recordour of Coventre is for the cite of Coventre, and it so in many places in Ingland'.[1] Thomas Yonge, who was returned eight times by Bristol and once by Gloucestershire, was a practising barrister, a member of the Middle Temple, and later a justice of Common Pleas and of King's Bench. His bold words in the parliament of 1451 probably served to enhance the bad reputation which the lawyer-member of parliament already enjoyed.[2] William Jenney also, as the context shows, was a lawyer, and in 1463 became serjeant-at-law. Henry Spilman, who sat for Norwich in 1467 and for Hindon in 1472, became recorder of Norwich in 1469. William Cumberford, returned by Newcastle-under-Lyme in 1442, was protonotary of the Court of King's Bench.[3] Richard Page, who sat for Plymouth, was the king's solicitor;[4] William Wode represented Winchester and was also recorder of the city.[5] London returned several lawyers. Thomas Urswyk was recorder; Thomas Bittyng was afterwards Chief Justice of the King's Bench; John Nedeham was Judge of Assize in Yorkshire.[6] Thomas Fitz-William, recorder of London, was returned by Lincolnshire to the

---

[1] *Paston Letters*, ii, p. 176. John Dam was returned by Norwich in 1450.
[2] See the article in *Dictionary of National Biography*.
[3] *Staffordshire Parliamentary History*, i, p. 226.
[4] *Cal. Patent Rolls*, 1467–77, p. 180.
[5] *Black Book of Winchester*, p. 196.
[6] Beaven, *Aldermen of London*, i, p. 287.

parliament of 1489, in which he was Speaker. The lawyer's expert knowledge made him a valuable ally, though a dangerous enemy, and a society which expended so much of its time and money on litigation found it impossible to keep him out of parliament.

Between the beginning of the reign of Edward I and the end of the reign of Edward IV, we see, then, a marked change in the quality of the burgess 'estate'. Edward I's parliaments are composed of well-to-do merchants and humbler townsmen, who appear at Westminster or elsewhere, answer the King's questions, accede to his demands, and return with all possible speed to their own homes. Neither they, nor their contemporaries outside parliament, conceive that they are in any respect essential to the High Court before which the King pleases to summon them. But the burgesses in the parliaments of Henry VI and Edward IV are of very different quality. We see them as a mixed assembly of merchants, gentlemen, and lawyers, men bound by partisan loyalties, zealous to retain their seats, restless, uneasy, set about with privy conspiracy and rebellion. In the parliaments of Edward IV we are closer in atmosphere to the days of the Stuarts than to the days of the Plantagenets. The usurpation of borough seats by the squirearchy has already prepared the way for the future greatness of the House of Commons.

VII

THE BURGESSES IN PARLIAMENT

TO the student of the parliament rolls it is easily apparent that it was the knights of the shire, and not the citizens or burgesses, that were the leaders of the Commons in the medieval parliament. The rolls have remarkably little to tell us of the activities of the burgesses. It would appear that despite their numerical superiority the part played by them in parliament was, if not insignificant, at least inconspicuous. No burgess was appointed Speaker before the reign of Henry VIII; and it is a rare exception for the name of an individual burgess to find its way into the official records of parliament. The education and traditions of the knights undoubtedly gave them advantages which few of the burgesses could hope to share, and it was natural that both king and magnates should look to the knightly class for advice on matters of general policy. Yet it is possible to lay too much emphasis on the argument *ex silentio*. The parliament rolls are not, and do not profess to be, an exhaustive record of all parliamentary transactions. Still less are they concerned to report those private deliberations of the commons which were not recognized as forming part of the official proceedings of parliament. The presence, in every parliament, of a group of men concerned in their daily lives with trade and finance must have been of inestimable advantage to the rulers of medieval England, harassed as they were by constant financial anxiety. As will be shown, it is hardly possible to doubt that the part played by the townsmen in parliament must have been of much greater significance than a cursory reading of the printed rolls might lead us to suppose.

Moreover, the work of the parliamentary burgesses has a twofold aspect. Those who elected and paid them were not accustomed to think in terms of public service. For the electors, the chief function of their representatives was, in the words of a Norwich record, ' to increase our liberties as they may be able'. Faced with the necessity of electing representatives and of paying them for their services, the governing bodies of the towns were determined to obtain value for their money. Thus, the representatives often found themselves burdened with the responsibility of pursuing the town's advantage in parliament by seeking confirmation of charters or favourable responses to petitions, and with the necessity of undertaking private business for their constituents in or near London. From the point of view of the Crown, the burgess comes to parliament in order that the borough may be bound by the measures to which he there gives assent; but from the local point of view he is his town's attorney, and his summons to parliament affords an opportunity of laying local grievances before a central assembly. It is impossible to appreciate the importance of the parliamentary citizens and burgesses without considering both aspects of their work.

Direct evidence as to the activities of the burgesses in parliament is very scanty. The author of the *Anonimalle Chronicle*, for example, in his description of the deliberations of the commons in the Chapter-house of Westminster Abbey in 1376, tells us only of the speeches made by the knights. The author of the *Chronicon Angliae*, describing the same parliament, throughout uses *milites* as a synonym for the Commons. Rarely do we find burgesses among those appointed to serve on parliamentary committees or to perform any other special public service. None, even of the great London merchants, is elected Speaker. A few appointments to committees, a few famous privilege cases, afford the sum total of direct information to be deduced from the parliament rolls. It seems reasonable to deduce the subordination of the burgesses to the knights—a natural adjustment in view of the increasing tendency among modern scholars to see the Commons as the spokesmen of the Lords rather than as the initiators of an independent policy.

The direct evidence, such as it is, may conveniently be examined a little more closely. In the parliament of March, 1340, twelve knights and six citizens and burgesses were elected by their fellow-commoners, at the King's command, to assist certain of the magnates in the hearing of petitions touching the clergy, and in the preparation of a statute to be based upon these petitions. The six burgesses chosen were Robert de Morewode of Nottingham, Philip de Cayly of Cambridge, John de Rattlesden of Colchester, John de Preston, probably of Wycombe,[1] Thomas But of Norwich, and Thomas de Wycombe, who, as his name does not appear among the returns to this parliament, may perhaps be identified with the Thomas Gerveys who was returned by the borough of Wycombe.[2] All six were men of some parliamentary experience. Thomas But had represented Norwich in every parliament since 1328, and John de Rattlesden had sat fifteen times. Robert de Morewode had served in four parliaments, Thomas Gerveys in three, Philip de Cayly and Jordanus de Preston in two. Yet it is remarkable that, with the exception of Norwich and Nottingham, the towns which they represented were all of the second rank. Possibly the representatives of London and the greater towns took pains to thrust the unwelcome burden of service upon their less powerful brethren, rather than to select those best fitted to sustain it. It is not until the beginning of Richard II's reign that we find some of the leading burgesses playing in parliament the parts for which they were qualified by their wealth and experience. In October, 1377, two of the representatives of the city of London—John Philipot and William Walworth—were appointed treasurers of the subsidy granted for the war with France. Together with certain other London merchants they lent the King £10,000 on the security of the crown jewels.[3] In the parliament of May, 1382, Philipot was a member of the committee of merchants appointed to consider the proposed loan for the King's excursion to France, and was at the same time made 'receiver and guardian' of the tonnage and poundage appropriated for the keeping of the seas.[4] The violence of party feeling in the city at this period and the interdependence of London and national politics gave the leaders of the gilds an unwonted prominence in parliament, but by the beginning of the fifteenth century they had relapsed into their former insignificance. The wealth of the Londoners never enabled

[1] Jordanus de Preston is the name on the return.
[2] Rot. Parl., ii. 113.
[3] Ibid., iii. 7.   [4] Ibid., iii. 123–4.

them to attain the leadership of their fellow-commoners. It was difficult for them to combine either with the knights, for whom a bourgeois remained a bourgeois whatever his wealth, or with the provincial burgesses, who envied their magnificence and resented their arrogance. No London representative was chosen to be Speaker of the Commons in this period.[1] William Staundon, alderman of Cheap, and Nicholas Wotton, alderman of Broad Street, were members of the committee appointed in the parliament of 1406 to be present during the compilation of the parliament roll;[2] Thomas Urswyk (then recorder) and Ralph Josselyn were members, in 1467, of a parliamentary committee chosen to inquire into a dispute about coinage.[3] The list of London's representatives contains several names—Nicholas Brembre, Walter Sibylle, John of Northampton, Richard Whittington—which won fame or notoriety elsewhere, but of the actions of these men in the parliaments to which they were returned neither the rolls nor the local records tell us anything.

If fame was rarely achieved by a parliamentary burgess, occasionally a temporary publicity was thrust upon him. The well-known privilege cases of 1429, 1451, 1460, 1472, and 1478 gave to those concerned in them a prominence which most of them would hardly have otherwise obtained. In 1429 William Lark, the servant of William Melreth, who represented London in the parliaments of 1427, 1429, and 1432, was arrested for trespass at the suit of one Margery Janyns, and brought by the officers of the Abbot of Westminster before his Piepowder Court. The case was thence removed to the Common Pleas and, on judgement being given against him, Lark was imprisoned in the Fleet. In petitioning for his release, the Commons reminded the King that Lark was, at the time of his arrest, in the service of William Melreth, member-elect for the city of London, and should therefore enjoy the privilege of freedom from arrest during the session of parliament, unless accused of

---

[1] Thomas Fitz-William, recorder of London and Speaker in the parliament of 1489, was originally returned for the City, but resigned that seat on being elected for Lincolnshire a few days later.

[2] *Rot. Parl.*, iii. 585.   [3] Ibid., v. 634.

treason, felony, or breach of the peace. They ask for a guarantee for the future that no member of parliament, whether peer, knight, citizen, or burgess, and no member's servant, shall be arrested or imprisoned during parliament, except for the causes aforesaid. The reply to the petition orders the release of Lark, coupled with elaborate provisions for the recovery of damages by the plaintiff after the dissolution, but the guarantee for the future is withheld.[1] The case of 1460 was concerned with the arrest of a member himself. Walter Clerk, burgess for Chippenham, was arrested for a fine owing to the King, and for damages of £20 owing to Robert Basset, and of £20 owing to John Payn. The Commons petitioned for his release 'so that he may tend daily of this youre parliament as his dute is to doo', and for the saving to themselves of 'their hole Libertees, Fraunchises and Privileges in alse ample fourme and manere as your seid Commons at eny time afore this day have had, used and enjoyed and oweth to have, use and enjoy'.[2] The King granted this petition and Clerk was released. Although returned by Chippenham, Clerk is probably to be identified with the Walter Clerk who sat for Southampton in 1455 and was mayor of the town in 1457.[3] John Payn, to whom he owed £20, sat for Southampton in 1435, 1447, and 1450, and was concerned in a riot there in 1460.[4] A similar petition was provoked by the arrest, in 1472, of another Chippenham burgess, William Hyde. Hyde was arrested at Lambeth at the suit of John Marshall, a London mercer, seeking to recover an alleged debt of £69, and taken to London 'by myschevous men, murtherers, unknowen for any officers', cast into Newgate, 'as and he had bee a Traitour', brought before the Bench and remitted to Newgate. The petition urges that his arrest is leading 'to grete delay and retardation of procedyng and goode expedition of such matters and bosoignes as for your Highnes and the commen wele of this your Reame in this present Parlement were to be doon and spedde',[5] thus implying the impossibility of conducting parliamentary

---

[1] *Rot. Parl.*, iv. 357–8.
[2] Ibid., v. 374–5.
[3] *Cal. Patent Rolls*, 1452–61, p. 410.
[4] Ibid., p. 639.
[5] *Rot. Parl.*, vi. 160–1.

business without the full complement of members. Hyde is described as 'squyer', and this title, coupled with the magnitude of his alleged debts in London, suggests that he, like Clerk, was not a native of Chippenham, though he had persuaded the burgesses to return him.[1] Probably he may be identified with the William Hyde, esquire, who in 1469 is described as being ' of Stepell Moreden, co. Cambridge, *alias* William Hide, late of London, and late escheator in the counties of Oxford and Berks '.[2] A fourth famous case in which a burgess was concerned was that of John Atwyll, member for Exeter in the parliament of 1478. While Atwyll was attending parliament daily, ' oon John Tayllour, callyng hym Merchaunt of the said Cite of Exeter', had obtained judgement by default in the Exchequer, Atwyll himself having no knowledge of the action. The Commons urged upon the King the pitiful condition of Atwyll, who ' may not have his free departyng from this present Parlement to his home, for doute that booth his Body, his Horses and his other Goodes and Catalles necessarie to be had with hym, shuld be put in Execution in that behalfe, contrarie to the Pryvilege due and accustumed to all the Membres usuelly called to the forseid Parlementes ', and the King accordingly granted the issue of writs of *supersedeas*, saving the rights of the suitor after the end of the session.[3]

In these four well-known cases it was the injustice suffered by burgesses which led to the presentation of a petition against breach of privilege, yet it does not appear that either Melreth, Clerk, Hyde, or Atwyll made any further impression upon their fellow-members. It is, however, possible that Clerk and Hyde, being not the insignificant countrymen which their position as members for Chippenham might suggest, but the one a leading citizen of a great port, the other a gentleman of some administrative experience, were themselves the successful instigators of the petitions on their behalf. No such obscurity clouds the name of Thomas Yonge, the central figure

---

[1] For similar instances see above, Chap. VI.
[2] *Cal. Patent Rolls*, 1467–77, p. 174.
[3] *Rot. Parl.*, vi. 191.

in the case of 1451, which concerned the privilege of freedom of speech.[1] Yonge, one of the members for Bristol and a staunch Yorkist, ventured to propose the settlement of the succession question by the definite recognition of Richard, Duke of York, as heir to the Crown.[2] The King and the Lords opposed the suggestion, which was supported by a number of the Commons, and as Somerset remained in power Yonge was sent to the Tower. Four years later he presented, on his own initiative, a petition to the Commons, which was transmitted to the Lords, asking for compensation for losses amounting to one thousand marks and more, and reminding them that ' by the olde liberte and fredom of the Comyns of this Lande, had, enjoyed and prescribed, fro the tyme that no mynde is, alle suche persones as for the tyme been assembled in eny Parlement for the same Comyn ought to have theire fredom to speke and sey in the Hous of their assemble, as to theym is thought convenyent or resonable, withoute eny maner chalange, charge or punycion therefore to be leyde to theym in eny wyse'. The reference to privilege is, for all its eloquence, incidental; the object of the petition is damages. The Lords of the Council were ordered to provide compensation at their discretion, but the general principle of freedom of speech was never specifically admitted, though it is arguable that it is implicit in the privilege of freedom from arrest.[3] Yonge was a man entitled to speak with authority. He had already sat in six parliaments, and was both a merchant, as the indenture of his election states, and a trained lawyer whose abilities subsequently raised him to the Bench.[4] To take the initiative in making a proposal relative to so delicate a matter as the succession, he must have been recognized as one of the leaders in the House of Commons.

These scattered instances do not, of course, represent the complete sum of the parliamentary activities of the burgesses.

---

[1] *Rot. Parl.*, v. 337.   [2] Stubbs, *Constitutional History*, iii. 171.

[3] Cf. J. E. Neale, ' The Commons' Privilege of Free Speech in Parliament ' (*Tudor Studies*, p. 265). 'A certain or more probably a very uncertain freedom of speech had evidently come to be regarded as a customary right.'

[4] See article in *Dictionary of National Biography*.

That they acted with the knights, withdrew with them for deliberation in the Chapter-house or elsewhere, assisted at the election of the Speaker, advised as to the amount of the subsidy which the Commons could sustain, and helped to frame the common petitions, is sometimes stated and must generally be assumed. The great number of petitions relating to the franchises of the towns and to matters of trade and finance must have been, at least in part, the work of the merchant classes. Occasionally we find traces of the recognition of the burgesses as a separate entity. At the time of the re-establishment of the home Staple in 1353, one copy of the document containing the reasons for the change was given to the knights, another to the citizens and burgesses.[1] Sometimes the term 'commons' is used to distinguish the citizens and burgesses from the knights. In April 1343 *the knights of the counties and the commons* were charged to assemble in the Painted Chamber and to consult among themselves as to the proposals for peace with France,[2] and again, in January 1348, *the knights of the counties and others of the commons* were ordered to consult together on the conduct of the war.[3] The author of the *Anonimalle Chronicle* writes of the assembling of the 'knights and commons' in the Chapter-house, during the parliament of 1376.[4] Such instances serve to remind us of the presence, in the medieval parliament, of a body of well-to-do townspeople, but they do not give us much help in estimating the significance of their presence there.

From the very beginning of representative parliaments one of the main preoccupations of the burgesses must have been with finance. Recent historical criticism has shown itself sceptical of the belief held by Hallam, Gneist, Stubbs, and other nineteenth-century writers, that Edward I was led to summon representatives to parliament largely by his desire to obtain their consent to taxation. The emphasis now laid upon other aspects of parliament, judicial and administrative, has tended to divert attention from the financial aspect. It has been pointed out that what we know of Edward's autocratic temper accords ill with the view that

---

[1] *Rot. Parl.*, ii. 246.   [2] Ibid., ii. 136.   [3] Ibid., ii. 164.
[4] *Anonimalle Chronicle*, p. 80.

he would willingly have sought the consent of his subjects to any tax which had hitherto been levied by kings at their own pleasure. The concessions granted by the *Confirmatio Cartarum* of 1297 are worded in general terms, and Edward's intention to evade them is shown by his appeal to Clement V to absolve him from his oath. Parliament was primarily and essentially the high court of justice, and the summoning of representatives might well justify itself on administrative grounds. Yet when due weight has been given to these considerations, neglected by an older generation of historians, the fact remains that one of the earliest functions of the Commons was to accede to money grants, and that it was in the sphere of taxation that they first won any appreciable degree of control over the Crown. When the King, in 1295, announces his intention to hold a colloquy with his earls, barons, and other magnates, *super remediis contra pericula quae eidem regno hiis diebus imminent providendum*, it is evident that the remedy which he has in mind is financial; and when the sheriffs are commanded to obtain the election of knights, citizens, and burgesses endowed with full and sufficient powers for themselves and the communities they represent, *ad faciendum quod tunc de communi consilio ordinabitur in praemissis*, it seems hardly less evident that it is to money grants which the words refer. Further, when the writ for the collection of the aid, issued in December of the same year, states that the earls, barons, knights, and others *liberaliter fecerunt undecimam de omnibus bonis suis mobilibus*, and that the citizens, burgesses, and other good men of the demesne, *septimam de omnibus bonis suis mobilibus . . . nobis curialiter concesserint et gratanter,*[1] it seems idle to dispute the importance of the financial motive or to deny that consent to taxation, however formal, was intimately connected with representation. Although the practice of Edward I shows that he never admitted his inability to tax certain classes of his subjects at will, yet the desirability of obtaining a general consent to taxation seems to have been early recognized. In the course of the fourteenth century such assent came to be regarded as an essential preliminary to direct taxation, and throughout the later

[1] *Foedera*, i, p. 833.

Middle Ages the voting of subsidies was among the most important parliamentary duties which the Commons had to perform. The King's need of money looms large in the opening sermon of almost every parliament, and the main preoccupation of the knights and burgesses is to secure that taxation shall not be intolerably heavy, and that a due share of it shall be paid by all classes.

To the burgesses, even more than to the knights, taxation was a matter of vital importance.[1] In Edward I's reign, the majority of the English boroughs formed part of the royal demesne, and were therefore legally subject to arbitrary tallage by the Crown. The tallage—which was not, of course, an exaction peculiar to England—seems to have been originally a tribute taken by the lord from his dependent peasants. When economic conditions changed and urban communities began to grow up on rural estates, such communities still remained subject to the lord's right of arbitrary tallage, unless he chose to relieve them from it. In England, the tallage was a Norman importation, but by the thirteenth century only the peasant of servile status remained subject to an arbitrary imposition, the freeholder having secured the right of paying a fixed annual sum. The position of the English towns was, however, peculiar. Most of them were on the royal demesne, but the Norman kings seem to have made no attempt to take an annual tallage such as was frequently levied by other lords of towns. It was, perhaps, hardly necessary for them to do so, since they inherited from their Anglo-Saxon predecessors the valuable land-tax known as the geld, to which all lands in England, unless specially exempt, were bound to contribute. For some time the towns continued to pay geld as in former days, but in the twelfth century the Saxon assessments were set aside, and 'aids', payable at a higher rate, gradually took their place. Henry II exacted from his boroughs special sums, called by various names—*dona, auxilia, assisa,* and finally *tallagia.* These sums were obtained by negotiation with the different communities, and were

---

[1] The substance of this paragraph is derived from Professor Carl Stephenson's essay on 'Taxation and Representation' in *Haskins Anniversary Essays in Medieval History,* pp. 291-312.

taken at irregular intervals, proving infinitely more profitable to the Crown than the antiquated geld. Legally, the boroughs had no defence against such impositions, but, actually, their arbitrary nature caused bitter and increasing resentment, as is shown by the famous protests of London in 1215 and in 1255. Such opposition was a menace to the Crown, and however unwilling Edward I may have been to relinquish his legal right to tallage, it was none the less obviously to his advantage to have his legal rights reinforced by voluntary consent. The co-operation of the moneyed classes arising in the towns was of more practical value than literal insistence on what was fast becoming an old-fashioned prerogative. A general grant made in a central assembly was a speedier and more convenient method of raising the money than a series of separate bargainings; and by summoning towns, irrespective of whether or not they were of his demesne, Edward was able to minimize the distinction between them, and ultimately to increase his revenue by assuming that all boroughs should pay at the same rate. There were many inducements to him to summon representatives of cities and towns to his parliaments in order that he might be able to state that the aid which he subsequently exacted had been granted by them all *curialiter et gratanter*. Other powerful motives there may have been; but Edward I, like all other medieval kings, valued the boroughs chiefly and primarily as a source of supply.

When tallage fell finally into disuse at the beginning of Edward III's reign, this liability of the towns to special taxation was perpetuated by their assessment, for the parliamentary subsidies, at a rate higher than that paid by the shires. In this way practical recognition was given to the fact that a great part of the movable wealth of the country was concentrated in the cities and boroughs. Before 1334, the taxation of movables was both complex and haphazard. The proportions levied varied greatly, and, as a new assessment was made each time a subsidy was voted, it was impossible for the government to foretell what sum it might expect to receive. But in 1334 it was agreed that the amounts paid towards the tenth and fifteenth in that year should be recognized as the future basis of taxation. Henceforth, when a tenth and fifteenth was voted by the Commons, the government knew what sum it should receive, and the towns knew how much each of them would have to pay. Such was the theory; but the practice fell very far short of it. If a town declined in prosperity, it became more and more difficult for its inhabitants to raise the allotted sum. Evasions were attempted or exemptions allowed, so that the revenue actually received from this source almost always fell short of the sum anticipated. Once the control of the Commons over direct taxation had been established, almost every parliament witnessed bargainings as to what grievances should be redressed before supplies were granted. In spite of the unusual character of the Good Parliament of 1376, the details of its proceedings, as given in the *Anonimalle Chronicle*, indicate what were probably the usual preliminaries to the grant of a tax.[1] Parliament opened with a speech from the Chancellor, in which he set forth the King's necessities and asked for a subsidy on movables and for the custom on wool and other merchandise. After listening to the speech, the Lords and Commons separated for consultation, the Commons meeting in the Chapter-house of the Abbey. A full discussion followed. Certain knights rose to emphasize the poverty of the Commons, the difficulty of making a large grant, and their dissatisfaction with the way in which public money was being wasted. The attack on the administration which followed was peculiar to the year 1376, but some such discussion of grievances and attempt to secure their redress were common features of many parliaments. Sometimes the Commons seem to have been doubtful of their competence to make a grant on their own initiative. In 1339, while admitting the King's need of a generous aid, they expressed a doubt whether they could well offer it without first consulting their constituents.[2] At Lynn, as probably in other towns, the constituents were kept in touch with the progress of events, and the parliamentary representatives occasionally wrote home to ask for advice on financial matters. In 1371, a messenger was sent from Lynn to London to inquire what progress

---

[1] *Anonimalle Chronicle*, pp. 79–94.   [2] *Rot. Parl.*, ii. 104.

was being made with the grant of the subsidy;[1] in 1426, the mayor of Lynn asked the Assembly if they wished the parliamentary burgesses to offer any money to the knights in order to procure a restriction of the subsidy.[2] Three years later, the mayor announced to the Assembly that the parliamentary burgesses had sent a letter reporting that the citizens of London, York, Bristol, Hull, and other towns proposed to work together with the knights for the same purpose.[3] Negotiations of this kind, naturally unrecorded on the parliament roll, must have claimed a great part of the time and energies of the burgesses.

The great importance of the 'estate of merchants' in the early part of the reign of Edward III is a commonplace of fourteenth-century history.[4] It was the merchants, with their controlling interest in the wool-trade, who financed the Hundred Years' War, and it was in the struggle to prevent the grant of taxes by colloquies of merchants that parliament won some of its most famous victories against the Crown. Councils of merchants were constantly summoned by Edward III, many of them when no parliament was sitting. In 1336, merchant assemblies were convened in May, in June, and again in September. The business discussed was the levy of a tax on wool, which was finally granted by the assembly at Nottingham in September. Again, in 1337, a body of merchants, speaking through their two elected representatives, Reginald de Conduit of London and William de la Pole of Hull, came to an arrangement with the King whereby he was to receive half the profits resulting from the exercise of a stringent monopoly of wool by the merchants. These and other similar arrange-

[1] Archives of the Corporation of King's Lynn. Chamberlains' Accounts, 44–5 Edward III, 'Item, de xiijs. iiijd. solutis Petro de Rollesby pro expensis suis uersus London ad inquirendum quomodo fecerunt in partibus illis de subsidio domini regis.'

[2] Assembly Book, 4 Henry VI : 'Et ibidem maior petit a congregacione si burgenses parliamenti expendere uellent super milites comitatum ad restringendum subsidium.'

[3] Ibid., 8 Henry VI : 'Et ibidem motum fuit per maiorem quod burgenses parliamenti miserunt litteram maiori, ut ciues London', Bristoll', Ebor', Hull et alii proponunt laborare militibus comitatum pro restrictione subsidii. Et petitum est quid in hac parte respondere uoluerint.'

[4] Unwin, *Finance and Trade under Edward III*, pp. 179–255.

ments became increasingly unpopular as the war progressed. In 1339, the magnates asked that the maltolte on wool should cease. In 1340, the King renounced his right to take more than the ancient custom on wool without the consent of parliament. When the pledge was broken and assemblies of merchants continued to be summoned for purposes of taxation, care was taken that such grants should receive subsequent parliamentary confirmation. Gradually the 'estate of merchants', as such, began to disintegrate. At the beginning of the reign the merchants appear as a body separate and distinct from the Commons, but by 1348 'the petitions emanating from the merchants, and representing a variety of different interests, are mingled with those of the Commons, and the many petitions of the Commons express to a large extent the grievances of the merchants'.[1]

It thus becomes evident that the rise and fall of the 'estate of merchants' is closely connected with the problem before us. The method of summons to the merchant assemblies was twofold. Greater merchants were summoned by writs addressed to them individually, lesser merchants by writs addressed to the sheriffs or to the mayors of cities and boroughs ordering the election of suitable persons. Great merchants like Reginald Conduit or William de la Pole or Henry Goldbetere were all, in their turn, elected members of parliament. The lesser members of the merchant assemblies were drawn from the same class and chosen in the same way as the parliamentary representatives, and many of them also served in both capacities. As parliament gradually deprived the merchant assemblies of the right to negotiate taxes privately, it was upon duly-elected merchant members of parliament that this and similar responsibilities came to fall. The 'parliament' of September 1353 affords an interesting illustration of an attempted compromise between the two kinds of assemblies. In addition to the magnates, eighty-two burgesses from forty-three selected towns, and one knight from each of the counties were summoned. Thus the merchant element predominated, while the inclusion of a number of knights might be thought to lend a parliamentary sanction to their decisions.

[1] Unwin, op. cit., p. 220.

For the Ordinances of the Staple, drawn up by this assembly, the merchants must obviously have been mainly responsible.

The establishment of the Calais Staple in 1363, which was regarded as a breach of the King's solemn pledges to Parliament, led to a strongly-worded protest from the knights of the shire together with certain borough representatives and other merchants, and the scheme was subsequently abandoned.[1] Again, in the legislation of 1363, the influence of the borough members may probably be discerned. Merchants and craftsmen were required to follow one chosen trade and no other—an attempt to undermine the wealth of the 'grossers' and to return to the principles of the craft gilds which, for a number of reasons, may well have had the support of many of the townsmen in parliament.[2] In short, it may be inferred that, with the passing of the old merchant assemblies, the main responsibility for directing the fiscal and mercantile policy of the country devolved upon the borough members of parliament in consultation with other merchants of the realm. It is not without significance that the third quarter of the century sees the rise of such great merchant members of Parliament as Philipot, Walworth, and Graa of York. A study of the functions of the merchants generally throughout the reign of Edward III makes it difficult to suppose that either the Rolls or the chroniclers give an adequate impression of the activities and importance of those same merchants as elected members of parliament.

When we turn to the local aspect of the representatives' work we become still more clearly aware of the responsibilities of their office. The manifold duties with which many towns entrusted their representatives fall roughly into three groups. First, the representatives were given the task of laying local grievances, in the form of petitions, before the central assembly; secondly, they were asked to undertake general business for the town; and, thirdly, they were often required to bring back to their con-

---

[1] Compare the discussion as to the location of the Staple in the York parliament of 1318. Tout, *Place of Edward II in English History*, p. 252 and n. 3.

[2] For suggested reasons see Unwin, op. cit., pp. 248–50.

stituents a report of the progress of events in parliament and of the liabilities to which the commons were committed. The national records are not concerned with these aspects of the burgesses' activities, but they may be fully illustrated from local sources.

There is evidence that the elected representatives, aided, it might be, by other responsible burgesses, were frequently entrusted with the furthering of parliamentary petitions. Thus, on 2 October 1377, Walter de Bixton and Peter de Alderford were elected by the city of Norwich to attend the first parliament of Richard II. At the time of the election, the four bailiffs and thirteen other citizens were deputed to consult with the elected representatives on matters touching the community.[1] The result of their deliberations was a petition in parliament whereby the poor citizens of Norwich asked for a confirmation of the charters, privileges, and customs granted and confirmed to them by former kings.[2] On 15 December, and again on 7 January, Walter de Bixton was sent to London with a companion to prosecute the confirmation of the charter.[3] The *inspeximus* and confirmation were finally granted on 26 February 1378.[4] In 1482, the citizens of Exeter presented a petition to parliament for the curtailment of the privileges of the Exeter Tailors' Gild.[5] That the elected representatives were in part responsible for it is shown by the payment of £3 19s. 8d. to one of them—John Attwyll—*pro negociis ciuitatis tempore parliamenti pro annullacione carte Scissorum.*[6] Again, Henry Betele and Thomas Morton of Lynn, at the time of their election to parliament in January 1377, were instructed to press the Council for the repayment of certain moneys lent to the King by the town, repayment to be made either in cash or by assignment of customs.[7] In consequence, a petition was presented to the Council from the poor commons of the borough asking for the repayment, in one or

---

[1] Hudson and Tingey, op. cit., i. 271.
[2] Ancient Petitions, no. 6443.
[3] Hudson and Tingey, op. cit., i. 271.
[4] *Cal. Charter Rolls*, v. 238.   [5] *Rot. Parl.*, vi. 219–20.
[6] Archives of Exeter Corporation. Receivers' Accounts, 22–3 Edward IV.
[7] Ingelby, *Red Register of Lynn*, ii. 128.

other of these forms, of the sum lent to the Crown during the treasurership of Brantingham.[1] The grant to the burgesses of Lynn, on 20 May 1414, of an *inspeximus* and confirmation[2] of the charter dated 16 March, 11 Henry IV, must almost certainly have been the result of a petition, now lost, presented by the parliamentary representatives, for at a meeting of the assembly on 31 May 1413, the mayor announced that William Hallyate and John Tylney had written more than once urging that the charter might be sent to London so that they might see it confirmed.[3] Similarly, the payment at Cambridge, in 1425, of £4 ' for confirmation of the King's charter' to William Weggewode, who represented the borough in the parliament of that year, was probably a reward for his energy in procuring a favourable reply to a petition.[4] Specific evidence of the activities of the elected representatives in furthering petitions is naturally scanty, but it is obvious that they would be expected to exert their influence to obtain favourable replies.

The subject-matter of these petitions from the towns is very various, but some financial grievance is usually at the root of them. Petitions for the confirmation of charters, especially on the accession of a new king, were commonly presented ' to the King and his Council in parliament', as were the frequent requests for a reduction of the *firma burgi*, for grants of pavage and murage, and for the regulation of trade and industry. Few petitions relate to matters of more than local interest, and fewer still throw any light on parliamentary problems. Even the London petitions, though naturally more numerous than those from lesser towns, are not noticeably wider in scope. The Londoners' petition of 1377, touching the education of Richard II during his minority,[5] is quite exceptional; the great majority of London's anxieties were purely local. Infringements of the franchise, the intrusions of alien

---

[1] Ancient Petitions, no. 6118. This petition is endorsed ? 1376, but there can be little doubt that it belongs to the following year.

[2] *Cal. Patent Rolls*, 1413–16, p. 191.

[3] Archives of the Corporation of King's Lynn. Gildhall Roll, 13 Henry IV–1 Henry V.

[4] Cooper, *Annals of Cambridge*, i, p. 173. [5] *Rot. Parl.*, ii. 436.

merchants and traders, impediments in Thames and Medway, increases in the price of fish: such were the main preoccupations of the Londoners. Even when a petition raises some wider constitutional issue, the root of the matter is always a local grievance. Thus, the well-known complaint of the burgesses of St. Albans against the abbot, that he is neglecting his due service of sending two burgesses to parliament, springs less from desire to secure representation than from the fear that the abbot is attempting to put them in worse servitude than before, *pur eux mettre en autre servage qe fere ne dusent*.[1] Similarly, a local grievance led the citizens of York to complain of the enhancement of prices due to the holding of parliament in the city in 1322,[2] and led them again, in 1451, to demand that no further letters patent be issued to citizens exempting them from holding certain offices, including that of member of parliament, and that exemptions already issued should be annulled.[3]

The furthering of petitions was only one of the parliamentary burgesses' responsibilities. Many towns expected their representatives to use the opportunity of their visits to Westminster to carry out a variety of local business. The records of King's Lynn afford remarkable evidence on this point. In 1413, John Spycer and John Brown, elected to parliament for the borough, were entrusted by their fellow-burgesses with a bond containing an acknowledgement by the King's serjeant-at-arms of a debt of forty marks owed by him to the mayor and commonalty of Lynn, and ordered to press for payment.[4] William Hallyate and John Tylney, elected to the second parliament of the same year, were given letters of attorney empowering them to conclude an agreement with the mayor, bailiffs, and burgesses of Southampton, in the matter of tolls.[5] During the session of the parliament of 1425, John Copnote and Thomas Burgh, representatives of Lynn, sent to

---

[1] Ancient Petitions, no. 8472.
[2] Ibid., no. 10148. [3] *Rot. Parl.*, v. 225.
[4] '... ad exequendum et inde execucionem faciendum.' Archives of the Corporation of King's Lynn. Gildhall Roll, 13 Henry IV–1 Henry V.
[5] Ibid.: '... ad concludendum et tractandum cum maiore, balliuis et aliis burgensibus uille de Suthampton pro toltis burgensium mercatorum de Lenne.'

the mayor, asking him for a letter of attorney under the common seal which should authorize them to receive the sum of £333 6s. 8d. from Henry V's executors, in repayment of a loan. In compliance with this request, a letter was read to the assembly of the burgesses and sealed publicly, authorizing John Copnote to receive this sum in the name of the town.[1] Three years later (1428) a similar question arose, when the assembled burgesses were asked if they would agree that the parliamentary representatives should receive £100 from the executors of the late King, since they were unable to obtain payment in full. This same assembly imposed a further responsibility upon the representatives. Finding themselves unable to agree whether the inhabitants of South Lynn should contribute towards the strengthening of the town's defences, the mayor and commonalty decided that the parliamentary burgesses should be ordered to investigate the relevant evidence.[2] Again, in 1439, the charter of the town was delivered to the parliamentary burgesses in order that a confirmation might be obtained 'if by the advice of the said burgesses of parliament it can conveniently be done'; and in 1442 the charter was confirmed 'by the labour and industry of Walter Curson, one of the burgesses of parliament'.[3]

Although the evidence from Lynn is unusually full, it is clear from the records of other towns that they too knew how to make use of their representatives. London seems to have developed, at an early date, the habit of 'instructing' her representatives. In 1472, a committee consisting of four aldermen and five commoners was appointed to discuss with the representatives such of the city's business as was to be brought before Parliament.[4] The city of York, in 1445, reimbursed John Thrisk and Richard Buksey for the extra expenses incurred by them in doing business for the city and having a scrutiny made

---

[1] *Hist. MSS. Comm., 11th Report*, Appendix 3, p. 158.

[2] Ibid., p. 160. (Lynn) Assembly Book I : '. . . ut burgenses parliamenti debent facere scrutacionem inter libros regios pro huiusmodi materia . . . '

[3] *Archaeologia*, xxiv, pp. 321, 322.

[4] Journal 9, fol. 12 : ' Assignati ad habendum communicacionem cum ciuibus nouiter pro parliamento etc. pro materiis ciuitatis erga parliamentum &c.'

of certain Exchequer rolls.[1] John Thrisk, in 1449, was paid £13 4s. in addition to his ordinary wages as member of parliament ' because of divers expenses incurred by him in seeking to preserve the liberties and franchises of the city aforesaid '.[2] In 1478, the payments to Miles Metcalf and Robert Amyas for service in parliament included the fees paid by them ' for the writing of a certain petition, as well as for a privy seal and a bill of array, and other expenses incurred by them for the common profit of the city '.[3] At Norwich in 1406, the parliamentary burgesses (Walter de Eton and John Alderford) were paid £5 for their expenses in producing the charter of the city before the King's Justices in the Court of Common Pleas.[4] John Gerard and Richard Monesle, citizens elected to the parliament of 1423, remained in London for two days after the dissolution to discuss the question of exemption from tolls and customs with the ' mayor and council ' of the city of London.[5] Thomas Ingham and Robert Toppes undertook so great an amount of business for the city of Norwich during the parliament of 1445 that at the time of his death, eight years later, Ingham had not been repaid.[6] Stephen Haym, who represented Winchester in the parliament of 1379, undertook business for the city for which he was paid £3 0s. 4d.[7] John Hoord, representative of Shrewsbury in the parliament of 1472, was recom-

---

[1] Archives of the Corporation of York. Chamberlains' Rolls of Accounts, 23 Henry VI: 'In diuersis expensis factis London' per dictos Iohannem et Ricardum pro causis et negociis ciuitatis . . . cum iijs. iiijd. pro scrutacione facta in scaccario domini regis . . . xxviijs. iiijd.'

[2] Ibid., 27 Henry VI: ' pro diuersis expensis per ipsum factis pro saluacione libertatum et franchesiarum ciuitatis predicte.'

[3] Ibid., 18 Edward IV: ' . . . tam pro scribendo cuiusdam supplicacionis quam pro priuato sigillo et billa de array ac aliis expensis per eos factis pro commune utilitate istius ciuitatis.'

[4] Archives of the Corporation of Norwich. City Chamberlains' Roll, 1406-7: ' Waltero de Eton et Iohanni Alderford pro allocacione carte libertatis ciuitatis Norwic' habenda coram Justiciis domini Regis in communi banco — c s.

[5] Chamberlains' Account Books, 2 Henry VI: ' . . . Pro expensis suis apud London' per ij dies in presencia maioris et consilii ciuitatis London' circa exoneracionem custumarum et toltarum . . . '

[6] City Chamberlains' Roll, 1453. For details of the account presented by Ingham's executors to the city see Appendix III.

[7] Archives of the Corporation of Winchester. Compotus Roll, 2 Richard II: 'Item, pro diuersis negotiis factis per Stephanum Haym in dicto parliamento—lxs. iiijd.'

pensed for his labour in resisting a bill for the payment of murage in this parliament.[1] During the second session of Henry VII's first parliament, the mayor of Southampton delivered up the charter to Thomas Overay, one of the elected representatives, in order that he might, if possible, see it confirmed.[2] Thomas Lane and John Sheldwych, representatives of Canterbury in the first parliament of Henry IV, demanded reimbursement from the city chamberlains for various expenses which they had incurred in serving the city in parliament. These included fees for letters patent confirming the liberties of the city, expenses in connexion therewith incurred in the Courts of King's Bench and Common Pleas, and also wine sent on different occasions to Sir Thomas Percy and the Marquis of Dorset.[3] In 1413, the assembly of the burgesses at Salisbury directed the parliamentary representatives to try to obtain an amendment of the Assize of Cloth, and advanced to them the sum of 100s. for this and other business.[4] In 1485, it was part of the duties of the Colchester burgesses to pay in the fee farm of the town at the Exchequer.[5]

A third important service rendered by the representatives to those who elected them was that of making some report on parliamentary proceedings. Here again the fullest and most interesting evidence is supplied by the

---

[1] Archives of the Corporation of Shrewsbury. Bailiffs' Account, 13 Edward IV : ' Et in denariis solutis Iohanni Hoord uni burgensium parliamenti pro diuersis custis et expensis factis pro resistenda bille pro muragio soluendo ad parliamentum predictum—iij*li*. x*s*. ij*d*.

[2] Archives of the Corporation of Southampton. Book of Remembrances, 1 Henry VII : ' Mem. that the last day of January, anno primo R. Henrici vij[i], the meir delyverd unto Thomas Overay esquyer, be the advice of . . . Massy Salmon, their Town bailly, and others, the new charter last confermyd and a roll of parchement writen for a copy of the grene wex to conferme if he may and to delyuere agen when he shall be requyred. And the same day he rode to the parlement ward.'

[3] Archives of the Corporation of Canterbury. Chamberlains' Accounts, 1 Henry IV : ' Pro expensis suis factis circa prosecucionem cuiusdam litterae patentis regie pro renouacione carte de libertate ciuitatis Cantuar'. Et pro uino misso diuersis uicibus domino Thome de Percy et Markisio de Dorsete . . . et pro expensis suis diuersis modis factis tam in banco regis quam in communi banco circa allocacionem carte de libertate ciuitate Cantuar', &c.'

[4] Archives of the Corporation of Salisbury, Ledger A. 1, 14 Henry IV.

[5] Benham, *Red Paper Book of Colchester*, p. 62.

records of Lynn. There can be little doubt that in London, as in many of the smaller towns, the representatives on their return from parliament were called upon for some report of what had taken place ; but these reports, possibly because informal news could easily be obtained day by day, were not entered among the proceedings of the Courts of Aldermen and Common Council. John de Grantham and John Prior, elected to the York parliament of 1328, sent several letters discussing events there,[1] but the only example from London of a detailed verbal report which has come down to us is that given by John Hadle and his fellows to the aldermen, common councillors and other good men of the city, specially summoned for the purpose after the Gloucester parliament of 1378.[2] This report is of great value in illuminating the details of the quarrel between the Court party and the city, yet for the historian of parliament it is inferior in interest to the reports delivered by the burgesses of Lynn. The Londoners confined themselves strictly to matters affecting the city ; but the men of Lynn tried to give their hearers some idea, however crude, of proceedings in parliament as a whole.

The records of Lynn contain many examples of these parliamentary reports. The descriptions suggest that the return of the representatives from parliament was regarded as an event of some importance, bringing numbers of burgesses to the Gildhall to hear the news and to learn what they were to be asked to pay. The *Red Register* contains the earliest brief reference to such a report. The clerk notes that, after the Good Parliament of 1376, a 'congregation was held for the promulgation of diverse acts of parliaments, &c.'[3] These reports are more fully summarized on the gildhall rolls and in the assembly books of the fifteenth century, though they, too, are often disappointingly meagre. In 1413, the burgesses delivered their report on the first parliament of Henry V :

'William Hallyate and Master John Tylney, burgesses of parlia-

---

[1] Thomas, *Calendar of Plea and Memoranda Rolls*, i, pp. 52–7.

[2] Riley, *Memorials of London*, pp. 427–8.

[3] *Red Register of Lynn*, ii. 124 : '. . . congregacio facta fuit ad promulgandum diuersos actus parliamenti, &c.'

ment in this year, arose and stood by the window in the northern part of the hall, and worthily declared the acts of the last parliament before the mayor and commonalty, point by point, from the beginning to the end, opening with the sermon of the reverend father the Bishop of Winchester, Chancellor of England, which he preached in the presence of the lord king of England, the text of which was *Ante omnem actum stabile consilium*, of which sermon he made three divisions. . . . Then the mayor asked William and John to restore to the commonalty the muniments and evidences which they had in their possession. And they delivered the royal charter . . . to the chamberlains. . . . Then the mayor asked the parliamentary burgesses why the charter of liberties had not been ratified. They answered that no charter in the whole of England had been ratified or confirmed by the Friday after St. Barnabas last past, not even the charter of the city of London, and they added that whereas the ratification of charters used to be granted for ten marks or £10, now £100 or one hundred marks is asked, which seems excessive . . .' [1]

The reliability of these reports is doubtful in view of the very inaccurate account delivered by Thomas Brygge and Andrew Swanton on their return from the parliament of

---

[1] Archives of the Corporation of King's Lynn. Gildhall Roll, 13 Henry IV– 1 Henry V: 'Deinde Willelmus Hallyate et Magister Iohannes Tylney, burgenses parliamenti hoc anno, surrexerunt et ad fenestram ex parte aquilonari in aula stete- runt et actus ultimi parliamenti ualde hic pronunciauerunt et coram maiore et communitate, de punctu in punctum a principio usque ad finem, incipientes ad collacionem reuerendi patris Episcopi Wyncestr', cancellarii Anglie, quam dixit in presencia domini nostri regis Anglie, unde thema et idem magister dixit "ante omnem actum stabile consilium" et inde fecit tres diuisiones seu distinctiones de materiis . . . Deinde dictum est prefatis Willelmo et magistro Iohanni per maiorem quod restituant coram communitate eiusdem uille de Lenn' munimenta et eui- dencia quae habent in sua custodia. Et cartam regis de priuilegiis et libertatibus Burgi de Lenn', ratificatam per dominum Henricum regem quartum post con- questum, in manus Iohannis Bucworth, Iohannis Maseye, et Willelmi Walden camerariorum uille de Lenn' ibidem existencium liberarunt . . . Quesitum est per maiorem a burgensibus parliamenti quare carta de priuilegiis et libertatibus Lenne Episcopi non sit de nouo ratificata. Dicunt quod nulla carta in tota Anglia die ueneris proxima post festum Sci Barnabi Apostoli ultimum elapsum est ratificata neque confirmata, neque carta priuilegiorum et libertatum ciuitatis London'. Quesi- tum est per maiorem qua sit causa. Dicunt quod ratificatio que solebat concedi pro x marcis uel x libris nunc petunt c marcas uel c libras quod uidetur excessum. Unde est consulendum.'

Rot. Parl. iv, p. 3 records the sermon of the Bishop of Winchester at the opening of the parliament, quotes the text *Ante omnem actum consilium stabile*, and refers to the threefold division of the sermon.

1420–1. They told their brethren that the Archbishop of Canterbury had preached a fine sermon (*unam collacionem nobilem*) from the text 'Justice and Peace have kissed each other',[1] whereas the preacher was the Bishop of Durham and his text was '*Inivit David consilium*'.[2] After the account of the sermon, Thomas Brygge went on to deliver what is possibly the earliest surviving description of the method of choosing the Speaker. 'He declared that Roger Hunte and Richard Russell were nominated as Speakers, but that when a scutiny was made Roger had the advantage with a majority of four votes, and he obtained the office of Speaker of the parliament.'[3] This brief account, though it leaves many problems unsolved, is of great interest, showing as it does that the election was closely contested, and suggesting that the Commons exercised greater freedom in the choice of their Speaker than has sometimes been supposed.[4] Hunte and Russell may, of course, have both been nominees of the Crown, and we are not told whether the voting was by heads or by constituencies. Of the two candidates, Hunte was one of the Bedfordshire knights, and if the Richard Russell who represented Dunwich may be identified as the second, it is remarkable to find a burgess from one of the smaller towns within four votes of the Speakership at such an early date.[5]

On their return from the parliament of May 1421, Bartholomew Systerne and John Parmenter of Lynn published their report on the news and acts (*noua et actus*) of parliament, 'as well as they were able to remember them' (*prout eorum sensus retinere potuerunt*).[6] Bartholomew, who was the spokesman, gave a description of the assembling of the

---

[1] 'Justitia et pax esculate [sic] sunt, &c.'   [2] *Rot. Parl.*, iv. 123.

[3] Gildhall Roll, 8–9 Henry V: 'Et dicit quod Rogerus Hunte et Ricardus Russell nominati fuerunt ibidem prolocutores, tamen, dicit, quod examinacionibus inde factis, Rogerus preualuit, et habuit plures uoces iiij^or &c. et optinuit officium prolocutoris parliamenti.' The presentation of Hunte as Speaker is recorded in *Rot. Parl.*, iv. 123.

[4] e.g. by Porritt, *Unreformed House of Commons*, i, pp. 432–3.

[5] He is the only Richard Russell in the Official List for this parliament; but more probably the unsuccessful candidate was John Russell, who sat for Herefordshire, and who held the office of Speaker in the parliaments of 1423, 1432, and 1450.

[6] Gildhall Roll, 8–9 Henry V.

members, 'saying that he entered the Star Chamber with great difficulty and discomfort because of the multitude of people, noble lords, citizens of cities and burgesses of boroughs; and they were among the first boroughs called because such was the order of the sheriff's return.'[1] The manner in which these reports were delivered differed from year to year. In 1421, John Waterden and Robert Brandon each gave half of the report;[2] in 1425, Thomas Burgh read aloud from a roll containing the acts of parliament, and John Copnote added explanatory comments;[3] in 1453, Henry Bermingham and William Pilton declared the acts of parliament, reduced them to writing, and then read them aloud;[4] in 1478, John Burbage, one of the two representatives, described the acts of parliament partly in writing and partly in words.[5] Occasionally partial reports or requests for instructions were sent down while parliament was still in session. Thus in November 1427, the parliamentary burgesses sent a letter to the town making mention that the Friars Preachers had contrived a certain malicious bill against the community.[6] In October 1429, the mayor read to an assembly of Lynn merchants a letter from the parliamentary burgesses in which they explained that the citizens of London, Bristol, York, Hull, and others were planning to join with the knights in pleading for a restriction of the subsidy, and asked what the community wished them to do in this matter.[7] In February 1437, the assembly

---

[1] '...dicens quod intrauit cameram Stellarum cum magna difficultate et duritate propter multitudinem gencium cum magnatibus proceribus, ciuibus ciuitatum et burgensibus burgorum; et fuerunt cum primis burgis uocati et eo quod retornum uicecomitis sic uoluit.' The last phrase is probably a reference to the customary 'call-over' of the Commons. The sheriff of Norfolk's return may have been one of the first which came to hand in reading over the list of names.

[2] Gildhall Roll, 8–9 Henry V: 'recitauerunt dicta et acta xvij dierum in parliamento, dont la. moyte par Robert et l'autre moyte par Jehan.'

[3] Assembly Book, 3 Henry VI: 'Et ibidem T. Burgh legebat gesta parliamenti intitulata in quodam rotulo et Iohannes Copnote declarauit plenius huius gesta.'

[4] Assembly Book, 31 Henry VI: '... declarauerunt actus parliamenti et in scripta reduxerunt quae lecta fuerunt.'

[5] Assembly Book, 18 Edward IV: 'Iohannes Burbage, unus burgensium parliamenti, declarauit acta parliamenti partim in scriptis et partim in uerbis.'

[6] *Hist. MSS. Comm. 11th Report*, Appendix 3, p. 160.

[7] *Supra*, p. 131, n. 3.

of the burgesses again listened to a letter sent to the mayor
by the parliamentary representatives, and when the letter
was fully understood, the assembly agreed that the mayor
should return an answer; the following April, the representatives 'well and discreetly' reported what they had done
for the mayor in parliament.[1]

The delivery of these reports on parliament seems to have
been recognized as forming part of the regular duties of
the elected representatives in several other towns. The *Red
Paper Book* of Colchester contains a transcript of a remarkably detailed account of the first parliament of Henry VII
delivered by the elected burgesses, Thomas Christemasse
and John Vertue. This transcript consists of a diary of the
proceedings as seen by the commons, and covers the whole
of the session from 7 November to the prorogation on
10 December.[2] John Saynton, who represented Grimsby in
one of the early parliaments of Henry VII, sent a friend
from London with authority to report, on his behalf, on
all that had passed in the parliament.[3] At Norwich, in
1421, Robert Dunston and Robert Baxstere 'declared the
whole intent and the business done in the lord king's parliament held at Westminster on Friday next after the Feast
of the Ascension'.[4] The servant of William Bastard, who
represented Shrewsbury in the Bury parliament of 1447,
brought letters from his master to the town while parlia-
was still sitting.[5]

Official copies of statutes and ordinances were often pro-
cured by the towns as a supplement to the verbal or written

---

[1] *Hist. MSS. Comm. 11th Report*, Appendix 3, p. 160 ; *Archaeologia* xxiv, p. 321.

[2] *Red Paper Book of Colchester*, pp. 60–4.

[3] His letter, which belongs probably to the year 1487, runs as follows (*Hist. MSS.
Comm. 14th Report*, App. 8, p. 251): 'Right worshipfull and w[t] all my hert entirely
belovyd maystre and frendez, I recomaund me to yow as hertely as I can, praying
you to gyff faithfull credence to my fellow and frend Thomas Broghton, youre
neighpur, the brynger hereoff, in all suche thyngez as he will say to you on my
behalff, as touchyng such . . . passid in the Parlement and for the worship and
wele off yo[r] toune for yo[r] franchez.   Written at London the xvj day of June.

yo[r] own man and frend
John Saynton.'

[4] Hudson and Tingey, op. cit., i. 276.

[5] Archives of the Corporation of Shrewsbury. Bailiffs' Account, 25 Henry VI :
'Item, in argento dato seruienti Willelmi Bastard uenienti cum litteris de parliamento tento apud Bury . . . vj*d*.'

reports of the representatives—Lynn paid two shillings for a copy of the statutes and ordinances issued in the Cambridge parliament of 1388,[1] and at the beginning of Henry IV's reign 6s. 8d. was paid 'for having a copy of the parliament' of the twenty-first year of Richard II.[2] Exeter paid 3s. 4d. for a 'copy of the parliament' of February 1388.[3] Norwich paid messengers for bringing copies of the statutes of the parliaments of 1423 and 1426,[4] and several towns had the statutes of various important parliaments transcribed at length among their official records.[5]

When we come to examine the sum of our information on the functions of the burgesses in parliament we cannot fail to be aware how much still remains to be discovered. Yet the knowledge we have is sufficient to show that the position of an elected representative was no sinecure. He took, and was expected by his fellow-townsmen to take, his duties seriously. Only a man of judgement and experience could rightly fill such a position of responsibility. Nor were his duties lightened by the fact that he was often an inconspicuous figure in parliament and that his concerns were as much local as national. Local business was often both complicated and important, and faithful service rendered to the small community was beneficial in its effects on the larger community, which the ordinary medieval townsman was perhaps as yet unable to visualize as the nation or the state.

---

[1] Archives of the Corporation of King's Lynn. Chamberlains' Account Roll 1389-90 : 'Et ijs. solutis pro una copia statutum et ordinacionum editorum in parliamento tento apud Cantebrigg.'

[2] Ibid., 1 Henry IV. Copies of the roll of this parliament and of that of 1387-8 may have been sold as propaganda. Cf. Dr. Tout's article 'The English Parliament and Public Opinion 1376-88,' in *Mélanges d'Histoire offerts à Henri Pirenne.*

[3] *Journal of the British Archaeological Association*, xvii, p. 315.

[4] Archives of the Corporation of Norwich. Chamberlains' Account Books 1423-4 and 1426-7.

[5] e.g. the York Memorandum Book, which contains copies of many statutes issued between 1381 and 1424.

APPENDIX I

Some Names of Burgess Representatives not included in the Blue Book of 1878

(*Italics* denote a printed source.)

Parliament.	Town.	Representatives.	Source of Information.
1296	Wallingford	Osbert de Nottlee	*Hist. MSS. Comm. 6th Rept.*, 591
1331	Shrewsbury	? Richard Russell	Bailiffs' Account
1332–3	,,	Nicholaus de Ser'	,,
1340 (Mar.)	Lynn	William de Snorryng	Chamberlains' Account
1340 (Sept.)	Norwich	Robert de Wyleby	*Norfolk Official Lists*
		John Fitz John	,, ,,
1343	Exeter	Philip de Bersham	Receivers' Account
,,	Norwich	John Ymme	*Norfolk Official Lists*
		John de Morle	,, ,,
1354	Lynn	Geoffrey Drewe	Chamberlains' Account
		John de Couteshale	,,
,,	Winchester	William Wynesflode	Compotus Roll
		Roger Germayn	,,
1357	Lynn	William Hanton	Chamberlains' Account
		Thomas Curson	,,
,,	Winchester	William Hazelwode	Compotus Roll
		Thomas Husee	,,

Date	City	Name	Source
1369	Norwich	John de Welborn	Hudson and Tingey, i. 268
		Thomas de Bumpstead	,, ,,
1371 (Feb.)	Exeter	John Bosoun	Receivers' Account
1371 (June)	Lynn	Geoffrey de Tolboothe	Chamberlains' Account
1372	Reading	John Hyde	Mayor's Account
1376	Exeter	John Hulle	Receivers' Account
		John Bozoun	
,,	Norwich	Bartholomew de Appelyerd	Hudson and Tingey, ii. 44
		William de Bliclyng	,, ,,
,,	Lynn	John Brunham	Red Register, ii, pp. 123-4
		Geoffrey Tolboothe	,, ,,
1379	Exeter	John Wadham	Receivers' Account
		Robert Hulle	,, ,,
,,	Winchester	Stephen Haym	Compotus Roll
		Hugo Cran	,, ,,
1380 (Nov.)	Reading	Richard Wycombe	Account Roll
		Richard Brompton	,, ,,
,,	Lynn	Richard Houtone	Red Register, ii, p. 154
		Henry de Betele	,, ,,
,,	Norwich	John Latymer	Norfolk Official Lists
		Robert de Bernham	,, ,,
1388 (Feb.)	Exeter	Thomas Reymund	Receivers' Account
1390 (Jan.)	Lynn	Robert de Waterden	Red Register, ii, p. 45
		John Wace	,, ,,
1390 (Nov.)	,,	John de Wentworth	Red Register, ii, p. 48
		Thomas de Waterden	,, ,,

Parliament.	Town.	Representatives.	Source of Information.
1390 (Nov.)	Norwich	William Appelyerd	*Norfolk Official Lists*
		Thomas Gerard	„
1394	Lynn	Thomas Drewe	*Red Register*, ii, p. 8
		Thomas Morton	„
„	Norwich	Henry Lomynour	*Norfolk Official Lists*
		William Everard	„
1397–8	Exeter	William Wilford	Receivers' Account
		William Frye	„
1399	„	Robert Coblegh	„
		Roger Golde	„
1400	Canterbury	Thomas Ikham	Chamberlains' Accounts, vol. i
		John Pirie	„
„	Lynn	Thomas Drewe	*Norfolk Official Lists*
		John Bolt	„
„	Norwich	Edmund Warner	„
		William de Crakeford[1]	„
1401 (Jan.)	Lynn	Robert Botkesham	„
		Thomas Waterden	„
1402 (Jan.)	„	Thomas Brigge	„
		Roger Galton	„
1402 (Sept.)	„	Thomas Faukes	„
		Robert de Brunham	„
„	Norwich	William Appleyerd	„
		William Crakeford	„

[1] The City Chamberlains' Roll gives Walter Eton in place of Crakeford.

Year	Place	Names	Source
1403–4	Exeter	William Wilford[1], Thomas Reymund[1]	Receivers' Account, "
"	Canterbury	Richard Beson[2], John Umfray[2], John Haute[2]	Chamberlains' Accounts, vol. i, ", "
"	Lynn	Thomas Drewe	Chamberlains' Account
"	Norwich	John Wentworth, William Everard, Walter de Eton	Norfolk Official Lists, ", "
1404	Exeter	John Lake, John Nywaman	Receivers' Account, "
"	Lynn	Thomas Drewe, John Brandon	Chamberlains' Account, "
"	Salisbury	John Wollap, Richard Jewel	Ledger A. 1, "
1410	Canterbury	Thomas Lane, Henry Lynde	Chamberlains' Accounts, vol. i, "
"	Norwich	Robert Dunston, William Ampulford	City Chamberlains' Roll, "
"	Salisbury	William Bayly, William Bourer	Ledger A. 1, "
1411	Norwich	Bartholomew Appleyerd, Thomas Gerard	Norfolk Official Lists, "
"	Salisbury	Richard Spencer, Walter Shirle	Ledger A. 1, "
1412–13	Canterbury	William Lane, John Sheldwych	Chamberlains' Accounts, vol. i, "

[1] At Westminster session only. [2] At Coventry session only.

Parliament.	Town.	Representatives.	Source of Information.
1412–13	Exeter	Thomas Eston Peter Sturte	Receivers' Account ,,
,,	Lynn	William Hallyate John Tylney	Chamberlains' Account ,,
,,	Norwich	John Alderford Bartholomew Appleyerd	Norfolk Official Lists ,,
,,	Winchester	Marcus le Fayre William Wode	Black Book of Winchester, p. 17 ,,
,,	Salisbury	Walter Shirley William Waryn	Ledger A. 1 ,, ,, ,, ,, ,,
1414 (Jan.)	Canterbury	Richard Water John Sheldwych	Chamberlains' Accounts, vol. i ,,
,,	Norwich	Robert Brasier John Alderford	Norfolk Official Lists ,, ,,
1415	Canterbury	John Sheldwych John Biskelee	Chamberlains' Accounts, vol. i
,,	Norwich	Robert Dunston	Norfolk Official Lists
1416 (Mar.)	,,	Henry Rafman William Sedman	,, ,, ,, ,,
,,	Winchester	Marcus le Fayre Walter Shirle	Compotus Roll
,,	Salisbury	Henry Man	Ledger A. 1 ,, ,,
1416 (Oct.)	Exeter	John Pollow Roger Golde	Receivers' Account
,,	Lynn	William Herford John Warren	Chamberlains' Account ,, ,,

Date	City	Name	Source
1416 (Oct.)	Norwich	William Appleyerd	*Norfolk Official Lists*
„		John Biskelee	„ „ „
„	Shrewsbury	Robert Horsley	*Owen and Blakeway* i, p. 548
„		William Horde	„ „ „
„	Canterbury	William Ikham	Chamberlains' Accounts, vol. i
„		William Benet	„ „ „
„	Winchester	William Reson	Compotus Roll „ „
„		Richard Turnaunt	„ „ „
„	Salisbury	Walter Shirle	Ledger A. 1
„		Thomas Mason, draper	„ „
1419	Lynn	Philip Frank	*Norfolk Official Lists*
„		Walter Curson	„ „ „
1421 (May)	Canterbury	John Sheldwych	Chamberlains' Accounts, vol. i
„		William Lane	„ „ „
1426	Lynn	John Parmenter	*Hist. MSS. Comm. 11th Rept.*, 3, p. 159
„		Bartholomew Petypas	„ „ „
1439	Exeter	Thomas Cook	Receivers' Account
„		Henry Hull	„ „ „
„	Canterbury	John Sheldwych	Chamberlains' Accounts, vol. i
„		John Lynde	„ „ „
„	Lynn	Thomas Burgh	*Archaeologia*, xxiv, p. 321
„		Thomas Salisbury	„ „ „
„	Salisbury	William Ludlow	Ledger A. 1
„		Richard Payn	„ „
1445	Canterbury	John Mulling	Chamberlains' Accounts, vol. i
„		William Osborn	„ „ „
„	Norwich	Thomas Ingham	*Hudson and Tingey*, ii. 70
„		Robert Toppes	„ „

Parliament.	Town.	Representatives.	Source of Information.
1445	Shrewsbury	Richard Stury / ?William Boerley	Bailiffs' Account
,,	Salisbury	William Hore / Richard Hayne	Ledger A. 1 ,,
,,	York	John Thrisk / Richard Buksey	Chamberlains' Account Roll ,, ,, ,,
1449 (Nov.)	Canterbury	John Mulling / John Winter	Chamberlains' Accounts, vol. ii ,, ,, ,,
1459	Exeter	John Hamley / John Netherton	Receivers' Account ,,
,,	Canterbury	William Sellow / Thomas Forster	Book of Accounts, vol. ii ,, ,,
,,	Lynn	Simon Pigott / William Pilton	Norfolk Official Lists ,, ,, ,,
,,	Norwich	John Chyttok / Richard Browne[1]	,, ,, ,,
,,	Salisbury	William Hore / Richard Hayne	Ledger B. 2 ,, ,,
1460	Exeter	William atte Will / John Aysshe	Receivers' Account ,, ,,
,,	Lynn	Henry Bermyngham / William Pilton	Norfolk Official Lists ,, ,,
,,	Ipswich	Richard Felaw / William Baldrey	Annalls of Ipswche, p. 118 ,, ,, ,,
,,	Salisbury	William Wayn / John Halle	Ledger B. 2 ,, ,, ,,

[1] The City Chamberlains' Roll gives Robert Toppe in place of Browne.

Year	City	Names	Source
1461	Exeter	John Coteler	Receivers' Account
"	Canterbury	William Duke Roger Brent	" Chamberlains' Accounts, vol. ii
"	Lynn	John Fremyngham Simon Pigott	*Norfolk Official Lists* "
"	Norwich	Henry Bermyngham Robert Toppes Edward Coteler	*Norfolk Official Lists* " "
"	Shrewsbury	?John Graston Thomas Stone	Bailiffs' Account "
"	Southampton	Richard Aysshe Andrew James	Stewards' Accounts, 1–2 Edward IV "
"	Ipswich	Richard Felaw William Baldree	*Annalls of Ipswche*, p. 119 " "
"	Salisbury	John Halle Richard Gilbert	Ledger B. 2 "
"	York	William Barclay Thomas Scansteby	Chamberlains' Account Roll " "
1463	Canterbury	Robert Bertyn Roger Brent	Book of Accounts, vol. ii
"	Lynn	William Caus Robert Thorisby	*Norfolk Official List* "
"	Norwich	Thomas Elys William Skippewith Roger Pontesbury	" " "
"	Shrewsbury	John Water William Worsop	Bailiffs' Account "
"	Ipswich	John Loppam	*Annalls of Ipswche*, p. 121 " "

Parliament.	Town.	Representatives.	Source of Information.
1463	Salisbury	Henry Swayn, Richard Freman } to York; Henry Swayn, John Wise } to Westminster	Ledger B. 2
,,	,,		,, ,,
1467	Shrewsbury	John Trentham, John Hoord	Bailiffs' Account
			,, ,,
1469	Canterbury	William Sellowe, Nicholas Faunt	Chamberlains' Account, vol. ii
,,	Lynn	John Braibroke, William Waales	Norfolk Official Lists ,, ,,
,,	Shrewsbury	?John Trentham	Bailiffs' Account ,, ,,
,,	Ipswich	John Timperley, jun., John Alfray of Hindley	Annalls of Ipswche, p. 129 ,, ,,
1470	Canterbury	Nicholas Faunt, William Sellowe	Book of Accounts, vol. iii
,,	Lynn	Henry Bermingham, Robert Braibroke	Assembly Book II ,, ,,
,,	Salisbury	Thomas Huse, Roger Holes	Ledger B. 2 ,, ,,
,,	York	William Scawsell, John Glassier	Chamberlains' Account Roll ,, ,,
1483	Exeter	John Attwyll, George Browne	Receivers' Account
,,	Canterbury	Roger Brent, Piers Curtes	Chamberlains' Accounts, vol. ii ,, ,,
,,	Leicester	John Roberdes	Leicester Records, ii, p. 304 ,, ,,

1483	Lynn	William Marche	*Norfolk Official Lists*
,,		Robert Thorisby	,, ,,
,,	Ipswich	James Hobard, esquire	*Annalls of Ipsweche*, p. 147
,,	Salisbury	John Timpetley, esquire	Ledger B. 2 ,, ,,
		William Eston	,, ,,
,,	York	John Hampton	*York Records*, p. 138
		Richard Yorke	,, ,,
		John Tonge	,, ,,
1484	Cambridge	John Wyghton	*Annals of Cambridge*, i, p. 230
		John Hessewell	,, ,, ,,
,,	Canterbury	Roger Brent	Chamberlains' Accounts, vol. ii
,,	Leicester	Thomas Atwode	*Leicester Records*, ii, p. 305
		John Roberdes	,, ,,
		Peers Curtes	,, ,,
,,	Lynn	William Marche	*Norfolk Official Lists*
		William Munke	,, ,,
,,	Norwich	Robert Thorp, senr.	,, ,,
		John Marleburgh	,, ,,
,,	Shrewsbury	Robert Wanternoure	*Owen and Blakeway*, i, p. 548
,,	Ipswich	Benet Caldwell	*Annalls of Ipsweche*, p. 150
		Thomas Baldry	,, ,,
,,	Winchester	Richard Bole	Compotus Roll
		Thomas Bowland	,, ,,
,,	Salisbury	William Becket, mayor	Ledger B. 2
		John Musgrove, esquire	,, ,,
,,	York	Richard York	*York Records*, p. 184
		Thomas Wrangwyssh	,, ,,
1485	Colchester	Thomas Christemasse	*Red Paper Book*
		John Vertue	,, ,,

Parliament.	Town.	Representatives.	Source of Information.
1485	Lynn	Robert Braibroke William Munke	*Norfolk Official Lists*
,,	Canterbury	Roger Brent Nicholas Sheldwych	,, ,, ,, Book of Accounts, vol. v
,,	Southampton	Thomas Raynold Thomas Overay	Stewards' Accounts ,,
,,	Norwich	John Paston, esquire Philip Curson	,, *Norfolk Official Lists* ,,
,,	Ipswich	Thomas Samson William Wimbill	,, ,, ,, *Annalls of Ipswche*, p. 152
,,	Salisbury	William Becket Roger Holes	Ledger B. 2 ,, ,,
,,	York	Robert Hancok Richard York	York House Book II ,, ,, ,,
1487	Colchester	Richard Heynes ?John Saynton	*Red Paper Book*, p. 124
,,	Grimsby		*Hist. MSS. Comm. 14th Rept.*, 8, p. 251
,,	Exeter	Robert Newton John Pring	Receivers' Account
,,	Norwich	Thomas Jenney Robert Thorp	*Norfolk Official Lists* ,, ,, ,,
,,	Lynn	Robert Thorisby John Tygo	,, ,, ,, ,, ,, ,,
,,	Salisbury	William Becket William Hall	Ledger B. 2 ,, ,,
,,	Canterbury	Thomas Atwode Nicholas Sheldwych	,, ,, Chamberlains' Accounts, vol. ii
,,	Bridgnorth	Thomas Wyldecote	*Hist. MSS. Comm. 10th Rept.*, p. 4

1487	York	Nicholas Lancaster	York House Book VI
		John Gilyot	" "
1495	Lynn	John Gryndyll	Norfolk Official Lists
		William Horwode	" "
"	Norwich	Stephen Bryan	" "
		Robert Thorp	" "
"	Canterbury	Edward Bolney	Chamberlains' Accounts, vol. ii
		William Atwode	" "
"	Ipswich	John Fastolf	Annalls of Ipswche, p. 169
		Edmund Bocking	"
"	Plymouth	William Thyckpenny	Worth, History of Plymouth, p. 169
		William Bree	"
"	Salisbury	John Hampton	Ledger B. 2
		Richard Eliot	" "
1497	Exeter	John Attwyll	Receivers' Account
		John Banaster	"
"	Canterbury	William Wode	Chamberlains' Accounts, vol. ii
		Edward Bolney	"
		Thomas Alvard	"
"	Ipswich	Richard Bayly	Annalls of Ipswche, p. 170
		Robert Thorp	"
"	Norwich	Robert Burgh	Norfolk Official Lists
			" "

APPENDIX II

Parliamentary Returns, illustrating Election Methods of the Fifteenth Century.[1]

1. *York. Election of citizens in a shire incorporate.*

Hec indentura facta inter Ricardum Shirwod et Willelmum Burton, uicecomites ciuitatis Ebor', ex una parte, et Ricardum Warter, Willelmum Bowes seniorem, Willelmum Ormeshede, Thomam Snawedon, Nicholaum Blakburn, Iohannem Bolton, Thomam Gare, Willelmum Bedale, Nicholaum Usflete, Nicholaum Urpyngton, Thomam Rydley, Thomam More, Willelmum Crauen, Iohannem Dodyngton, et Iohannem Warde, ciues ciuitatis predicte, ex parte altera, testatur quod predicti uicecomites, in presencia comitatus predicti, ad proximum comitatum ciuitatis predicte tentum ibidem proximum post recepcionem cuiusdam breuis domini Regis huic indenture consuti, uidelicet ad comitatum ciuitatis predicte tentum ibidem die lune in uigilia Natalis domini anno regni Regis Henrici sexti post conquestum Anglie quintedecimo, proclamacionem fecerunt de quodam parliamento domini Regis apud Westmonasterium tenendo, uicesimo primo die Ianuarii tunc proximo futuro, et ibidem eligi fecerunt duos ciues de discrecioribus et magis sufficientibus de ciuitate predicta, uidelicet Willelmum Bowes, juniorem, et Ricardum Louth, plenam et sufficientem potestatem pro se et communitate ciuitatis predicte habentes, ad essendum ad parliamentum predictum et ad faciendum et consentiendum hiis que tunc ibidem ordinari contigerit, deo dante. In cuius rei testimonium partes predicte partibus huius indenture sigilla sua separatim apposuerunt. Datum apud Ebor' die et anno supradicto. Et quoad habendum aliud breue de parliamento, sicut istud breue in se exigit, nullum aliud breue nobis liberatum fuit, etc.

2. *Leominster. Election of burgesses in the borough court.*

Hec indentura facta inter Ricardum Wynnesley balliuum libertatis abbatis Radyng de Leomynstre, ex una parte, et Iohannem Walter balliuum burgi de Leomynstre, Iohannem Bradford, Walterum Walker, Iohannem Sherer, Thomam Morton, Thomam Olnet, Iohannem Astald, Iohannem Kyngislane, Thomam Hode, Iohannem Corbet, Thomam Strete, et Thomam Knott, burgenses

[1] P.R.O. Parliamentary Writs and Returns, Bundle 15.

burgi predicti, ex parte altera, testatur quod predicti burgenses ex assensu tocius communitatis eiusdem burgi, die ueneris proximo ante festum Epiphanie domini, anno regni regis Henrici sexti post conquestum quintodecimo, in Guyhald eiusdem burgi, elegerunt Willelmum Rabys et Iohannem Crewe, burgenses burgi predicti, ad essendum ad parliamentum domini regis apud Westmonasterium tenendum, uicesimo primo die Ianuarii proximo futuro, habentes secum plenam et sufficientem potestatem pro se et communitate eiusdem burgi, ad tractandum, monendum et consentiendum hiis que de communi consilio regis Anglie, favente domino, ordinari contigerit super negociis inibi tractandis et mouendis. In cuius rei testimonium huic parti indenture predicti burgenses sigilla sua alternatim apposuerunt. Datum die et anno supradictis.

3. *Devonshire. Election, in the shire court, of knights of the shire, citizens for Exeter city, and burgesses for several boroughs.*

Hec indentura facta in pleno comitatu Devon' tento in castro domini regis ciuitatis Exon' die martis xxviij° die Decembris, anno regni Regis Henrici sexti quintedecimo inter Thomam Beaumont militem, uicecomitem comitatus predicti, ex parte una, et Willelmum Wonard, Iohannem Copleston, Iohannem Mulys, Ricardum Holand, Iohannem Holand, Adam Somaister, Iohannem Coteler, Stephanum Giffard, Rogerum Baron, Iohannem Harry, Nicholaum Tyrant, Thomam Bonde, Iohannem Kyton, Iohannem Gyffard, Henricum Whityng, Willelmum Bysshop, Iohannem Henstecote, Thome (*sic*) Giffard et Willelmi (*sic*) Bleuthe, uirtute cuiusdam breuis domini regis eidem uicecomiti directi et huic indenture consuti super eleccionem militum, ciuium et burgensium comitatus predicti ad essendum ad parliamentum domini regis tenendum apud Canteb' xxj° die Ianuarii proximo futuro, factaque proclamacione de die et loco prout in predicto brevi fit mencio, testatur quod predicti Willelmus Wonard et Iohannes Coplestone, et alii elegerunt Iohannem Speke, militem, et Rogerum Champernoun milites ad essendum ad parliamentum predictum ad diem et locum predictos pro communitate comitatus predicti, et Thomam Cooke et Walterum Pope, ciues ciuitatis Exon', et Iohannem Serle et Ricardum Strode burgenses burgi de Plympton, et Thomam Ayssheldon et Iohannem Walsshe burgenses burgi de Dertemouth, et Iohannem Wolston et Iohannem Sprye, burgenses burgi de Tavystoke, et Iohannem Worthy et Iohannem Wyche, burgenses burgi de Tottenes, et Iohannem Bearl et Hugonem Champernoun burgenses burgi de Barnestaple, iuxta formam dicti breuis. In cuius rei testimonium, predicti Willelmus Wonard et Iohannes Copleston, et omnes alii infrascripti qui eleccioni illi interfuerunt, sigilla sua presèntibus apposuerunt. Alteri parti istius indenture penes prefatum uicecomitem remanenti predictus uicecomes sigillum suum apposuit. Datum die, loco et anno suprascriptis.[1]

[1] The names of the knights and burgesses, with their sureties, are written on a separate sheet, attached to the return. The sureties may have been fictitious, judging by the list of their surnames, which reads as follows: Comb, Moys, Loir, Roos, Gy, Couper, More, Gay, Mayn, Moys, Wey, Motte, Fox, Ritte, Gay, Coy, Joy, More, Moys, Ware, Rous, Hore, Lacy, More, Fitz, Hore, Moys, Man.

APPENDIX III

A Bill for Parliamentary Expenses (1445–6)

(From the Norwich City Chamberlains' Roll for 1453)

'THIS Bill remembreth the dette of the Mair and Coẽs of the Citee of Norwich that is due to John and Walter Ingham, by reson of their fader and testator Thomas Ingham, late Citeceyn and Alderman of Norwich.[1]

First, it is remembrid that to the parliament of our soveraign lord kyng Henry the vj^te holden at Westm' the xxiij year of his reigne, Robt Toppes and the seid Thomas the xxij^mo day of Feverer redyn, whoes beyng oute contynued unto the Wednesday nexte after Seynt Marke the Evangelist and in the day of Seynt Marke the seid Robert and Thomas redyn ageyn to the seid parliament and contynued there unto the v^te day of June, that is xlij^mo dayes.

Item, the seid parliament was prolongid unto the xx^mo day of October the whiche was the Wednesday next after Seynt Luke the Evangelist. Item, fro the v^te day of June after the parliament was prolongid the seid Robert and Thomas contynued there to seke upon the good lordship of the Lord of Suff' and othir lords and in their comyng hoom fro the parliament viij dayes.[2]

Item, the seid Thomas payed to the seid Robert in the Cheker of our soveraign Lord at Westm' for the comyssion for the Alienes ijs ijd. Item, to Depden of the seid Eschar for writyng of copies xvjd.

Item, at the first labour to the parliament the seid Robert and Thomas hadde w^t theym to London, Walter Jeffereys[3] forasmoche as he hadde gret undirstandyng in the euidencez of the citee, to the whiche Walter the seid Thomas payed vs. And also to Moyll' the Kyng Sergeaunt in lawe for his counsall iijs iiijd. Item, payed for wyn to hym goven. vd. Also payed by the seid Thomas to the clerk of the parliament xvjd. Item, for parchemyn iijd.

Item, at the comyng hoom fro the parliament payed for the cost of the comyng up of John Intewode[4] and Thomas Grafton[5] in the

---

[1] Thomas Ingham represented Norwich in the parliaments of 1427, 1429, and 1445.
[2] The parliament of 1445–6 sat from 25 February to 15 March; from 29 April to 5 June; from 21 October to 15 December 1445; and from 24 January to 9 April 1446: *Rot. Parl.*, v, pp. 66 sq.
[3] Sheriff of Norwich in 1459.
[4] Sheriff of Norwich in 1443, 1444, 1445, 1446, and 1447.
[5] Sheriff of Norwich in 1431.

first vij dayes of May, for mete and drynk to theym and to their ij servauntz, vjs jd.

Item, payed for ther cost whanne they redyn with the seid Robert, and Thomas Ingham to Fernham to the Lord of Suff' iiijs iiijd. Item, payed by Thomas Pert for a letter of instruction and for a copy of the patent xijd. Item, payed for billes writtyng ijs xjd. Item, payed for boot hire and for wyn whanne Thomas Catworth, the seid Robert, and Thomas Ingham laborid by water to Lord Cromwelle, vijd. Item, payed to juryman of court for makyng of the bille for the patent, the whiche shulde have be put in to the lord of Suff', vs.

Item, payed to the seid Thomas Grafton whanne he, the seid Robert, and Thomas Ingham, redyn to Fernham, for his man and hors, in his beyng oute xjs iiijd.

Item, payed for burgeys for comyng up of John Intewode, thanne beyng Shirreve of Norwich, xjs iiijd. Item, payed by the advyse of John Jennay [1] to Moyll, the King's sergeaunt for his counsell iijs iiijd. Item, delyvered to John Intewode for John Jennay and William Aleyn vjs viijd. Item, payed to Burgeys for a testimoniall vjd. Item, for a copy of burgeys patent, xiijd.

Item, payed to John Intewode for to delyvere to lerned counceyll Rampage the Kyng's attorne, for to repleyn to the fee ferme in the Cheker, and also for Burgeys matier xxxs.

Item, payed to Walter Jeffereys at his comyng oute of prisoun, vs, and for his fynes iiijs. Also, payed for hise boord at London by iij weks in Lent and for xiiij dayes after Estere.

Item, the seid Robert and Thomas Ingham labourid toward the seid parliament the xvij day of Octobr unto the xx day of Octobr that was the Wednesday next after Seynt Luke the Evangelist, and contynued there till the Wednesday next after Seynt Lucy the Virgyns and by iij dayes after in ther comyng hoom, and the parliament was prolongid unto the xxiiij day of Jan^y, and fro thanne it contynued foorth unto the ix day of Aprill the whiche was palme Sonne evyn and fro that time by iij dayes in their comyng hoom.

Item, payed to counsell lerned for burgeys matier first to the said John Intewode xs. Item, to William Aleyn iijs iiijd. Item, to Wangford of Greyes Inne vjs viijd. Item, for writyng of billes vjs vd. Item, spent upon counsell lerned in a pyke and wyn, ijs vd.

Item, payed for sute for Thomas Catworth,[2] first for a bille, the whiche was delyuered to the Lords of the parliament, iiijd. Item,

---

[1] Returned for Norwich to the parliament of 1453.
[2] Thomas Catworth was royal warden of Norwich in 1446 and 1447, when the liberties were in the King's hands.

payed in the Rolles for a copy of Sir John Blyston patent, ijs. Item, to the pryue seall for a warrant vjs viijd. Item, in the Chauncery for writyng of the patent vjs viijd. Item, to his clerk xijd. Item, to the clerk of the hanaper ijs. Item, for the enrollyng of the patent ijs. Item, for a writte of discharge of Sir John Blyston ijs. Item, for the seall vjd. Item, for a bille and a letter sent hoom and for boot hire to Lambehithe and ageyn xiiijd. Item, payed for costs of a man and of an hors iijs iiijd. Item, payed for cariage of euydence viijd. Item, payed for iiij quart of cole ijs viijd. Item, for candell xjd ob. Item, for rysshes iiijd. Item, for wyn iiijd.

Item, in the somme of all the dayes of the parliament with iij dayes allowed outeward and iij dayes hoomwerd is $\frac{xx}{x}$ xv [215] dayes. And the seid Robert and Thomas Ingham abyden v dayes for to speke with the Lord of Suff' and other lords for to sue to their grace and to knowe their will.'

BIBLIOGRAPHY

A. Manuscript Sources.

Public Record Office. Ancient Petitions.
Exchequer Lay Subsidies.
Parliamentary Writs and Returns.
Municipal Archives. Canterbury. Chamberlains' Accounts, 2 vols., 1393–1506; Books of Accounts, 5 vols., 1400–1499.
Exeter. Receivers' Account Rolls, 1340–1500.
King's Lynn. Chamberlains' Account Rolls, 1 Edward IV–1 Henry VII; Gildhall Rolls, 9 Richard II–10 Henry V; Assembly Books I, II, III.
London. London Letter-Books, A to L. Journals 1–9. Husting Proceedings, vol. I.
Norwich. Book of Proceedings of the Municipal Assembly, 1434–1491; Chamberlains' Books of Accounts, 1384–1448, 1470–1491; Bailiffs' Accounts, 1342 and 1350; City Chamberlains' Rolls, 1375–1464; Rolls of the City Assembly, 1365–1426. Various Taxation Rolls.
Reading. Account Rolls (various).
Salisbury. Ledgers A. 1 and B. 2.
Shrewsbury. Taxation Rolls (various); Bailiffs' Accounts, 1276–1498.
Southampton. Stewards' Book of Accounts, 1432–1500; Book of Remembrances, 1445 to James I.
Wallingford. Miscellaneous Deeds.
Winchester. Compotus Rolls, 27 Edward III–15 Henry VII.
York. Corporation House Books, Vols. I–VIII; Chamberlains' Rolls of Accounts, I–IV; Chamberlains' Books of Accounts, I, I A.

B. General Printed Sources.

(1) *Records.*

Calendar of the Charter Rolls preserved in the Public Record Office. *Rolls Series.* London. 1903, &c.
Calendar of the Close Rolls preserved in the Public Record Office. *Rolls Series.* London. 1902, &c.
Calendar of the Patent Rolls preserved in the Public Record Office. *Rolls Series.* London. 1891, &c.
Collectanea Topographica et Genealogica, ed. J. G. Nichols. 8 vols. London. 1834–1843.
Foedera, ed. Thomas Rymer. 20 vols. London. 1704–1735.
Inquisitiones Nonarum temp. regis Edwardi III. *Record Commission.* London. 1807.
Memoranda de Parliamento (1305), ed. F. W. Maitland. *Rolls Series.* London. 1893.

Parliamentary Writs (Edward I–Edward II), ed. F. W. Palgrave. *Record Commission.* 2 vols. London. 1827–1834.

Proceedings and Ordinances of the Privy Council, 1386–1542, ed. Harris Nicholas. *Record Commission.* 7 vols. London. 1834–1837.

Reports of the Royal Commission on Historical Manuscripts. *Parl. Papers.* London. 1870, &c.

Return of the name of every member of the lower house, 1213–1874. *Parl. Papers.* 3 vols. London. 1878.

Rotuli Parliamentorum, 1278–1503. 6 vols. Index. 1832.

Select Charters and other illustrations of English Constitutional History, ed. W. Stubbs and H. W. C. Davis. Oxford. 1913.

Statutes of the Realm. 11 vols. London. 1810–1828.

(2) *Chronicles and Letters.*

Annales Monastici, ed. H. R. Luard. *Rolls Series.* 5 vols. London. 1864–1869.

Annales Ricardi Secundi et Henrici Quarti (1392–1406), ed. H. T. Riley. *Rolls Series.* London. 1866.

The Anonimalle Chronicle of St. Mary's, York, ed. V. H. Galbraith. Manchester University Press. 1927.

Chronicle of London, 1089–1483. London. 1827.

Chronicles of London, ed. C. L. Kingsford. Oxford. 1905.

Chronicles of the Reigns of Edward I and Edward II, ed. W. Stubbs. *Rolls Series.* London. 1882.

Chronicon Angliae, 1328–1388, ed. E. M. Thompson. *Rolls Series.* London. 1874.

Cotton, Bartholomew. Historia Anglicana, ed. H. R. Luard. *Rolls Series.* London. 1859.

Eulogium Historiarum sive temporis, ed. F. S. Haydon. *Rolls Series.* 3 vols. London. 1858–1863.

Fabyan, Robert. The New Chronicles of England and France, ed. H. Ellis. London. 1811.

Fitz-Thedmar, Arnold. De antiquis legibus liber: cronica maiorum et vicecomitum Londoniarum, ed. T. Stapleton. *Camden Society.* London. 1846.

Hemingburgh, Walter of. Chronicon de gestis regum Angliae, ed. H. C. Hamilton. *English Hist. Soc.* 2 vols. London. 1848–1849.

Higden, Ranulf. Polychronicon, ed. Babington and Lumby. *Rolls Series.* 9 vols. London. 1865–1886.

Historia vitae et regni Ricardi secundi, ed. T. Hearne. Oxford. 1729.

Historical Collections of a Citizen of London in the Fifteenth Century, ed. J. Gairdner. *Camden Society.* London. 1876.

Knighton, Henry. Chronicon, ed. J. R. Lumby. *Rolls Series.* London. 1889–1895.

The Paston Letters, ed. J. Gairdner. 6 vols. London. 1904.

Rishanger, William. Chronica, ed. H. T. Riley. *Rolls Series.* London. 1865.

Three Fifteenth-Century Chronicles, ed. J. Gairdner. *Camden Society.* London. 1880.

Trokelowe, John of. Annales, ed. H. T. Riley. *Rolls Series*. London. 1866.
Walsingham, Thomas. Historia Anglicana, ed. H. T. Riley. *Rolls Series*. 2 vols. London. 1863–1864.

C. LOCAL HISTORIES AND PUBLICATIONS OF LOCAL RECORD SOCIETIES.

Barnstaple. Chanter, J. R., and Wainwright, T. Reprint of the Barnstaple Records, 2 vols. Barnstaple. 1900.
   Gribble, J. B. Memorials of Barnstaple. Barnstaple. 1830.
Bath. Green, E. 'A Poll-Tax in Bath, 2 Richard II'. (*Bath Natural History and Antiquarian Field Club, Proceedings*, vol. vi. Bath. 1889.)
Bletchingley. Lambert, U. History of Blechingley, 2 vols. London. 1921.
Bristol. Bickley, F. B. Calendar of Deeds relating to Bristol. Edinburgh. 1899.
   Bickley, F. B. The Little Red Book of Bristol, 2 vols. Bristol. 1900.
   Latimer, J. Calendar of the Charters, &c. of the City and County of Bristol. Bristol. 1909.
   Lucas, S. Illustrations of the History of Bristol. Bristol. 1853.
   Ricart, R. The Maire of Bristowe is Kalendar, edited L. T. Smith (*Camden Society*). London. 1872.
   Seyer, S. Memoirs of Bristol, 2 vols. Bristol. 1821–1823.
Cambridge. Cooper, C. H. Annals of Cambridge, 5 vols. Cambridge. 1842–1908.
   Muskett, J. J. 'The Cambridgeshire Lay Subsidy of 1327.' (*East Anglian*, 3rd *Series*, vols. 10–12. Norwich. 1904–1908.)
Colchester. Benham, W. G. The Red Paper Book of Colchester. Colchester. 1902.
   Benham, W. G. The Oath Book or Red Parchment Book of Colchester. Colchester. 1907.
   Harrod, H. Report on the Records of the Borough of Colchester. Colchester. 1865.
   Harrod, H. Repertory of the Records and Evidences of the Borough of Colchester. Colchester. 1865.
   Rickword, G. 'Taxations of Colchester in 1296 and 1301.' (*Essex Archaeological Society, Transactions. New Series*, vol. 9. Colchester. 1906.)
Cornwall. Maclean, J. 'The Poll-Tax Account for Cornwall, 51 Edward III.' (*Journal of the Royal Institution of Cornwall*, No. IV. Truro. 1872.)
Coventry. Poole, B. Coventry, its history and antiquities. London. 1870.
   Whitley, T. W. Charters and Manuscripts of Coventry, 2 pts. Warwick. 1897–1898.
   Whitley, T. W. The Parliamentary Representation of Coventry. Coventry. 1882–1894.
Dartford. Coates, R. P. 'Valuation of the Town of Dartford, 29 Edward I.' (*Kent Archaeological Society, Archaeologia Cantiana*, vol. ix. London. 1874.)

Derby. Cox J. C. 'Derbyshire in 1327–1328; a Lay Subsidy Roll.' (*Derbyshire Archaeological and Natural History Society, Journal* xxx. London. 1908.)

Dorchester (Dorset). Mayo, C. H. Municipal Records of Dorchester. Exeter. 1908.

Exeter. Reichel, O. J., and Mugford, W. E. An Old Exeter Manuscript. Exeter. 1907.

Shillingford, John. Letters and Papers of John Shillingford, Mayor of Exeter, 1447–1450, ed. S. A. Moore. (*Camden Society.*) London. 1871.

Gloucester. Gloucestershire Subsidy Roll, 1 Edward III. Middle Hill Press. 1832.

Stevenson, W. H. Calendar of the Records of the Corporation of Gloucester. Gloucester. 1893.

Hampshire. 'Taxation of the Tenth and Fifteenth in Hampshire in 1334.' (*Collectanea Topographica et Genealogica*, Vol. I. London. 1834.)

Hull. Hadley, G. A new and complete history of the town of Kingston-upon-Hull. Hull. 1788.

Ipswich. Bacon, N. The Annalls of Ips^{wche}, ed. W. H. Richardson. Ipswich. 1884.

Wodderspoon, J. Memorials of Ipswich. Ipswich. 1850.

Lancashire. Pink, W. D., and Beaven, A. B. The Parliamentary Representation of Lancashire, 1258–1885. London. 1889.

Leicester. Bateson, Mary. Records of the Borough of Leicester, 1103–1603. 3 vols. Cambridge. 1899–1905.

Fletcher, W. G. D. 'The Earliest Leicestershire Lay Subsidy Roll, 1327.' (*Associated Architectural Societies, Reports and Papers*, Vol. XIX. Lincoln. 1887–1889.)

Lincoln. Birch W. de G. Catalogue of Royal Charters, &c., belonging to the Corporation of Lincoln. 2 parts. Cambridge. 1906.

London. Beaven, A. B. Aldermen of the City of London. 2 vols. London. 1908–1913.

Birch, W. de G. Historical Charters of the City of London. Revised edition. London. 1887.

'Lay Subsidy Roll for London, 1412.' (*Archaeological Journal*, Vol. XLIV. London. 1887.)

Norton, G. Commentaries on the History of the City of London. London. 1869.

Pulling, A. The Laws, Customs, Usages, and Regulations of the City and Port of London. London. 1854.

Riley, H. T. Munimenta gildhallae Londoniensis: Liber Albus, Liber Custumarum, et Liber Horn. 3 vols. *Rolls Series.* London. 1859–1862.

Riley, H. T. Memorials of London and London life. London. 1868.

Sharpe, R. R. London and the Kingdom. 3 vols. London. 1894–1895.

Sharpe, R. R. Calendar of Letters from the Mayor, &c., of London. London. 1885.

Sharpe, R. R. Calendar of the Letter-Books (A–L) of the City of London. London. 1899–1912.

Sharpe, R. R. Calendar of Wills proved and enrolled in the Court of Husting, 1256–1688. 2 parts. London. 1889–1890.

Thomas, A. H. Calendar of Plea and Memoranda Rolls, 1323–1381. 2 vols. Cambridge. 1926–1929.

Unwin, G. The Gilds and Companies of London. London. 1908.

Lynn. Harrod, H. Report on the Deeds and Records of the Borough of King's Lynn. King's Lynn. 1874.

Hillen, H. J. The Borough of King's Lynn. 2 vols. Norwich. 1907.

Ingleby, H. The Red Register of King's Lynn. 2 vols. King's Lynn. 1919–1922.

' Extracts from a Manuscript containing portions of the proceedings of the Corporation of Lynn Regis etc.' (*Archaeologia*, Vol. XXIV. London. 1832.)

' Extracts from the Chamberlains' Book of Accounts, 14 Henry IV, in the possession of the Corporation of Lynn Regis.' (*Norfolk Archaeology*, Vol. II. Norwich. 1849.)

Newcastle-under-Lyme. Pape, T. Medieval Newcastle-under-Lyme. Manchester. 1928.

Norfolk. Hudson, W. ' The Assessment of the Townships of the County of Norfolk for the King's Tenths and Fifteenths.' (*Norfolk Archaeology*, Vol. XII. Norwich. 1895.)

Le Strange, Hamon. Norfolk Official Lists. Norwich. 1890.

Northampton. Hartshorne, C. H. Historical Memorials of Northampton. Northampton. 1848.

Markham, C. A. The Liber Custumarum of the Town of Northampton. Northampton. 1895.

Markham, C. A., and Cox, J. C. The Records of the Borough of Northampton. 2 vols. Northampton. 1898.

Norwich. Hudson, W. Leet Jurisdiction in Norwich. *Selden Society*, Vol. V. London. 1892.

Hudson, W., and Tingey, J. C. The Records of the City of Norwich. 2 vols. Norwich. 1906–1910.

Nottingham. Blackner, J. History of Nottingham. Nottingham. 1815.

Stevenson, W. H. Records of the Borough of Nottingham. London. 1882–1900.

Stevenson, W. H. Royal Charters of Nottingham. London. 1890.

Oxford. Salter, H. E. Munimenta Civitatis Oxonie. (*Oxford Historical Society Publications*, LXXI. Oxford. 1917.)

Thorold Rogers, J. E. Oxford City Documents, 1268–1665. (*Oxford Historical Society Publications*, XVIII. Oxford. 1891.)

Plymouth. Worth, R. N. History of Plymouth. Plymouth. 1890.

Reading. Coates, C. The History and Antiquities of Reading. London. 1802.

Guilding, J. M. Reading Records, Vol. I, 1431–1602. Reading. 1892.

Salisbury. Benson, R., and Hatcher, H. Old and New Sarum. 2 vols. Salisbury. 1822.

Scarborough. Rowntree, A. The History of Scarborough. London. 1931.

Shaftesbury. Mayo, C. H. Municipal Records of Shaftesbury. Sherborne. 1889.

Shrewsbury. Calendar of the Muniments and Records of the Borough of Shrewsbury. Shrewsbury. 1896.

Fletcher, W. G. O. 'The Poll-Tax for the Town and Liberties of Shrewsbury, 1380.' (*Shropshire Archaeological and Natural History Society, Transactions,* 2nd Series, Vol. II. Shrewsbury. 1890.)

Forrest, H. E. The Shrewsbury Burgess-Roll. Shrewsbury. 1924.

Owen, H. and Blakeway, J. B. A History of Shrewsbury. 2 vols. London. 1825.

Somerset. Dickinson, F. H. 'A Tax-Roll for Somerset, 1 Edward III.' (*Somerset Record Society Publications,* No. III. London. 1889.)

Southampton. Chapman, A. B. W. The Black Book of Southampton. (*Southampton Record Society.* 3 vols. Southampton. 1912–1915).

Davies, J. S. A History of Southampton. Southampton. 1883.

Gidden, H. W. Charters of Southampton. (*Southampton Record Society.* 2 vols. Southampton. 1909.)

Horrocks, J. W. Assembly Books of Southampton. (*Southampton Record Society.* 4 vols. Southampton. 1917.)

Studer, P. The Oak Book of Southampton. (*Southampton Record Society.* 3 vols. Southampton. 1910.)

Staffordshire. Wedgwood, J. C. Staffordshire Parliamentary History. 2 vols. London. 1919.

Wrottesley, G. 'The Subsidy Roll of 1327.' (*William Salt Archaeological Society, Collections for a History of Staffordshire,* Vol. VII, Part I. London. 1886.)

Wrottesley, G. 'The Subsidy Roll of 1332–1333.' (*Ibid.,* Vol. X. London. 1890.)

Surrey. Smith, J. E. The Parliamentary Representation of Surrey, 1290–1924. London. 1927.

Surrey Taxation Returns, 1332. (*Surrey Record Society,* No. 18. London. 1923.)

Wallingford. Hedges, J. K. The History of Wallingford, 2 vols. London. 1881.

Warwick. 'Subsidy Roll of Warwickshire for 1327.' (*Midland Record Society, Transactions,* Vols. III–VI. Birmingham. 1899–1902.)

'Lay Subsidy Roll for 1332.' (*Dugdale Society, Publications,* Vol. VI. Stratford-on-Avon. 1925.)

Winchester. Bird, W. H. B. The Black Book of Winchester. Winchester. 1925.

Furley, J. S. City Government of Winchester from the Records of the XIVth and XVth Centuries. Oxford. 1925.

Worcester. Eld, F. J. Lay Subsidy Roll for the County of Worcester. (*Worcestershire Historical Society, Publications.* Oxford. 1895.)

York. Brown, W. 'The Yorkshire Lay Subsidy of 1301.' (*Yorkshire Archaeological Society, Record Series,* Vol. XXI. Leeds. 1897.)

Davies, R. Extracts from the Municipal Records of the City of York during the reigns of Edward IV, Edward V, and Richard III. London. 1843.

Park, G. R. The Parliamentary Representation of Yorkshire. Hull. 1886.

Sellers, Maud. York Memorandum Book. Part I, 1376–1419; Part II, 1338–1493. (*Surtees Society Publications.* Durham. 1912–1915.)
Sellers, Maud. York Mercers and Merchant Adventurers. (*Surtees Society Publications.* Durham. 1918.)

D. GENERAL MODERN WORKS.

Adams, G. B. The Origin of the English Constitution. New York. 1912.
American Historical Review. Vol. XIX (1914). 'Some Early Instances of the Concentration of Representatives in England,' by A. B. White.
Baldwin, J. F. The King's Council. Oxford. 1913.
Ballard, A. British Borough Charters. Vol. I, 1042–1216. Cambridge. 1913.
Ballard, A., and Tait, J. Borough Charters. Vol. II, 1216–1307. Cambridge. 1923.
Bateson, Mary. Borough Customs. (*Selden Society.* 2 vols. London. 1904–1906.)
Bulletin of the Institute of Historical Research. Vol. III, No. 7 (1925). Select Documents, I. A Parliamentary Election in 1298. E. J. D.
Vol. III, No. 8 (1925). Select Documents V. Parliamentary Representation in 1294, 1295, and 1307.
Vol. III, No. 9 (1926). Select Documents VII. List of Members of the Fourth Parliament of Henry VII.
Vol. V, No. 15; Vol. VI, Nos. 17 and 18 (1928–1929). The Early Records of the English Parliament, by H. G. Richardson and G. Sayles.
Vol. VIII (1931). The Parliaments of Edward III, by H. G. Richardson and G. Sayles.
Cox, Homersham. Antient Parliamentary Elections. London. 1868.
Davies, J. C. The Baronial Opposition to Edward II. Cambridge. 1918.
Dowell, S. A History of Taxation and Taxes in England. 4 vols. London. 1888.
English Historical Review. Vol. XXV (1910). 'The First Parliament of Edward I,' by C. H. Jenkinson.
Vol. XXVIII (1913). 'The Taxes upon Movables of the Reign of Edward I,' by J. F. Willard.
Vol. XXIX (1914) 'The Taxes upon Movables of the Reign of Edward II,' by J. F. Willard.
Vol. XXX (1915). 'The Taxes upon Movables of the Reign of Edward III,' by J. F. Willard.
Vol. XL (1925). 'Representation of Cities and Boroughs in 1268,' by G. O. Sayles.
Vol. XLVI (1931). 'The Common Council of the Borough,' by J. Tait.
Essays in Medieval History presented to T. F. Tout. Manchester. 1925.
Gneist, R. Englische Verfassungsgeschichte. Berlin. 1882.
Gross, C. Bibliography of Municipal History. Harvard Historical Studies, V. Cambridge. 1915.
Gross, C. The Gild Merchant. 2 vols. Oxford. 1890.
Haskins Anniversary Essays in Medieval History. Boston. 1929.

History. Vol. XI (1926). 'History, English and Statistics,' by A. F. Pollard. 'Re-Election and the Medieval Parliament', by J. G. Edwards.

McIlwain, C. H. The High Court of Parliament and its Supremacy. New Haven. 1910.

Madox, T. Firma Burgi. London. 1726.

Maitland, F. W. Township and Borough. Cambridge. 1898.

Mélanges d'histoire offerts à Henri Pirenne. Brussels. 1926.

Mitchell, S. K. Studies in Taxation under John and Henry III. Yale Historical Publications, Studies II. New Haven. 1914.

Pasquet, D. An Essay on the Origin of the House of Commons. Translated by G. Lapsley. Cambridge. 1925.

Petit-Dutaillis, C. Studies Supplementary to Stubbs' Constitutional History. 3 vols. Manchester. 1911–1929.

Pollard, A. F. The Evolution of Parliament. 2nd edition. London. 1926.

Pollock, F., and Maitland, F. W. History of English Law. 2nd edition. 2 vols. Cambridge. 1923.

Porritt, E. The Unreformed House of Commons. 2 vols. Cambridge. 1903.

Prynne, W. A brief register, kalendar and survey of the several kinds of all parliamentary writs. 4 parts. London. 1659–1664.

Ramsay, J. H. The Revenues of the Kings of England. 2 vols. Oxford. 1925.

Reports of the Deputy-Keeper of the Public Records. Vols. II and III. London. 1841–1842.

Reports from the Lords' Committees touching the dignity of a peer. 5 vols. London. 1820–1829.

Riess, L. Geschichte des Wahlrechts zum englischen Parlament im Mittelalter. Leipsic. 1885.

Scofield, Cora L. The Life and Reign of Edward IV. 2 vols. London. 1923.

Stubbs, W. The Constitutional History of England. 5th edition. 3 vols. Oxford. 1891.

Tait, J. The Study of Early English Municipal History. (*Proceedings of the British Academy.* London. 1922.)

Tout, T. F. The Place of the Reign of Edward II in English History. Manchester. 1914.

Tout, T. F. Medieval Town-Planning. Manchester. 1917.

Tout, T. F. Chapters in Medieval Administrative History. 5 vols. Manchester. 1920–1930.

Transactions of the Royal Historical Society. 4th Series. Vol. VIII (1925). 'Devonshire Ports in the Fourteenth and Fifteenth Centuries,' by Frances A. Mace.

Vol. XI (1928). 'The Origins of Parliament,' by H. G. Richardson.

Tudor Sudies, ed. R. W. Seton-Watson. London. 1924.

Unwin, G. Finance and Trade under Edward III. Manchester. 1918.

Victoria History of the Counties of England, ed. H. A. Doubleday, W. Page, and others. Westminster. 1900, &c.

INDEX OF PERSONS

Abraham (*Habraham*), William, 50 n. 2.
Acclom, Robert, 105.
Alderford, John, 138, 150.
Alderford, Peter de, 134.
Aleyn, John, 62, 63, 111.
Aleyn, Thomas, 49 n. 3.
Aleyn, William, 162.
Alfray, John, of Hindley, 38, 154.
Alvard, Thomas, 157.
Ampulford, William, 149.
Amyas, Robert, 138.
Aport, John, 95.
Appelyerd, Bartholomew de, 147, 149, 150.
Appelyerd, William, 148, 151.
Apsle, John, 108, 116.
Arblaster, James, 62, 63.
Aschewy, Stephen, 14, 15.
Astald, John, 158.
Atwode, Thomas, 154–6, 157.
Atwode, William, 93.
Atwylle, John, 105, 124, 134, 154–7.
Aubry (*Awbry*), John, 88.
Aysshe, John, 152.
Aysshe, Richard, 153.
Ayssheldon, Thomas, 159.
Ayssheton, Ralph, 109.

Bacon, Nathaniel, 34.
Bagot, John, 103.
Baldrey (*Baldree*), William, 152, 153.
Baldry, Thomas, 155.
Bam (*Bamme, Bain*), John, 109.
Banaster, John, 151.
Barantyn, Drew, 102.
Barclay, William, 153.
Baron, Roger, 159.
Barton, Henry, 49 n. 3.
Basset, Robert, 50 nn. 3 and 4, 123.
Bastard, William, 144.
Baxstere, Robert, 144.
Bayly, Richard, 157.
Bayly, William, 149.
Bearl, John, 159.
Beaumont, John, Viscount, 62, 63.
Beaumont, Thomas, 159.
Becket, William, 155, 156.
Bedale, William, 158.
Bedyngton (*Benyngton*), Simon de, 40.
Bekenham, Thomas, 88.
Benefeld, Simon, 42.
Benet, William, 151.
Berkeley, Maurice, 104 n. 2.
Berkeley, William, Lord, 104 n. 2.
Bermyngham, Henry, 143, 152, 153, 154.

Bernard, Richard, 42.
Bernham, Robert de, 147.
Bersham, Philip de, 146.
Bertyn, Robert, 153.
Beson, Richard, 149.
Betele, Henry, 134, 148.
Bettoyne, Richard de, 85, 101.
Billyng, Thomas, 50 n. 2.
Birlyngham, John, 41 n. 1.
Biskelee, John, 151.
Bittyng, Thomas, 117.
Bixton, Walter, 41 n. 3, 42, 104, 134.
Blakburn, Nicholas, 158.
Bleuthe, William, 159.
Bliclyng, William de, 147.
Blyston, Sir John, 163.
Bocking, Edmund, 157.
Boerley, William, 152.
Bold, William, 93.
Bole, Richard, 155.
Bolney, Edward, 93, 156.
Bolt, John, 148.
Bolton, John, 158.
Bonde, Thomas, 159.
Bonnyngton, John, 64.
Botiller, John, 49 n. 4.
Botkesham, Robert, 148.
Bourer, William, 149.
Bowes, William, senior, 158.
—— junior, 158.
Bowland, Thomas, 155.
Boyton, William de, 76.
Bozoun, John, 92, 147.
Bozoun, Sibilla, 92.
Bradford, John, 159.
Braibroke, John, 154.
Braibroke, Robert, 154, 156.
Brandon, John, 149.
Brandon, Robert, 143.
Brasier, Robert, 87.
Bree, William, 157.
Brembre, Nicholas, 31, 102, 122.
Brent, Roger, 153, 154, 155, 156.
Brews, Robert, 108.
Brigge (*Brygge*), Thomas, 141, 142, 148.
Brittany, John of (*John le Breton*), 14, 15.
Broghton, Thomas, 144.
Brompton, Richard, 147.
Brown, John, 136.
Brown, Richard, 63.
Browne, Sir George, 93, 94 n. 1, 110, 154.
Browne, Richard, 152.
Brunham, John de, 90, 147.
Brunham, Robert de, 148.

Bryan, Stephen, 157.
Buckingham, Thomas, Earl of, 102.
Bucworth, John, 141 n. 1.
Buksey, Richard, 86, 87, 137, 152.
Bumpstead, Robert de, 87.
Bumpstead, Thomas de, 146.
Burbage, John, 143.
Burgh, Robert, 151.
Burgh, Thomas, 136, 143, 151.
Burton, William, 158.
But, Thomas, 41 n. 3, 121.
Bymster, Robert, 91.
Bysshop, William, 159.
Bytteryng, Richard de, 87.

Calcote, Joan, 115.
Caldwell, Benet, 155.
Camel, Thomas, 39.
Cantebrigge, William, 49 n. 4.
Cantelowe, William, 50 n. 2.
Canterbury, Archbishop of (Henry Chichele), 142.
Canynges, William, 103.
Carpenter, John, 49 [50] n. 6.
Catour, William, 73.
Catworth (Catteworth), Thomas, 50 n. 2, 64, 162.
Caus, William, 153.
Causton, John de, 102.
Cayly, Philip de, 121.
Champernoun, Hugo, 159.
Champernoun, Roger, 159.
Chaundeler, Rauff, 62, 63.
Chichele, Henry, 109.
Chichele, Robert, 49 n. 3.
Chichele, William, 49 n. 3.
Chittok (Chyttok), John, 88, 152.
Christemasse, Thomas, 97, 144, 155.
Cinte, Robert, 109.
Clement V, Pope, 127.
Clerk, Thomas, 105.
Clerk, Walter, 97, 123.
Clerk, William, 108, 116.
Clopton, Robert, 49 [50] n. 6.
Coblegh, Robert, 148.
Cokesford, John de, 89.
Conduit, Reginald de, 131, 132.
Cook, Philip, 50 n. 3.
Cook, Simon, 87 n. 6.
Cook (Cooke), Thomas, 151, 159.
Copleston, John, 159.
Copnote, John, 136–7, 143.
Corbet, John, 158.
Cornburgh, Alured, 109.
Coteler, Edward, 153.
Coteler, John, 153, 159.
Coventre, John, 49 n. 4.
Crakeford, William de, 148.
Cran, Hugo, 147.

Cranthorne, Robert, 91.
Crathorn, Thomas, 86.
Craven, William, 158.
Crewe, John, 159.
Cromwell, Lord, 162.
Crowmere, William, 49 nn. 3 and 4.
Cullebere, Simon, 104.
Cumberford, William, 117.
Curson, Philip, 89–156.
Curson, Thomas, 146.
Curson, Walter, 137, 151.
Curteys, Peers, 57, 154, 155.
Curteys, Peter, 112.

Dacres, Giles, 111.
Dam, John, 63, 117.
Daventre, Simon, 37.
Davers, Thomas, 111.
David of Wales, see Wales.
Denton, Thomas, 98.
Denys, Walter, 45.
Derby, John, 50 n. 2.
Derby, Walter de, 103.
Derneford, Henry, 103.
Despenser, see Norwich.
Devon, Earl of (Thomas de Courtenay), 61.
Dockyngge, John, 90 n. 3.
Dodyngton, John, 158.
Dorset, Marquis of (John Beaufort), 139.
Drewe, Geoffrey, 89, 146.
Drewe, Thomas, 148, 149.
Duke, William, 153.
Dunston, Robert, 87, 144, 149, 150.
Durham, Bishop of (Antonius de Beck), 13.
—— (Thomas Langley), 142.

Edward I, ix, x, xi, 1–23, 24, 26, 66, 104, 118, 126, 127, 128, 129.
Edward II, ix, xi, 10, 24, 26, 27, 28, 41, 42, 101, 104, 106.
Edward III, 24, 27, 28, 41, 66, 69, 72, 82, 102, 103, 106, 129, 131, 133.
Edward IV, 44, 100, 107, 112, 113, 116, 118.
Edward V, 44 n. 1, 52, 86.
Edward, the Lord, see Edward I.
Edward, Prince, see Edward II.
Eland, Sir William, 107.
Eliott, Richard, 157.
Elys, Thomas, 87, 153.
Erley, Richard, 111.
Essex, William, 31, 40.
Estfeld, William, 49 [50]n. 6, 83.
Eston, Thomas, 150.
Eston, William, 155.
Eton, Walter, 87 n. 6, 138, 148 n. 1, 149.
Everard, William, 148, 149.

Exeter, Anne, Duchess of, 109.
Exeter, Duke of (Henry Holland), 61.

Fastolf, John, 157.
Fauconer, Thomas, 49 nn. 3 and 4, 64.
Faukes, Thomas, 148.
Fauld, Ralph de, 105.
Faunt, Nicholas, 154.
Fayre, Marcus le, 150.
Felaw, Richard, 152, 153.
Feldyng, Geoffrey, 49 [50] n. 6, 50 n. 2.
Ferror, Richard, 88.
Ferthyng, Robert, 94 n. 2.
Fitzjohn, Elias, 10, 22.
Fitzjohn, John, 146.
Fitz Thedmar, 1.
Fitz-William, Thomas, 64, 117, 122 n. 1.
Flemyng (Flemmyng), Richard, 50 n. 4.
Fogge, Sir John, 93, 109.
Fogge, John, 109.
Forster, Thomas, 152.
Fowler, Thomas, 111.
Frank, Philip, 151.
Fraunceys, Adam, 40.
Fray, John, 49 n. 4.
Freman, Richard, 154.
Fremyngham, John, 153.
Frestlyng, Bartholomew, 40.
Frowyk (Frowik), Henry, 50 n. 2, 64, 109.
Frye, William, 91–148.
Fulsham, Benet de, 83, 84.
Furnes, Christopher, 110.
Fyneux, John, 109.

Gale, Thomas, 105.
Galeys, Henry le, 101.
Galton, Roger, 148.
Gamel, Thomas, 27.
Gare, Thomas, 158.
Gawtron, Walter, 64.
Gay, Sir John, 110.
Gaynesford, Nicholas, 107, 110, 116.
Gaysle, William de, 42.
Gedney, John, 49 n. 3.
Gerard, John, 87 n. 6, 138.
Gerard, Thomas, 148, 149.
Germayn, Roger, 146.
Gervays, Thomas de, 121.
Giffard, Stephen, 159.
Giffard, Thomas, 159.
Gilbert, Richard, 153.
Gildeney, Henry, 32, 51.
Gilyot, John, 157.
Girlington, William, 86.
Gisors, John de, 82.
Glassier, John, 154.
Godknave, William, 21, 22.

Goldbetere, Henry, 103, 132.
Golde, Roger, 92, 148, 150.
Graa, Thomas, 42, 103, 133.
Graa, William, 42.
Grafton, Thomas, 161, 162.
Grantham, John de, 102, 140.
Graston, John, 153.
Gregory, William, 50 n. 2.
Gryndyll, John, 157.
Gubbe, Richard, 85.
Gyffard, John, 159.

Habraham, see Abraham.
Haddon, Lawrence, 37.
Hadle, John, 40, 42, 140.
Hadlegh, Peter, 91.
Hakethorn, Henry of, 27.
Hall (Halle), John, 96, 152, 153.
Hall, William, 156.
Hallyate, William, 135, 136, 140-1, 150.
Hamond, John, 110.
Hampton, John, 64, 95, 96, 155, 157.
Hampton, Sir William, 50 n. 4, 107.
Hancok, Robert, 86, 156.
Hanley, John, 105, 152.
Hanton, William, 146.
Hardgill (Hardgyll), Edward, 96, 108.
Harry, John, 159.
Harum, William, 106.
Hattefeld, Richard, 109.
Haute, John, 149.
Haute, Richard, 108.
Haym, Stephen, 138, 147.
Hayne, Richard, 152.
Hazelwode, William, 146.
Henle, Walter, 39.
Henry II, 128.
Henry III, 17.
Henry IV, 36, 37, 44, 48, 69, 72, 102, 139, 145.
Henry V, 44, 45, 92.
Henry VI, 44, 45, 87, 107, 112, 113, 118, 158-9, 161.
Henry VII, 44, 45, 87, 89, 139.
Henry VIII, 98, 118.
Henrys, John, 39, 40.
Henstecote, John, 159.
Henstede, William, 104.
Hereford, William de, 14, 15.
Herford, William, 150.
Hessewell, John, 155.
Heyberare, William, 116 n. 1.
Heynes, Richard, 97, 156.
Highham, John, 49 n. 4.
Hobard, James, 155.
Hode, Thomas, 158.
Hodelston, Alan of, 27.
Holand, John, 159.

Holand, Richard, 159.
Holes, Roger, 96, 154, 156.
Hoo, Thomas, 107, 110.
Hoord, John, 138, 139 n. 1, 154.
Hopton, Roger, 108.
Horde, William, 151.
Hords, John, 110.
Hore, William, 96, 152.
Horn, Edward, 93.
Horsley, Robert, 151.
Horwode, William, 157.
Houtone, Richard, 147.
Hull, Henry, 151.
Hulle, John, 147.
Hulle, Robert, 147.
Hulyn, William, 50 nn. 2 and 4.
Hunte, Roger, 142.
Huse, Thomas, 154.
Husee, Thomas, 146.
Hyde, John, 147.
Hyde (*Hide*), William, 123, 124.

Ikham, Thomas, 148.
Ikham, William, 151.
Ingham, John, 161.
Ingham, Thomas, 88, 138, 151, 161–3.
Ingham, Walter, 161.
Intewode, John, 161, 162.
Irlond (*Irlonde*), Sir George, 50 n. 4, 110.
Isabella (Queen of Edward II), 101.

James, Andrew, 153.
Janyns, Margery, 122.
Jay, Richard, 111.
Jeffrey (*Jeffreys*), Walter, 63, 161, 162.
Jenney, Edmund, 108.
Jenney, John, 62, 63, 162.
Jenney, Thomas, 111, 156.
Jenney, William, 63, 117.
Jewel, Richard, 149.
Jopson, Thomas, 97.
Josselyn, Ralph, 50 n. 4, 102, 122.

Karlill, Adam, 40, 41 n. 1.
Kebill, Thomas, 109.
Keleseye, Robert de, 83, 85.
Kene, John, 116 n. 1.
Kent, Simon, 105.
Knolles, Thomas, 49 n. 4.
Knott, Thomas, 158.
Knyvett, Sir William, 107, 111, 116.
Kyngislane, John, 158.
Kyton, John, 159.

Lake, John, 149.
Lamb (*Lombe*), John, 90, 104.

Lambard (*Lambert*), John, 50 n. 4.
Lancaster, Nicholas, 157.
Lane, Thomas, 94, 139, 149.
Lane, William, 149, 151.
Langedon, John, *see* Rochester.
Langedon, Thomas, 64.
Langley, John, 51.
Lark, William, 122, 123.
Latymer, John, 147.
Lee, Richard, 50 n. 4.
Lenthorp, Laurence, 110.
Leukenore (*Lewkenore*), Richard, 107, 110, 116.
Leukenore (*Lewkenore*), Thomas, 115.
Leyre, William de, 83.
Limnor (*Lomnor*), William, 62, 63.
Lomynour, Henry, 104, 148.
Loppam, John, 153.
Louth, Richard, 158.
Ludlow, William, 151.
Lynde, Henry, 149.
Lynde, John, 151.
Lytfot, John, 21, 22.

Man, Henry, 150.
March, Roger, Earl of, 101.
Marche, William, 155.
Marleburgh, John, 155.
Marowe, William, 50 nn. 3 and 4, 64.
Marshall, John, 123.
Maseye, John, 141 n. 1.
Mason, Thomas, 151.
Mauncell (*Mansel*), Thomas, 112.
Meade, Philip, 104.
Melcheburne, Thomas de, 89.
Melreth, William, 122, 124.
Merlawe, Richard, 49 n. 3, 64.
Merston, William, 110.
Meryvale, Richard, 49 n. 3.
Metcalf, Miles, 138.
Michell, John, 49 n. 4, 64.
Milford, William, 109, 116.
Monesle, Richard, 138.
Montfort, Simon de, 1, 2, 3, 7.
More, John, 94 n. 5.
More, Thomas, 158.
More, William, 31, 40.
Morewode, Robert de, 121.
Morgan, Philip, 111.
Morle, John de, 146.
Morley, Nicholas, 112.
Mortimer, *see* March.
Morton, Thomas, 32, 90 n. 3, 134, 148, 158.
Mulling, John, 151, 152.
Mulys, John, 159.
Munke, William, 155, 156.
Musgrove, John, 64, 155.
Mynors, John, 105.

Nedeham, John, 117.
Nedeham, Richard, 50 n. 3.
Netherton, John, 151.
Nevyle, Robert, 111.
Newton, Robert, 156.
Norbury, Richard, 31.
Norfolk, John Mowbray, Duke of, 114.
Norman, John, 50 nn. 2 and 4.
Northampton, John de, 102, 122.
Norton, Thomas, 65.
Norton, William, 49 n. 3.
Norwich, Bishop of (Henry Despenser), 102.
Nottlee, Osbert de, 98, 146.
Nywaman, John, 149.

Olnet, Thomas, 158.
Olney, John, 50 n. 2.
Organ, John, 40.
Ormeshede, William, 158.
Osborn, William, 151.
Oulegreve (Oulegrave), Thomas, 50 n. 4.
Overay, Thomas, 139, 156.
Oxney, Salamon, 49 n. 4.

Page, Richard, 109, 117.
Parmenter, John, 142, 151.
Parveys, John, 49 n. 4.
Paston, Sir John, 62, 63, 107, 114.
Paston, John, 46, 62, 63, 109, 117, 156.
Paston, William, 108, 111, 116.
Pattesle, John, 50 n. 2.
Payn, John, 123.
Payn, Richard, 151.
Pekeryng, John, 64.
Penne, John, 49 nn. 3 and 4.
Percy, Sir Thomas, 139.
Pert, Thomas, 162.
Pestell, William, 107, 111.
Petypas, Bartholomew, 151.
Phelip (Philip), Matthew, 50 n. 4.
Philipot, Sir John, 40, 85, 102, 121, 133.
Pilton, William, 91, 143, 152.
Pirie, John, 148.
Plente, Roger, 91.
Pole, John, 111.
Pole, Richard de la, 102.
Pole, William de la, 103, 131, 132.
Pollow, John, 150.
Pontesbury, Roger, 153.
Pope, John, 115.
Pope, Walter, 159.
Powtrell, Thomas, 109.
Prestecote, John, 91.
Preston, John de, 121.
Pring, John, 156.

Prior, John, 140.
Prout, John, 110.
Pygott (Pigott), Simon, 91, 152, 153.
Pyrie, Andrew de, 21, 22, 104.
Pyrie, Thomas, 95.
Pytte, Simon atte, 91.

Rabys, William, 159.
Radyng, Abbot, 158.
Rafman, Henry, 150.
Rattlesden, John de, 121.
Rawlyns, Richard, 37.
Raynold, Thomas, 156.
Reinwell (Renwell, Rounwell), John, 49 n. 3, 64.
Reson, William, 151.
Reymund, Thomas, 147, 149.
Richard II, 24, 25, 29, 30, 32, 35, 39, 42, 43, 45, 69, 72, 76, 90, 91, 96, 103, 121, 135, 145.
Richard III, 44, 52, 108.
Rideley (Rydeley), Thomas, 86, 158.
Rivers, Anthony, Earl, 108.
Roberdes, John, 154, 155.
Rochester, Bishop of (John Langedon), 64.
Rokesle, Gregory de, 101.
Rollesby, Peter de, 131 n. 1.
Russe, John, 62, 63.
Russell, John, 142 n. 5.
Russell, Richard (of Dunwich), 142.
Russell, Richard (of Shrewsbury), 146.

Salisbury, Thomas, 151.
Salter, John, 92.
Samson, Thomas, 156.
Saynton, John, 144, 153.
Scantesby, Thomas, 156.
Scawsell, William, 154.
Scot, Sir John, 110.
Scot, Thomas, 50 n. 4.
Sedman, William, 150.
Seebald, Simon, 49 n. 3.
Sellow (Sellowe), William, 152, 154.
Ser', Nicholas de, 146.
Serle, John, 159.
Sevenok, William, 49 n. 4.
Seward, Thomas, 39.
Sextayn, John, 93.
Shaplegh, John, 92.
Sheffield, Robert, 111.
Sheldon, Richard, 109.
Sheldwych, Nicholas, 156.
Sheldwyche (Sheldwych), John, 109, 139, 149, 150, 151.
Sherer, John, 158.
Shipward, John, 104.
Shirle (Shirley), Walter, 149, 150, 151.
Shirwood, Richard, 158.

Sibylle, Walter, 122.
Skinner, John, 115.
Skinner, Richard, 115.
Skippewith, William, 153.
Smalecombe, Richard, 92.
Snawedon, Thomas, 158.
Snorryng, William de, 146.
Somaister, Adam, 159.
Speke, John, 159.
Spencer, Richard, 115, 149.
Spilman, Henry, 111, 117.
Sprye, John, 159.
Spycer, John, 136.
Spycere, Thomas, 91.
Spynk, Thomas, 104.
Stable, Adam, 41 n. 1.
Standolf (Standelf), John, 49 n. 3.
Staundon, William, 122.
Stodeye, John de, 102.
Stokton, William, 86.
Stone, Thomas, 153.
Stone, William, 97.
Strecche, John, 39.
Strete, Thomas, 158.
Strode, Richard, 159.
Sturte, Peter, 150.
Stury, Richard, 106, 152.
Suffolk, John de la Pole, Duke of, 161,
    162, 163.
Suliard, John, 111.
Swanton, Andrew, 141.
Swayn, Henry, 154.
Swerdeston, Nicholas, 90.
Systerne, Bartholomew, 142.

Tatersall, Robert, 49 n. 4.
Tayllour, John, 124.
Tayllour (Taillour), 50 n. 4.
Temple, Thomas, 94 n. 5.
Thorisby, Robert, 153, 155, 156.
Thorp, Robert, 155, 156, 157.
Thrisk, John, 86, 87, 137, 138, 152.
Thyckpenny, William, 151.
Tolboothe, Geoffrey de, 147.
Tonge, John, 154.
Toppes (Toppe), Robert, 138, 151, 152 n. 1,
    153, 161-3.
Tornegold, John, 40.
Townsend, Roger, 110.
Trentham, John, 154.
Tresawell, Thomas, 109.
Turnaunt, Richard, 151.
Twynyo, William, 116.
Tygo, John.
Tylney, John, 135, 136, 140, 150.
Tymperley, John (junior), 108, 110, 114,
    115, 154.
Tymperley John (senior), 111, 116, 155.

Tyndale, William of, 29.
Tyrant, Nicholas, 159.

Uffenham, John, 111.
Uffenham, Roger, 111.
Umfray, John, 149.
Urpyngton, Nicholas, 158.
Urswyk, Thomas, 64, 103, 117, 122.
Usflete, Nicholas, 158.
Uvedale, Thomas, 108, 116.

Verney, Sir Ralph, 110.
Vertue, John, 144, 155.
Veske, Peter, 111.
Veysey, Robert, 92.

Waales, William, 154.
Wace, John, 147.
Wadham, John, 147.
Waget, Richard, 109.
Walden, William, 141 n. 1.
Waldern, William, 49 nn. 3 and 4.
Wales, David of, 6, 7.
Walker, Walter, 158.
Walsshe, John, 159.
Walter, John, 158.
Walter, Thomas, 93.
Walworth, William, 102, 121, 133.
Wanternoure, Robert, 155.
Warde, John, 41 n. 1, 158.
Warenne, John, Earl, 13.
Warner, Edmund, 148.
Warren, John, 150.
Warter Richard, 158.
Waryn, William, 150.
Water, John, 153.
Water, Richard, 93, 150.
Waterden, John, 143.
Waterden, Robert de, 147.
Waterden, Thomas de, 147, 148.
Wayn, William, 152.
Waynfleet, William, 90.
Wayte, William, 62, 63, 117.
Weggewode, William, 135.
Welborn, John de, 146.
Welles, John, 64.
Wentworth, John de, 147.
Westmorland, Ralph Neville, Earl of, 62.
Wetherby, Thomas, 87.
Whitingham (Whityngham), Robert, 49 nn.
    3 and 4.
Whittokesmede, John, 110, 115.
Whityngton (Whittington), Richard,
    49 n. 3, 102, 122.
Whityngton, Thomas, 108.
Wifold (Wyfold), Nicholas, 50 n. 2.
Wilford, William, 91, 149.

Will, William atte, 152.
Wilton, Harry, 63.
Wilton, Henry, 88, 89.
Wimbill, William, 156.
Winchester, Bishop of (Henry Beaufort), 141.
Winter, John, 152.
Wise, John, 154.
Wode, William, 117, 150, 157.
Wollap, John, 149.
Wolseley, Ralph, 107, 114, 116.
Wolston, John, 159.
Wonard, William, 159.
Worsop, William, 110, 153.
Worthy, John, 159.
Wotton, Nicholas, 49 n. 3, 64, 122.
Wrangwyssh, Thomas, 155.

Wychampton, William, 42.
Wyche, Hugh, 50 n. 4.
Wyche, John, 159.
Wycombe, Richard, 147.
Wyghton, John, 153.
Wygston, John, 57.
Wyldecote, Thomas, 156.
Wyleby, Robert de, 146.
Wylford, Robert, 91.
Wynesflode, William, 146.
Wynnesley, Richard, 158.
Wyting, Nicholas, 91.

Ymme, John, 146.
Yonge, Thomas, 63, 65 n. 1, 117, 124–5.
York, Richard, Duke of, 125.
York, Richard, 86, 154, 155, 156.

INDEX OF PLACES

Alcester, 5. Alresford, 8 n. 3. Alton, 8 n. 3, 10, 11. Amersham, 10. Andover, 8 n. 3, 10, 17. Appleby, 19, 29, 54, 55, 57, 110, 112. Arundel, 108, 116. Ashburton, 45, 77. Axbridge, 19, 77.

Bannockburn, 26. Banstead, 77. Barnstaple, 19, 39, 74, 75 n. 1, 77, 97, 109, 116, 159. Basingstoke, 8 n. 3, 10, 11, 17. Bath, 3, 10, 17, 77, 110. co. Bedford, 5, 8, 75 n. 5, 142. Bedford (borough), 5, 10 n. 2, 19, 42, 54, 104. Bedwyn, 8 n. 1, 28, 107, 108, 111, 116. Berkhampsted, 26. co. Berks, 9, 19 n. 1, 58, 59, 124. Berwick, 8 n. 6. Beverley, 8 n. 2. Bideford, 77. Biggleswade, 5. Birmingham, 5. Bishop's Stortford, 26. Bletchingley, 77, 107, 112 n. 5, 116. Bodmin, 19, 109. Bradford-on-Avon, 8 n. 1. Bradninch, 26, 77. Bramber, 108, 110, 116. Bridgnorth, 75 n. 5, 107, 108, 110, 116, 156. Bridgwater, 19, 77. Bristol (Bristowe), 3, 6, 10, 17, 18, 19, 22, 25, 32, 41, 42, 48, 51, 52, 63, 65, 68, 100, 103, 117, 125, 131, 143. Bristowe, see Bristol. Brittany, 102. Bromsgrove, 9. co. Buckingham, 8, 9, 10, 17, 111, 112. Bury St. Edmunds, 3, 8, 10, 20, 74, 86, 144. Byfleet, 77.

Calais, 107, 133. Calne, 8 n. 1, 26 n. 2, 42, 106, 107, 110. co. Cambridge, 109,

124. Cambridge (borough), 3, 19, 22, 34, 54, 55, 61, 70, 75 n. 5, 76, 83, 96, 98, 121, 135, 145, 155, 160. Canterbury, xii, 3, 6, 10, 19, 38, 48, 54, 56, 64, 71, 72, 93, 94, 98, 107, 108, 112, 113, 139, 148, 150, 151, 152, 153, 154, 155, 156, 157. Carlisle, 7, 11, 19, 54, 55. Castle Rising, 107. Chard, 26, 77. Chester, 7, 8. Chicheley, 112. Chichester, 3, 14 n. 3, 26, 75. Chippenham, 8 n. 1, 19, 107, 108, 111, 123, 124. Chipstead, 115. Christchurch, 11. Cinque Ports, 25, 45 n. 1. Cockermouth, 19. Colchester, 7, 10, 11, 12, 13, 17, 18, 19, 22, 26, 46, 75 n. 5, 76, 97, 121, 139, 144, 155, 156. Cold Harbour, 115. Coleshill, 5. co. Cornwall, 17, 19 n. 2, 20, 59, 69, 74, 109. Coventry, 3, 5, 19, 48, 54, 63, 84, 93, 117. Crediton, 77. Cricklade, 5, 8 n. 1, 28, 107, 110, 112. co. Cumberland, 9, 11, 19 n. 3.

Dartmouth (Dertemouth), 75 n. 1, 77, 105, 159. co. Derby, 109. Derby (borough), 19, 54, 56. Dertemouth, see Dartmouth. Devizes, 8 n. 1, 28, 110, 111. co. Devon, 20, 39, 40, 59, 74, 77, 111, 159. Dodbrooke, 77. Dorchester, 19, 54, 109. co. Dorset, 8, 12, 13, 20, 39, 59, 116. Downton, 8 n. 1, 110, 111, 112 n. 5. Dudley, 9. Dunstable, 5 n. 2, 26. Dunster, 77. Dunwich, 3, 9, 11,

28, 45, 59, 97, 107, 108, 111, 112, 114, 116, 142.

East Grinstead, 107, 110, 112, 116. Ebor', see York. Egremont, 19. Eltham, 109. Ely, 3, 9. co. Essex, 12. Evesham, 9. Exeter, xii, 3, 6, 19, 60, 61, 71, 75 n. 1, 76, 77, 91, 93, 98, 105, 110, 112 nn. 7 and 8, 124, 134, 145, 146, 147, 148, 149, 150, 151, 152, 154, 156, 157, 159–60.

Farnham, 25. Fleet Prison, 122. France, 121, 126. Fremington, 28 n. 2.

Gatton, 46, 77, 107, 111, 114, 115, 116. co. Gloucester, 108, 116 n. 1, 117. Gloucester (city), 3, 10, 19, 54, 57, 58, 70, 75 n. 5, 85, 116 n. 1, 140. Godalming, 115. Grantham, 46. Grimsby, 7, 11, 17, 19, 22, 26, 62, 63, 75 n. 5, 112, 144, 156. Guildford, 19, 22, 75 n. 5, 77, 110, 112 n. 5, 116.

Hampshire, see co. Southampton. Hedon, 8 n. 2. Helston, 109, 116. Hereford (city), 3, 6, 19, 21, 22, 58, 69, 75 n. 5, 112 n. 5. co. Hertford, 8, 12. Hertford (borough), 10, 12, 17, 75 n. 5. Heytesbury, 46, 111. High Wycombe, see Wycombe. Hindon, 46, 111, 112 nn. 5, 6, and 7, 116, 117. Honiton, 77. Horsham, 75, 107, 110, 112 n. 5, 116. Hull, 48, 53, 60, 96, 103, 107, 131, 143. Huntingdon (borough), 19, 54, 57, 75 nn. 5 and 6.

Ilchester, 77. Ipswich, 3, 11, 19, 22, 26, 28, 34, 38, 58, 61, 107, 108, 110, 112, 116, 152, 153, 154, 155, 156, 157.

Kenilworth, 3. co. Kent, 19 n. 5, 56, 109. Kidderminster, 9. Kingsbridge, 77. King's Lynn, see Lynn. Kingston-on-Hull, see Hull. Kingston-on-Thames, 26, 77.

Lambehithe, see Lambeth. Lambeth (Lambehithe), 123, 163. Lancaster, Duchy of, 115. Langport, 77. Launceston, 19, 109. Ledbury, 19. co. Leicester, 8, 9. Leicester (borough), 9, 10, 19, 54, 57, 58, 60, 73, 75 n. 5, 83, '154, 155. Leominster, 19, 75 n. 5, 158–9. Lewes, 2, 22, 110, 112. Lichfield, 3. co. Lincoln, 26, 117, 122 n. 1. Lincoln (city), 1, 3, 6, 10, 19, 27, 28, 48, 53, 70, 75 n. 5, 83, 101, 111, 112 n. 7. Liskeard, 109. Liverpool, 9. London, xii, 1, 2, 3, 5, 6, 7, 8, 9, 14–16, 25, 30–2, 35, 40, 42,

48–51, 52, 64, 68, 70, 71, 75, 82–6, 98, 100, 101–3, 106, 110, 111, 112, 117, 120, 121, 122, 123, 124, 130, 131, 134, 135, 137, 138, 140, 141, 143, 144 n. 3, 161, 162. Lostwithiel, 74, 109. Ludgershall, 8 n. 1, 28, 111. Ludlow; 45, 46, 100, 107. Lydford, 77. Lyme Regis, 9, 10, 11, 12. Lynn, xii, 3, 6, 10, 17, 19, 26, 33, 34, 39, 58, 72, 76, 89–91, 98, 104, 116, 130, 131, 134, 135, 136–7, 140–4, 145, 146, 147, 148, 149, 150, 151, 152, 153, 154, 155, 156.

Maldon, 28 n. 2, 62, 63, 78, 107, 108, 111, 114. Malmesbury, 8 n. 1, 28, 107, 108. Malton, 8 n. 2. Marlborough, 8 n. 1, 28, 111, 112. Marlow, 10. Meath, 112. Melcombe Regis, 10, 12, 111, 116. co. Middlesex, 4, 5, 8, 9, 109. Midhurst, 21, 107, 110. Milborne Port, 26 n. 2, 77. Milverton, 77. Modbury, 28 n. 2, 77. Montacute, 77. Much Wenlock, 45, 46, 100, 106, 108, 110, 116.

Nether Stowey, 77. Newcastle-on-Tyne, 7, 19, 22, 27, 28, 48, 53, 69, 75 n. 5. Newcastle-under-Lyme, 28 n. 2, 105, 111, 115, 116, 117. Newgate Prison, 123. Newport (I.o.W.) 8 n. 3. New Woodstock, 46. co. Norfolk, 7, 58, 59, 107, 108, 110, 111, 114, 116. co. Northampton, 11, 19 n. 6. Northampton (borough), 3, 6, 19, 36, 37, 58, 75 n. 5. co. Northumberland, 19 n. 7, 26, 28, 29. Norwich, xii, 3, 6, 19, 35, 36, 41, 42, 48, 52, 60, 63, 65, 68, 69, 70, 71, 76, 87, 88, 89, 91, 98, 104, 111, 113, 116, 117, 119, 121, 134, 138, 144, 145, 146, 147, 148, 149, 150, 151, 152, 153, 155, 156, 157, 161–3. Nottingham (borough), 7, 19, 48, 53, 54, 55, 79, 89, 121, 131. Nuneaton, 5.

Odell, 5. Odiham, 10, 11, 17. Okehampton, 77. Old Sarum, 8 n. 1, 111. Overton, 8 n. 3. co. Oxford, 124. Oxford (city), 3, 19, 21, 22, 33, 58, 60, 75 n. 5, 80, 104, 108.

Pershore, 9. Pickering, 8 n. 2. Plymouth, 96, 109, 117, 157. Plympton, 77, 159. Pontefract, 8 n. 2. Poole, 28 n. 2. Portsmouth, 8 n. 3, 10, 19, 26, 107, 108, 112, 116. Prussia, 103.

Reading, 10 n. 2, 19, 42, 58, 60, 73, 75 n. 5, 85, 96, 105, 110, 147. Reigate, 77, 112, 114, 115, 116. Rhuddlan, 6.

Richmond (Yorks.), 28 n. 2. Ripon, 8 n. 2. Rochester, 3, 19, 26, 37–8, 54, 56, 97, 109, 112. co. Rutland, 8, 9.

St. Albans, 10, 12, 17, 136. Salisbury, xii, 8 n. 1, 19, 22, 36, 59, 61, 64, 68, 70, 71, 76, 94–6, 107, 108, 110, 111, 112 n. 10, 139, 149, 150, 151, 152, 153, 154, 155, 156, 157. Scandinavia, 104. Scarborough, 7, 8 n. 2, 13, 19, 22, 26, 28, 42, 105. Scotland, 29. Shaftesbury, 39, 111, 112, 116. Sheen, 77. Shefford, 5, 75 n. 5. Shoreham, 42, 107, 111, 112, 116. Shrewsbury, 3, 6, 19, 22, 58, 73, 75 n. 5, 91, 97, 106, 138, 144, 146, 150, 151, 153, 154, 155. co. Somerset, 8, 11, 12, 13, 20, 39, 59, 69, 75, 77, 109. co. Southampton, 8, 9, 11, 59, 108, 110, 111, 116. Southampton (borough), 3, 8 n. 3, 10, 11, 17, 19, 26, 48, 53, 68, 97, 123, 136, 139, 153, 155. South Molton, 77, Southwark, 19, 75 n. 5, 77, 107, 112 n. 5, 116. co. Stafford, 107, 114, 115. Stafford (borough), 9, 105, 107. Staines, 5. Stamford, 3, 22. Stepell Moreden, 124. Steyning, 107, 108, 116. Stoke Courcy (*Stogursey*), 28 n. 2, 77. Stratford-on-Avon, 5. co. Suffolk, 7, 58, 76, 108, 116. co. Surrey, 19 n. 8, 29, 75, 77, 107, 113, 114, 116. co. Sussex, 29, 59, 75, 107, 108, 112, 113, 114, 116. Sutton Prior, 77.

Tamworth, 5. Taunton, 10, 17, 77. Tavistock, 75 n. 1, 77, 109, 110, 111, 112, 116, 159. Thirsk, 8 n. 2. Tickhill, 8 n. 2. Tiverton, 77. Tonbridge, 9. Torrington, 19, 75 n. 1, 77, 78. Totnes, 19, 77, 109,

112, 159. Tregony, 17. Truro, 109. Tutbury Castle, 115.

Uxbridge, 5.

Wales, 6. Wallingford, 9, 58, 74, 75 n. 5, 97, 107, 112 n. 6, 146. Wareham, 109, 111, 116. co. Warwick, 5, 8. Warwick (borough), 5, 19, 54, 55. Weare, 77. Wells, 77. Wendover, 10. Weobley, 26 n. 2. Westbury, 46, 111. Westminster, 4, 78, 86, 91, 95, 118, 120, 136, 158, 159, 161. co. Westmorland, 13, 19 n. 9, 29, 55. Weymouth, 26, 116. Wigan, 9. Wilton, 8 n. 1, 54, 59, 107, 110, 111. co. Wilts., 8, 9, 11, 20, 28, 36, 59, 74, 107, 108, 110, 111, 114. Winchester, xii, 3, 6, 8 n. 3, 19, 53, 54, 55, 68, 69, 71, 96, 98, 108, 117, 138, 146, 147, 150, 151, 155. Windsor, 10, 58, 109. Witley, 77. Woodmansterne, 115. Woodstock, *see* New Woodstock. Wootton Bassett, 46, 107. co. Worcester, 9, 12. Worcester (city) 3, 6, 12, 19, 54, 57, 102. Wycombe, 10, 17 n. 5, 76, 111, 112, 121.

Yarm, 8 n. 2. Yarmouth (I.O.W.), 8. Yarmouth (*Yernemouth*), 3, 6, 8 n. 3, 9, 10, 17, 19, 22, 42, 59, 62, 63, 68, 69, 107, 111, 112, 116. Yernemouth, *see* Yarmouth. co. York, 8, 9, 18 n. 3, 19 n. 10, 22 n. 1, 74, 111, 117. York (city) (*Ebor*'), 1, 3, 6, 8 n. 2, 9, 10 n. 3, 19, 22, 27, 32, 41, 42, 48, 52, 65, 68, 70, 82, 83, 85, 86, 87, 89, 100, 102, 103, 131, 133, 136, 137, 140, 143, 151–3, 154, 155, 156, 158.